D1029665

Dangerous Games

Dangerous Games

The True Story of a Convicted
Murderer on Death Row Who
Changed His Sex and
Won Her Freedom

Robert L. Bentley

A Birch Lane Press Book
Published by Carol Publishing Group

A Birch Lane Press Book
Published by Carol Publishing Group
Birch Lane Press is a registered trademark of Carol Communications, Inc.
Editorial Offices: 600 Madison Avenue, New York, N.Y. 10022
Sales and Distribution Offices: 120 Enterprise Avenue, Secaucus, N.J. 07094
In Canada: Canadian Manda Group, P.O. Box 920, Station U, Toronto, Ontario M8Z 5P9
Queries regarding rights and permissions should be addressed to Carol Publishing Group,
600 Madison Avenue, New York, N.Y. 10022

Carol Publishing Group books are available at special discounts for bulk purchases, for
sales promotions, fund-raising, or educational purposes. Special editions can be created to
specifications. For details, contact Special Sales Department, Carol Publishing Group, 120
Enterprise Avenue, Secaucus, N.J. 07094

Manufactured in the United States of America
10 9 8 7 6 5 4 3 2 1

Library of Congress Cataloging-in-Publication Data

Bentley, Robert L.
    Dangerous games : the true story of a convicted murderer on death row who changed
his sex and won her freedom / by Robert L. Bentley.
        p.   cm.
    ISBN 1-55972-180-4
    1. Perez, Leslie Elaine—Biography. 2. Transsexuals—United States—Biography.
3. Sex change—United States—Biography. 4. Criminals—United States—Biography.
I. Title.
HQ77.8.P47B46   1993
305.3—dc20   92-39499
                                                                                                        CIP

To my parents and Frances

. . . anyone who ever had a heart
They wouldn't turn around and break it
And anyone who ever played a part
They wouldn't turn around and hate it
—Lou Reed
"Sweet Jane"

Acknowledgments

Many people searched their memories to give me their version of the events in this book. I want to express my special gratitude to Leslie Perez and Sylvia Ayres; Jim Ayres; Ted Kipperman; Clyde Woody and Judge Neil McKay, who were both generous with their time; Lloyd Lunsford; James Hippard Sr.; Judge Miron Love; Judge Truman Roberts; Richard "Racehorse" Haynes; and Martha Terrill.

Judge John R. Brown received me in his chambers during August 1992. He was eighty-two years old, still working as a senior judge on the U.S. Fifth Circuit Court of Appeals. Early in his tenure as an outnumbered jurist on the southern court, he wrote many dissents favoring integration and voting rights for African-Americans. His views eventually prevailed with the Supreme Court, and he rose to serve as chief judge of the Fifth Circuit for thirteen years. Speaking of the stay of execution he signed for Leslie Douglas Ashley and Carolyn Ann Lima, Judge Brown told me, "Of all the decisions I made in my entire career, I've never been more positive I was right than I was about this one. I still feel that way today." Judge Brown died on January 23, 1993. I want to thank Ms. Kathy Hulce for arranging my interview with him.

Although I tried to contact him many times personally and through intermediaries, Frank Briscoe declined to be interviewed. Leslie Sherman Ashley did not wish to discuss his child. Mae Lima was courteous but not cooperative.

Court and legal records were retrieved from the Harris County District Clerk's files, the Texas Court of Criminal Appeals in Austin, the U.S. Fifth Circuit Court of Appeals in New Orleans, and the federal government's Southwest Regional Archives in Fort Worth. At the Coryell County courthouse, District Clerk Carolyn Pollard and Charl Dean Harrington found a treasure trove of material that had wound up there due to the change of venue that sent Leslie's last trial to Gatesville. Judge Phillip Ziegler reminisced about attending that trial during his summer vacation from college.

The journey of Fred A. Tones/Salvadore Pasquale/Salvador Pascual was found in records kept by the Immigration and Naturalization Service and the U.S. government's New England Regional Archives in Waltham, Massachusetts. A skeletal army-service background for him was reconstructed at the National Personnel Records Center in Saint Louis despite the 1973 fire there. In Houston, Diane Aubert of Forest Park Cemetery led me to his grave. Major David Georgi of the Office of Army Public Affairs in Los Angeles deciphered the abbreviations on his headstone.

Mary Haisten of the Houston Police Department's public affairs office worked to release the HPD's homicide investigation report to me. Thanks also to Officer Denny Hair of the HPD museum, as well as to Charles Brown and Misty of the Texas Department of Correction's public information office in Huntsville, where the electric chair referred to as Old Sparky is on display a few blocks from the Walls at the Texas Prison Museum.

My appreciation as well to Ray Hill; Andrew Edmonson of the splinter ACT UP Houston chapter; Dr. Cary Wintz, professor of history at Texas Southern University; Victor Borgeson of the Houston Metropolitan Research Center at the Houston Public Library; and Steve Kerbow of *The New Voice* in Houston.

I also relied on newpaper accounts in the *Post, Chronicle* and *Press*, the dailies published in Houston when these events happened. Whenever possible, I compared the newspaper articles to interviews and transcripts from the official record. When they clashed, I usually went with the record. Any mistakes are mine.

Jon Schwartz deserves a special nod for compiling many of the newspaper records in the beginning. Also, he was good company and endlessly patient during a number of research trips to Houston and beyond. Thanks to my agent, Mike Hamilburg, for selling this book; to Hillel Black for buying it; and to Denise O'Sullivan for editing the manuscript with a keen eye and a sharp pencil. I hope anyone I have overlooked will forgive me.

Finally, my parents deserve more gratitude than I can give them for encouraging me through all the ups and downs for so many years. And this book could not have been written without my wife, Frances Hayden. Her legal knowledge and research skills were irreplaceable. Even more, she tolerated my beastly moods. She should be beatified.

Los Angeles
February, 1993

Prologue

"Take a condom, save a life." Conventioneers streaming up the hot sidewalk dodged the gift. "Take a condom, save a life. . . . Take a condom, save a life."

A blue-haired woman beyond Social Security age laughed. "I haven't needed one of those things in fifteen years."

"Darlin'," the affable demonstrator said, grinning, "you're never too old to practice safe sex."

The blue-haired woman was not amused by the joke. She glared at the condom and a Red Cross pamphlet titled *Men, Sex, and AIDS*. Buttons for conservative causes and candidates covered her dress. "You think I oughta shoot him?" she asked, snickering, but her escort did not laugh.

"If you queers kept your mouths shut there wouldn't be any AIDS," he snapped.

Republicans poured into the God and Country rally inside a hotel across the street from the Astrodome. Delegates from around the country were in Houston to nominate George Bush for a second term in the White House and to celebrate right-wing values. The prayers and patriotic speeches drew the evangelical flank of the GOP. Exuberant Christian soldiers wearing red give-away Right to Life straw cowboy hats rushed past the small group of protestors.

The demonstrators made a lot of noise with whistles and chants. "ACT UP! FIGHT BACK! STOP AIDS! . . . BUSH AND QUAYLE SIDE BY SIDE, WE CHARGE YOU WITH GENOCIDE!" they yelled. Some wore stickers on their shirts that said BUTTFUCKING IS FUN; LOVE ME; LOVE MY PUSSY; I FUCK TO COME, NOT TO CONCEIVE.

The stickers and shouts, the anger and aggravation, all caused most of the rallygoers to hurry toward the air-conditioned comfort of the hotel ballroom and the security of a like-minded audience, yet the blue-haired woman and her escort stood like stones in the current. They gaped at the whirling activist who had tried to give them a condom.

"Honey," the escort said in astonishment, "I don't think that's a man."

"Darlin', you're so good-looking you better take a rubber."

The startled youngster, a husky poster boy, for an all-beef diet, jumped off the curb to avoid the taboo donation.

The voice, a smoker's bass created by nearly forty years of cigarettes, was deep even for a male. But a pair of breasts were obvious under the vertical black-and-white striped blouse that looked like a referee's uniform. Although there was no trace of rouge or lipstick, thick mascara and a layer of eyeshadow were concealed behind the dark, oversized feminine sunglasses. Long, straight red hair pulled back in a ponytail fell waist-length from beneath a rayon Mao cap. Unpolished fingernails, chewed low, were stained from nicotine. A couple of inches short of six feet, she wore flat, hard-soled moccasins that were the right length for a man her size.

Her audience was not receptive. Some delegates, who automatically grabbed every giveaway at the convention, snatched the condoms, then realizing what they had taken, shoved the invitations to sin back into the heretic's hand. Teenagers only took the condoms if their parents were not watching. Traditional kids follow traditional roles. Boys quickly stuffed the rubbers into their pockets, acting like they had an illicit use for the sidewalk samples. Tall girls with perfect posture studied the packages to get a fix on the unfamiliar key to forbidden fruit.

Leslie Elaine Perez was an expert. Sex had been her profession. She had started before she was a teenager, long before she was a woman. Leslie expected the God and Country crowd to despise her. She thrived on their fury, whether they masked their ire by muttering "bless you, bless you" between clenched teeth or just came right out and yelled, "You fags deserve to die." Making the most from rancor was a critical survival skill she had mastered, but she also found support from a friendly face nearby

The old woman wearing a frosted wig, who had a thin white scar across her throat, also reveled in the fun. "I always tell Leslie to keep it up, just keep it up," Sylvia Ayres said as she passed out condoms. "This is the way you get to the people," she explained with a voice raspy from thyroid surgery.

Leslie had spent most of her life living with or near her mother, Sylvia. They were separated when Leslie was on the lam from a murder charge and during her stretches in prison and an insane asylum, but they always returned to each other. Sylvia enjoyed giving away condoms as much as Leslie did. "This is the most wonderful thing I've ever done," she bubbled. Strong words from a mother who credited herself with saving her child from execution.

"I love to do this because it's so positive." Sylvia chuckled as she found another teenager willing to take a condom and an AIDS pamphlet.

They didn't have many allies left. Although Leslie had started the Houston chapter of the militant AIDS activist group ACT UP, she was no longer welcome in the ranks that had split from her failed attempt at leadership. She was a tyrant, alienated members charged, and never listened to anyone but herself. Critics said the demonstrations she planned were botched farces.

"I never could get nobody to turn out for nothing," Leslie admitted. Rival AIDS activists complained that her bad grammar, missing teeth, and tendency to get sidetracked damaged their cause. "They think I should go find a rock to crawl under and hide," she said.

Despite her troubles in the gay community, Leslie ran to head the local Democratic party machinery in 1990, and again in 1992. Election analysts think her name misled voters who believed they were casting ballots for a Hispanic female. The confusion boosted her into a runoff election to chair the Harris County branch of the party, but recognition brought media attention that exposed her forgotten past. "Killer Transsexual . . . former Death Row inmate . . . convicted of murder as Leslie Douglas Ashley."

In emotions, if not money, the trajectory of Leslie's life has matched the boom-and-bust pendulum in Houston, a city where the local economy went through the fiscal equivalent of a sex change by risking so many chips on a thrill ride with oil. Her identity switch also parallels the fabric of her hometown, which cannot decide if it is part of the Bible Belt or Sin City, brazenly trumpeting its wicked side. Palatial strip joints with million-dollar decor ("high-class titty bars" in local slang) service a population that buys more boxes of Girl Scout cookies than any other city in America.

Police maneuvers signaled the rally inside was about to break up, ending the lull in the bright afternoon. The weather was milder than anyone expected, "a record-low high for the day" Houston boosters crowed, ten degrees below normal for August. But the fierce Texas sun was still strong enough to simmer tempers in people unacclimated to the city's mind-bending dog-day heat and humidity. The police did not want sweaty demonstrators colliding with conservatives pumped high by pep talks from their heroes.

Squads of riot-control cops deployed themselves along both sides of the narrow sidewalk, an overkill display of force that took the steam from protestors by sheer numbers. The demonstrators were pressed into a thin space between the long rows of police officers who were wearing black rubber gloves sealed tight at the wrist by elastic cuffs, a standard precaution for confrontations with AIDS activists. With the protestors hemmed in, the top-ranking officer gave an order: "Everyone on the sidewalk must keep moving. Anyone who stops will be arrested for loitering."

The demonstrators could either march back and forth between the rows of menacing police or leave. Most of them left quickly, before the God and Country crowd emerged from the hotel, but Leslie remained. She picked up a sign she had brought along that carried the slogan WHAT ABOUT AIDS printed across a map of the United States. She raised the sign above her head and began pacing up and down the sidewalk. With every lap she took, her stride lengthened and her hips swayed more.

The cops were mesmerized by her prancing. One officer had heard about Leslie, but he had never seen her. "Is that Perez?" he muttered.

The cop beside him just grunted with an inflection that meant yes. Leslie seemed to be traveling back through the years, picking up the steps she left in her youth, when she had sashayed across the stage at drag bars or wiggled her wares at customers when she was hooking on the street. This was Leslie in full flower.

ONE

The Human Torch

1

On February 6, 1961, a young man in Houston came home to his mother's house in a neighborhood misnamed Magnolia Park. Nearby oil refineries poured out noxious fumes and the stink from a paper mill was awful when the wind blew off the Gulf of Mexico. Then and now, Magnolia Park was part of a larger barrio known as the East End. Anyone driving along Navigation Boulevard, a wide avenue beside the narrow sleeve of filthy sludge in the Houston Ship Channel, could see the wealth of the city came from the East End, but few of those dollars have ever been reinvested in the community.

From the street in front of his mother's house on Avenue I, Robert Reyna could see the source of that fugitive prosperity. Freighters from around the world were berthed at warehouses near the turning basin at the foot of the ship channel. Steam and gas flares churned from towers in the vast petrochemical complex that stretched beyond the horizon to Galveston Bay.

It was a cold night, almost freezing, and the street was wet from two days of rain. At around 8:30 that night, Reyna saw a sudden flash of fire in a vacant lot on the far side of 78th Street. He was not the first person who noticed the flames. A neighbor named Nick Valdez lived closer to the lot. His son had told him about the blaze, but Valdez just shrugged it off. People dumped garbage in the neglected property where the weeds grew five-feet high. Valdez assumed someone was burning a pile of trash.

The entire East End was dotted with tank farms that stored flammable liquids in residential neighborhoods. Zoning was still a dirty word in Houston. Although the ground was soaked, Robert

Reyna worried the flames might spread to tanks that were on the lot, so he called the fire department, which dispatched Number Twenty-two Pumper Company to a "grass fire" on the north side of the 7800 block of Avenue I.

One truck carrying four firemen responded. A thirty-one-year veteran named F. E. Blysard took the lead. Blysard grabbed a small water pump and walked into the weeds. A soggy mound of trash, however, was not what was burning. Nearby, about eight feet from the edge of the curbless asphalt street, he spotted the fire. As he stepped closer, he saw flames rising from the water in a drainage ditch. Then he recognized a familiar shape blazing in the tall, unmowed grass.

At first, Blysard thought the burning lump was a mannequin lying face down. The hair was on fire. Blysard put his foot beneath the sprawled figure and rolled it over. The body was nude, except for socks and an undershirt.

"We knew then it was a man," the firefighter said. "He was burned pretty bad."

Madeline Harlan woke up the next morning in her duplex cottage miles away from the patch of scorched grass left by the burning body in the vacant lot. Her small home faced Griggs Road, a busy four-lane thoroughfare where heavy traffic and the lack of zoning restrictions encouraged property owners to convert their houses into businesses. Mrs. Harlan was a widow in her fifties who supported herself by renting the spare half of her cottage.

For the past year, her tenant had been a small-time real estate agent named Fred A. Tones, who sold houses in the neighborhood. Mrs. Harlan answered his phone when he was out. She called herself his saleslady. Although she did not draw a salary and he did not need her, she did have an incentive for keeping an eye on him. His rent checks were her income and his cash flow had diminished lately. A few months before, Tones cut his expenses by subletting a room in his offices to a man whose occupation was unknown to her. In January, a FOR RENT sign appeared in the strip of grass along the curb in front of her duplex.

On that Tuesday morning in February, the radio weather report warned a norther was on the way. The frigid wind would blow away the rain, while plunging temperatures would kill tender shrubbery and small pets left outside. The morning news also reported a torch murder in the East End. No one knew the name of the victim, who had apparently been stripped, soaked with gasoline, and lit on fire.

Mrs. Harlan left her half of the duplex to open the Tones Realty office at about 9:00 A.M. Normally, the rooms were dark if she arrived before anyone else, but this morning the hallway light was on. "I was looking at the light and wondering why it was on," she said. "Later, I missed the television." A portable TV usually sat on a desk in a corner of the front office, which had been a living room when the unit was a residence. "After I missed the television, I looked down and saw some blood on the floor."

Mrs. Harlan remembered noises she heard coming from the office during the previous evening. "I thought he was over there working," she recalled. "I thought he was hammering." Perhaps the blood came from a cut Tones suffered while he was fixing something. Or, Mrs. Harlan could picture him hurting himself if he dropped the TV, then taking it with him without cleaning up. He might have been in a rush to take care of that cut.

She decided to tidy up the mess. Tones used the office kitchen as a storeroom for lawn signs and stacks of yellow newspapers, as well as for housekeeping supplies. Mrs. Harlan found a mop and washed away the blood. More dark stains on a mat inside the door puzzled her. Then she saw Tones's hat and tie in a bedroom he used as his private office. Mrs. Harlan had never met her tenant's wife, although they spoke once in a while over the telephone. Mrs. Tones looked up the number of an insurance agency downtown where Dorothy Tones worked as a clerk. The call came just after she arrived at the office. The realtor's wife was already frightened because her husband had not come home the night before. She hurried to Griggs Road.

The women introduced themselves at the duplex, then called the police. Mrs. Tones dialed the number herself. The solo officer who arrived was not trained to make a detailed investigation, but he noticed skidmarks made by large tires that ran across the driveway. The tracks looked like a big car must have backed up to the front door of the Tones Realty office.

For most people in Houston, February 7, 1961 was not a special day. The torch murder was background noise during a humdrum morning. But three hundred fifty miles to the east, the city of New Orleans was getting ready for the climax of the Mardi Gras season.

A mammoth white 1960 Lincoln Premiere, with sleek tail fins and heavy chrome, stopped in front of the Golden Age Mansion, a senior citizens home on the rundown fringe of the Garden District. The old folks home was operated by Mrs. Hortense Cooke, a roly-poly version of Blanche DuBois twenty years after the final curtain of *A Streetcar Named Desire*. She put poetry into everything she saw, including the business she ran. "A discriminating clientele of golden agers resides in the stately main building," she boasted. Mrs. Cooke saved less desirable rooms for travelers. "The annex I rent to transients." In New Orleans, these rear buildings are called slave quarters.

A young couple emerged from the Lincoln; they locked a German shepherd and a toy poodle with a fake jewel collar in the car as they walked to the front door. "They came in wearing dungarees and asked for a room," Mrs. Cooke remembered. "I sat and talked to them on the settee for quite awhile because I won't allow just anyone to stay here." She found the couple to be "lovely and polite."

The young man made a favorable impression on her. Mrs. Cooke admired his "golden auburn hair . . . red and long on his neck like a playwright." His complexion was "smooth and nice." She adored his smile, "He had teeth like pearls." A minor detail bothered her, "The only odd note was the way he giggled. He giggled all the time, like a schoolgirl." She decided the nervous affliction was friendly laughter.

Mrs. Cooke offered them room 8, with a private bath, for fifteen dollars a week, a stay that would extend until the following Tuesday, the crescendo of the carnival, Fat Tuesday. "It was the only room I had left," she said. Room 8 had just become available; she had checked it earlier that morning to make sure it was clean and ready to rent. The couple was lucky to find any vacancy, but they wanted to discuss their decision.

Mrs. Cooke recalled, "They went out and came back in about twenty minutes." They agreed to take the room and paid cash for a week in advance. Mrs. Cooke wrote out a receipt for Mr. and Mrs. Charles Adam, a name they gave her without identification, although she normally used Social Security cards to register her elderly guests. "They said they had none, that they had never worked, so I took them for people of means and didn't worry about them."

Her houseboy showed the couple to their room upstairs in the slave quarters behind the boarding house. Mrs. Cooke watched them wheel the big Lincoln into the garage beneath their room. License plates on the luxury car fueled her belief that her guests were wealthy young Texans who didn't have to earn a living. Everything she saw confirmed her notion. "They had some lovely clothes . . . a whole lot of beautiful clothes, no tinselly cheap evening clothes, but expensive ones . . . lovely clothes, beautiful clothes that glittered and shimmered in the sun as they took them upstairs." Their portable television also attracted her attention, "It was crème, with a little touch of gray."

About an hour after the couple settled into their room, they came down to the dining room for lunch. The girl, a teenager with a silver brace on her upper teeth, brought her poodle to the table and ate quietly. According to Mrs. Cooke, she "was very affectionate toward the dog, like a mother taking care of her child."

Charley Adam called his companion Joan. He was a few years older, in his early twenties, but was "giddy and acted childish, talking incessantly" as he entertained the senior citizens. "They thought he was a honeymooner," Mrs. Cooke said. She decided her guests were rich Texas newlyweds who had come to Mardi Gras to celebrate their marriage. They seemed so happy, she never suspected they were fugitives running from a torch murder.

Police officers swarmed through the duplex on Griggs Road. Lab experts scraped dry blood from the floor and the sidewalk outside, collected hair samples, and dusted the furniture for fingerprints. A team of homicide detectives talked to Mrs. Harlan, who described the bumps and thuds she had heard on the other side of the duplex wall during the previous evening, but she was too upset to give a detailed statement. Mrs. Tones was distraught. She could only tell the police that her husband's car, a white 1960 Lincoln Premiere, was missing. She had no idea why anyone would want to kill him. She said her husband was "friendly and well liked."

A cop tossed the bloody mop and soiled floormat into his car. An old-fashioned military bayonet with an eighteen-inch blade was in the victim's private office. A lab expert thought he saw the bayonet on a window shelf; a homicide detective believed it was on top of a filing cabinet. "It was dusty," Detective John Thornton said. "It seemed to me like it had gone quite awhile without being touched." He said that he carried the bayonet to a fingerprint specialist, who decided the potential weapon did not merit a microscopic examination.

The bayonet was not taken into custody. The police decided it was not relevant, but that long knife would resurface at the center of another life-or-death struggle where the losers might burn, except this battle would be fought in a courtroom.

Before the sleuths left the scene, they appointed Officer C.D. Mitchell to stay behind to deflect reporters and nosy neighbors.

He had been shivering in front of the Griggs Road duplex for about three hours when the solution to a mystery unfolded before him. It was about 4:30 and Officer Mitchell must have thought the man striding across the driveway was another snoop. Clinton McDaniel lived next door in a duplex that was almost identical to the cottage that Officer Mitchell was guarding. McDaniel was a pharmacy student at the University of Houston. He had been at the campus since seven-thirty that morning, almost two hours before Mrs. Harlan found the bloodstains. The cop and a radio station's mobile van (a "news wagon" to McDaniel) piqued his curiosity and he went over to see what had happened.

Before Officer Mitchell could order him to move along, McDaniel told the patrolman that he had seen a young couple enter the office around five o'clock the previous afternoon when he came home from school with a classmate. He and his friend drove past the duplex as the eyecatching couple walked toward the realty office. McDaniel had nudged his buddy to scope out the exotic pair. "It looked like two girls from the rear," the classmate remembered. The skinny man's tight Levi's stuck in his memory.

McDaniel knew the couple. By sheer coincidence, they were regulars at a drugstore where he worked part-time. They were inseparable and spent endless hours kibitzing at the soda fountain or browsing through the hair dyes and cheap cosmetics. McDaniel even gave Officer Mitchell their names. The "honeymooners" on the lam in New Orleans were Leslie Douglas Ashley and Carolyn Ann Lima, shutterbugs who constantly shot pictures of themselves. The pharmacy student steered the cops to a roll of undeveloped film the pair had brought to his drugstore over the weekend. The clerks always got a big kick out of peeking at the couple's snapshots. The photos were an under-the-counter joke because a fair share of the pictures always showed the unforgettable young man decked out in drag.

The language in the police report did not need words to describe him. "Ashley appeared to be a 'Q.' " An initial was enough. It was an obvious code for queer.

2

Leslie Douglas Ashley had met Carolyn Ann Lima in a lesbian bar. "She was just a baby," Leslie remembered. Carolyn was only seventeen and living with her mother in a little house perched on cinder blocks halfway between Harvard and Yale streets in the Heights, a lower-middle-class enclave bypassed during Houston's postwar boom. The files at Alexander Hamilton Junior High listed her IQ at 72, far below the broad 90 – 109 "normal intelligence" band. Being slow was not the only reason for her bad grades. An elementary school teacher sent home a dismal report card with the comment, "She doesn't seem to care."

Carolyn grew up in a Sun Belt soap opera. She was the third child in the marriage of Frank and Mae Lima. At the age of three, when her mother was pregnant with her little brother, Carolyn's father announced that he was in love with another woman. "I think he wanted to take me with him," Carolyn recalled, "but mother told him he'd have to take all four of us, so he just walked off." Frank Lima abandoned the family, and six weeks after Mae delivered her fourth child she enrolled at beauty school. "To learn how to make a living," Mae said. She soon opened a hair salon in her home and started to work.

"Mother was too busy to pay attention to me," Carolyn complained. "She wasn't too busy to pay attention to big sister though, she liked her."

Mae defended herself, "I never showed any partiality. I helped the one who needed me most."

Carolyn was not convinced. "Mother doesn't love me. She never did," Carolyn charged in an angry moment. "And the last

10

time I saw Father I was four years old."

Those brief visits usually came at court appearances when Mae dragged Frank before the law to pay for an appendectomy or braces for the older children. Then Frank moved west to escape those obligations. Mae had trouble keeping up with him; sometimes she thought he was in Arizona and other times she believed he was in Gallup, New Mexico. She knew he had a second family with three new children.

When she was twelve, Carolyn did not come home one night and Mae called the police, who listed her as a runaway. Carolyn refused to see any love in Mae's concern: "She caught me. She didn't much care, but she caught me." After that brief rebellion, they reached a truce. On the surface, Carolyn was obedient. She washed the dishes after dinner and came home before her ten o'clock curfew. Every Sunday, Mae took her children to a Church of Christ. Carolyn followed the hymns that were always sung a cappella, according to the strict doctrine of that faith. As an infant, she had been christened as a Catholic, her father's religion; in her teens, she was dunked in water and baptized into the Church of Christ.

Switching denominations did not help Carolyn's performance at school. Mae thought the only way to improve her daughter's grades might be "to sit in the classroom with her." Carolyn hid her defiance behind a shield of indifference. "She never said much or reacted strongly to things," Mae recalled. "She didn't have many friends. She'd just have one at a time. Maybe she talked about the others or something. She seemed popular enough. She just wasn't close to people."

Carolyn became a convincing liar. "I'd tell mother I was going to see some girls and slip off to meet a cute freckle-faced boy at the movies. Of course, I'd just cuddle with them, nothing bad. Mother never caught on. . . . She was working all the time."

Mae Lima had to work hard. Sixty or seventy dollars was a good week at the beauty parlor. With that paltry income, she supported four children and kept her family together. Mae paid the hefty dental bills for a false front tooth anchored by a silver brace that was put into Carolyn's mouth after a childhood playground accident.

Mae saw Carolyn as a dutiful daughter. Carolyn knew better. She liked to think of herself as "a real mean little bebopster . . .

hell on wheels." Five feet seven inches tall with hazel eyes, Carolyn's svelte figure rivaled Natalie Wood's in *Rebel Without a Cause*. She finished her first year at John H. Reagan Senior High, where Dan Rather had walked the halls before her, but Carolyn did not follow his fast-track footsteps. She had to carry a full load at summer school and was two years behind the other kids her age. To compensate, she signed up for morning classes at Reagan in the Heights, and registered at another school across town that offered classes at night.

Adding to her burden, Carolyn spent the scorching summer afternoons learning to be a hairdresser. Mae had scraped together $150 to pay the tuition for a six-month course at an "academy of beauty culture" in the Montrose area, which had been the city's best address prior to the Great Depression. By the summer of 1960, the money and status had moved on. Montrose was a mix of stubborn geriatrics unwilling or unable to leave and nonconformist newcomers creating a haven of bohemian tolerance. Homosexuals were building a refuge in Montrose that they were unable to build anywhere else in Houston.

Carolyn did not tell Mae that she quit her morning courses at Reagan the day she started beauty school. She spent more and more time talking about hairdos and fashion trends with her new friends, "older people" Mae called them. Getting away from her insular neighborhood and hanging out with the beauty school crowd liberated Carolyn. She was seventeen with a wild streak. Fear was not part of her personality, and she was willing to look in dark corners to find herself.

When she met Leslie Douglas Ashley, Carolyn forgot about her casual engagement to a Heights boy who was off in the army. "He let me have my own way about everything. I couldn't stand that. . . . I wanted a man to put his foot down." Leslie was different. "He puts his foot down if I lie. I lie lots. . . . " Carolyn couldn't praise Leslie enough. "I love him very much. He's kind, considerate, an ideal man."

3

"I was the first true drag queen this town ever saw," Leslie bragged. Leslie Douglas Ashley was twenty-two when he met Carolyn Ann Lima, and he had dressed in women's clothes since puberty. His favorite name was Renée "Cookie" LaMonte, but he insisted that his mother call him Bette Davis if he was feeling like a prima donna. When he wasn't wearing drag, his family knew him as Douglas. His life had been a wild ride of gender confusion, with constant mood swings veering between high camp hilarity and bottomless depression.

"I didn't know if I was a boy or a girl," Leslie remembered. He was an outcast, ridiculed and reviled, an unmistakable fairy in a city where a beer belly and the bone-crushing grip of a man's handshake were considered critical character traits.

His mother had left her own nest at age seventeen. Sylvia Kipperman's parents owned a shoe shop in Hot Springs, Arkansas. The quaint resort spa attracted visitors to soak in healing waters along a picturesque row of Victorian bathhouses while police winked at gambling in the illegal casinos that flourished from the Roaring Twenties until reformist politicians cleaned up Hot Springs in the 1960s. Joe and Elizabeth Kipperman were mortified when their only daughter, Sylvia, succumbed to the permissive winds and married a good-looking *goy*, a teenager named Leslie Sherman Ashley.

Almost immediately, their worst suspicions about mixed marriage were confirmed. Leslie Sherman Ashley found his friends on the wild side of town. He was arrested for stealing a brand-new Plymouth with one of his pals and sentenced to hard labor for two

13

years. Sylvia spent a year fending off that disgrace before he was paroled early. They had a son on January 3, 1938, a little more than nine months after Leslie Sherman was released. They named their baby Leslie Douglas Ashley, but the infant did not renew the floundering bond between his parents.

Sylvia claimed Leslie Sherman neglected their infant. He doubted the child was his, she said. According to her, he had an ex-convict's typical suspicions about his wife's fidelity while he was locked up. He also had an ex-convict's typical trouble finding work. The Ashleys were dirt poor. Sylvia said her baby never had enough to eat and she had to take him to the charity hospital, where he was treated for malnutrition. The frail child developed a heart murmur, which spurred Sylvia to coddle him even more.

Leslie Sherman Ashley joined the army, leaving his wife and son to shift for themselves. Sylvia could not turn to her parents because the useless fight to save their shoe shop during the Depression had left Sylvia's father with debilitating heart problems. Joe Kipperman died barely a year after his grandson was born. Sylvia went to work in a laundry and Leslie Douglas spent his days with babysitters. Even after her husband returned from the army with an honorable discharge that helped to restore his reputation, Sylvia considered him unreliable. Her anxiety and isolation made her personality more fragile, so she clung more tightly to her child.

Their relationship tightened as Leslie Douglas began to grow and the facial resemblance between mother and son increased. "I wanted him to be a boy, but I guess I should have wanted him to be a girl because he looked so much like me," Sylvia confessed. They marveled in front of mirrors, and posed together for photos that captured two smiles that were impossible to tell apart.

The obsessive bond between mother and son was another strain on a marriage already in distress. Sylvia and her husband bickered and separated constantly for ten years before they split up for good. Sylvia took her son to greener pastures in Houston, where her mother and only sibling, a brother ten years her junior, had moved after Joe Kipperman died. Sylvia did not stay single very long. Her new groom was from Tennessee, but he liked to be called Tex. Jim Ayres was in the photography business with her brother, and he ran a small advertising agency out of the boarding house where the Kipperman clan lived. He was six years younger than Sylvia, just thirteen years older than his stepson.

"There was a jealousy," Sylvia remarked. She referred to her son by his middle name as did all his family, "Douglas didn't like [Jim] because he didn't like the attention I gave him. . . . And I think Douglas resented him because he was young." Jim Ayres accepted that judgment, "I was too young to be seriously accepted by him as a father so I spoiled him, gave him what he wanted. . . . I tried to give him everything."

Instead of feeling pampered, Leslie felt displaced. Before he was a teenager he began staying out all night. At twelve, he was picked up by the police with a man he had met near one of the city's bus terminals. "The cops got us in different rooms," Leslie recalled. "They'd ask one of us if we did such and such, then they'd run and ask the other one." The adult was charged with molesting Leslie. Sylvia blamed her son's problems on the incident, but Leslie minimized that night, "It wasn't the first time." At twelve, Leslie was familiar with fleeting sexual exchanges around bus terminals. He was already looking for his niche in the shadows.

Sylvia said Leslie had nightmares. She thought he became more nervous as the sun went down and that his fear of terrifying dreams gave him insomnia that often kept him awake until dawn. Typical teenage jobs like an afternoon newspaper route or ushering at a movie theater turned into brief fiascos. He developed a high-pitched nervous giggle he was unable to control, and minor frustrations triggered childish temper tantrums.

His uncle, Ted Kipperman, thought Leslie might have been molested by the babysitters who watched him as a young child while Sylvia worked in the laundry. Jim Ayres believed there was a different cause behind Leslie's troubles, "My wife grew very close to him, too close. She overprotected him." Leslie described himself as "a sissified child." No one in the family was trained to diagnose the complicated mix of environment and biology that was shaping him.

At an early age, Leslie played dress up with his mother's clothes. Around the time he turned thirteen, he started collecting his own female outfits. The possibility that he could have been born different was not a topic for debate inside or outside the circle of medical science during his childhood.

Because Leslie could not cope with his problems at home, he

frequently ran away. "Constantly running," Sylvia moaned. Once he ran all the way to Hot Springs; another time, when Leslie was in the ninth grade, Sylvia agreed to let him live with his father. "There were always indications that he needed psychiatric treatment, but people are funny," Leslie Sherman remembered. "I guess we always thought it would clear itself up. It didn't . . . but my son was never violent. He went to the other extreme. He loved pets and growing things. He became over-attached to them, too sentimental."

Jim Ayres said Sylvia kept her son "from sports and other manly pursuits." Leslie Sherman Ashley tried to make up for that absence, "I love to hunt. . . . I bought him a rifle, but he couldn't stand to use it. My son didn't want to kill then. He had many things wrong with him, but he wasn't aggressive." Leslie took up the clarinet instead.

School was torture for him because his effeminate mannerisms made him a social outcast. He was skinny with dark eyes above high cheek bones, and his face was scarred by teenage acne that thrived on his emotional disturbance. Leslie's most distinctive physical feature was his hair. "He had gorgeous hair," Martha Terrill remembered. She and Leslie were classmates at San Jacinto High School when Leslie came back to Houston to start the tenth grade. "It was long and wavy, and he dyed it a different color almost every week. Black, red, orange . . . " Unaware of his afterschool dress habits, she said, "Leslie was a nice boy. He was pretty quiet, except for the giggling."

Martha Terrill and Leslie were in biology class together. "Miss Babbs had suffered a stroke and she couldn't remember the students' names, so she assigned everybody a seat and a number according to the alphabet. . . . Leslie sat on the front row and he was Boy Number One." His compulsive giggle distracted the whole class. "Miss Babbs was always saying, 'Boy Number One, stop giggling!' " Leslie tried to explain that he was not giggling for any reason, but he couldn't stop. "He said it was a nervous condition," Martha Terrill remembered.

"Everybody knew Leslie was peculiar," Martha Terrill continued, "but he was avoided, not persecuted, at least by the girls. I can't say about the boys."

Leslie's mother pictured her son differently, "He always had a persecution complex. He always felt like people were talking about him and nobody liked him."

Leslie said he never made a single friend during his entire childhood, "not one running buddy," but he didn't change to win acceptance. While at San Jac, Leslie was arrested when he went to a Halloween party in drag. "I saw the handwriting on the wall then," Jim Ayres said. Boy Number One would not grow out of this phase.

After the tenth grade, Leslie quit school. Algebra stumped him. "Biology too," Leslie said, wincing. "All those bugs, and dissecting animals."

Life at home could be chaotic too. Leslie's grandmother lived with them. Elizabeth Kipperman suffered from a muscular coordination problem, but her children had not consulted a neurologist. An osteophath called her "spastic." She had a speech defect that worsened as her condition deteriorated. And the extended family shared the same roof with Sylvia's brother, Ted, just nine years older than Leslie, who owned Kipperman's Camera Shop, a store that became the umbrella for the family enterprises. Sylvia worked as the business manager, keeping the books. Jim Ayres had a job there as well.

Before the camera shop became their realm, the family had consolidated its commercial ventures around Douglas Studios, a portrait salon that drummed up customers with a boiler-room telephone crew of middle-aged women who sold on commission. Leslie went to work hand-tinting photographs in the years just before cheap color film made that skill obsolete. And he also worked as a delivery boy, running eyeglasses around downtown Houston for an optical company. He also learned to grind lenses, but Leslie did not have the patience for time-consuming, detailed work and he lacked any incentive to serve a life sentence hunched over a workbench.

Instead, he discovered prostitution and began working the streets in drag when he was still a teenager. He fooled a lot of tricks who paid for French dates, slang for fellatio, but the police caught on to him. When he was picked up as a juvenile, they released him to the custody of his family. After he turned seventeen, vice officers charged him with loitering eight times within two years.

The year after the police began booking him as an adult, Sylvia took Leslie to see the family's general practitioner. Because Leslie was against the visit, he got into an argument with Sylvia during the exam. Dr. H. Newell Taylor concluded the emotional outburst "had the characteristic of one much younger" and labeled it "an immaturity type of reaction." He also diagnosed a moderate hyperthyroid condition that overstimulated Leslie's metabolism, but the medications he prescribed were not intended to treat the anguish that fueled Leslie's tantrums.

"He obviously was suffering. He displayed marked tension even when he wasn't in the midst of an emotional outburst." Dr. Taylor suggested psychiatric help, but Sylvia said no. "Economics were given as her reason," Dr. Taylor recalled. Without psychiatric advice, Leslie's difficulty remained the same. For three years, Sylvia brought him to the general practitioner. She never lost faith in Dr. Taylor's medical skill, but she always ignored his unwavering recommendation to take her son to a psychiatrist. It was a contradictory rut that canceled any hope of relieving Leslie's emotional pain.

"I had no money and I was afraid they might take him and put him in a mental institution." Sylvia had another fear as well, "I was ashamed. . . . I was afraid of what they might tell me."

Without professional counseling, Leslie continued to run away whenever pressure overwhelmed him. Now that he was older, he traveled farther. San Francisco. Chicago. "Always running, always running," Sylvia wailed.

Leslie worked the streets as a transvestite prostitute. "I went to L.A. too, but I couldn't make it there." New York was his favorite destination. He kept thumbing back to the Big Apple, where he hustled on the Upper West Side. "I had my hair real long and I stuck a fall on top of that." Leslie liked to hook in fake leopard skin pedal pushers and tight sweaters. Three dollars bought a French job in a nearby restroom. For five dollars, Leslie took his dates to his room. He was proud of his technique, especially his speed. "I was up and down them tubes like nobody's business."

As much as he enjoyed his life on the streets in New York, he never stayed long. "I always came back to mother," Leslie said, "but I was way too much for my family to handle."

In Houston, he tried living on his own in cheap apartments. He went without food so he could buy his favorite statues, especially fat Buddhas with their arms raised in exaltation. His private environment was a kitschy jungle filled with Asian statues and tall plants, both real and plastic. He populated his secret world with a zoo of cats and dogs rescued from animal shelters. Leslie's menagerie was not housebroken. Flies buzzed on excrement and plates of spoiled pet food. A putrid stench filled his apartments. Sylvia once found a dead chicken neglected on the floor. As soon as a landlord discovered the filthy conditions, Leslie was evicted. Sylvia would pack up his treasures and Leslie would move back home until he could find another apartment for himself.

Whether he lived with his family or on his own, Leslie's torment constantly simmered and always threatened to boil over. He scarred his wrists with the blade on a tape dispenser in a half-hearted effort to kill himself. In another fit of despair, he took an overdose of pills. During a period when he rented an apartment next to a service station, his mind dropped into a deep depression. He called Sylvia and begged her to come over, but she refused. Leslie threatened to kill himself if she did not change her mind, but Sylvia stood her ground. Later, she had second thoughts and began to worry. She called the attendant at the service station, who agreed to check on Leslie. The attendant found him groggy inside the apartment with gas hissing from the stove.

Leslie wanted a sex change operation from the time he heard the procedure was possible, when he was around seventeen, but the surgery was out of the question for a Texas teenager during the mid-1950s. Sylvia thought Dr. Taylor had given her son some medical advice that did not require a scalpel. Somehow she came to believe Dr. Taylor had prescribed marriage as a remedy for Leslie's troubles. Dr. Taylor later dismissed that idea as a figment of her imagination. Leslie was much too immature to be a husband, and Dr. Taylor presumed his patient was gay with no interest at all in the opposite sex, but Leslie was willing to try any solution to ease his mental turmoil.

At eighteen, he got involved with a girl he called his "wife." Their romance did not last, but a couple of years later he tried again. Leslie set his sights on a young Mexican-American woman he met through his family's photography business. Her name was Rosemary, which she usually shortened to Rose. She fell for him too. Leslie might have seemed to be an unlikely spouse, but he could deflect hostility and pain with his quick, camp wit. And women loved his beautiful hair.

Leslie married Rose and moved into her East End neighborhood, far from Sylvia, in a corner of Houston known as Magnolia
Park near the heavy industry along the ship channel. Late in the
spring of 1959, Rose became pregnant. Leslie had enough trouble
being a breadwinner, but the prospect of becoming a father
strung him even tighter. He and Rose fought constantly. During
one battle, he threw a television across the room. Time after
time, he left Rose at her mother's house and drove away, but he
always returned after a few hours and they always made up.

In 1960, Rose gave birth to their baby. The burden of a child
made the marriage worse. Leslie slapped Rose during one argument before he dumped her with her mother. They reconciled
after a day apart, but Sylvia persuaded them to seek counseling
from the Jewish Family Service.

According to the case history, this was not the first time Leslie
had hit his wife during an argument. The counselor was very clear
about the reason for the marital problems. "The difficulty lies in
his recreational activities. He seems drawn to those places where
queers hang out, and where people are queers. He invites them
to his home and takes his wife to these places. She has been very
upset about this, and this is the greatest reason for their quar-
rels." The director of the Jewish Family Service cleaned up the
language in the final prognosis. The union was destined to col-
lapse because Leslie was "unable to adjust to normal married
life."

The unhappy couple split up in the summer of 1960. Leslie
moved back to a smothering mother, a stepfather he resented, an
uncle who was ashamed of him, and a handicapped grandmother
verging on senility with an illness that was finally diagnosed as
cerebral palsy. Home was hardly a sanctuary where he could
recover from his failure.

Gay old-timers remember the early sixties in Houston as the
era of "Park in the dark and sprint for the bar." Leslie was too
flamboyant to be discreet. "I never hid nothing," Leslie gloated.
"I was always wide open."

The Pink Elephant and the Desert Room were the most popular "show bars" for female impersonator acts. Despite Leslie's
boast, he was not the city's first drag queen, much less its most

popular. One of his detractors noted a basic handicap, "Leslie was
never one of the world's great beauties." The detractor gave him
credit for persistence, "Leslie tried and tried and tried." To com-
pete with the other female impersonators, he needed a retinue.
Life would have been much easier with a seamstress to sew his
gowns, as well as a hairdresser to keep his wigs combed, and his
own long tresses dyed a beautiful color.

Leslie met Carolyn Lima just two months after his disastrous
marriage ended. Although she could not make costumes, Carolyn
knew how to care for hair and she quickly became much more
than his beautician. Jim Ayres remembered that Leslie "was all
broken up by the divorce. He and Carolyn formed this strange
attachment. I think she sort of became his mother in a pyschologi-
cal way." They both were tenth-grade dropouts and children from
broken marriages during a time when divorce still carried a
stigma. Their sexuality was up for grabs, and they locked on to
each other like Hansel and Gretel skipping into a Grimm fairy
tale. A mutual trance made them oblivious to any reality beyond
the spell they cast on each other.

"We were very sexually compatible," Leslie said. "I really
learned to satisfy her. She was oversexed with me."

They were looking for ways to distance themselves from their
families. Just before Thanksgiving, less than a week after Leslie
received his divorce decree, they found the right place. Using
Ashley as their last name, Leslie and Carolyn rented their new
home at 1205 Truxillo as brother and sister. It was a spacious
unfurnished apartment costing forty-five dollars a month in a clus-
ter of three white-frame buildings owned by a widow.

Madge Duncan Staples, the landlady, lived upstairs in one of
the buildings that she referred to as her "estate." Her small
domain on the corner of the block was overgrown with vegetation
and the buildings had begun to buckle. She managed her estate
like a proper cash-poor dowager while her mind dwelled on the
past. The address had been fashionable many years before when
she and her husband bought the property, but that bygone era
had vanished along with bathtub gin and raccoon coats. Now, pot-
holes cratered the boulevards and the derelict mansions seemed
haunted.

For Carolyn, the move instantly granted her most urgent
desire—independence. Busy at her beauty parlor miles away,

Mae Lima never went to inspect her teenage daughter's first apartment away from home. At first, Carolyn said she had moved in with girlfriends. She finally told Mae about Leslie at a Christmas dance for beauty parlor operators. Carolyn said they were engaged. When she eventually got around to introducing her mother to Leslie, Carolyn claimed they were not living in sin because they had eloped. Mae never raised an eyebrow, although Leslie wasn't exactly the dreamboat image of a perfect son-in-law.

Mae believed that she kept her brood under close supervision. "I was always strict with my children. Carolyn hadn't missed church in two or three years until she was married." Mae lived by the philosophy: What I don't know won't hurt me. That delusion, however, would soon be destroyed.

Leslie could not break away from his mother as easily. Sylvia said she "very rarely, very very rarely" went a day without seeing her son. Less than a five-minute car ride separated Leslie's apartment from his family's red-brick bungalow on Wentworth, which was just outside the boundaries of Riverside Terrace. The city's most prosperous Jews congregated in Riverside because they were excluded from River Oaks, Houston's playpen for oil barons. Jewish life revolved around this golden ghetto of splendid mansions, but the neighborhood had begun to unravel. The NAACP targeted Riverside for integration in the 1950s. Blockbusting by well-heeled African-Americans launched a wave of white flight that turned the golden ghetto into the real thing. Houston wouldn't see real estate values fall so far and so fast until oil prices cratered in 1986 when the whole city went up for sale at bargain-basement prices.

By the end of 1960, the fate of the house on Wentworth was sealed. It was only a matter of time before integration made the short leap from Riverside, but no one in Leslie's family could predict the hysteria that was about to grip their hearts. Their trauma would have nothing to do with racism or the long-range future of property investments. Very soon, this family and a single mother in the Heights would have to scrape together every penny they could beg or borrow. They would need all the money they could raise to keep Leslie and Carolyn from being strapped into the electric chair.

4

Carolyn practiced her beauty school assignments on Leslie. He was a patient model and spent hours in curlers. Carolyn tried new styles on him. She said he was her guinea pig. She dyed his gorgeous hair a different tint every Saturday night, and he encouraged her to experiment with bright Crayola colors that made his elaborate coiffures look pink like cotton candy or as yellow as a stick of margarine.

His family called him Douglas, but to Carolyn he was Cookie, a nickname that was part of his persona when he took the stage to lip-sync popular tunes at the Desert Room or Pink Elephant as the Amazing, Dynamite Renée "Cookie" LaMonte! Leslie loved to pose in drag, so they flashed roll after roll of snapshots of each other. Because they didn't own a car, Leslie and Carolyn walked their undeveloped film a few blocks to a Walgreen's drugstore, where the soda fountain became one of their favorite haunts. They spent long afternoons sipping soft drinks and yakking about wigs or costume jewelry. Their lives became a lazy blur of homemade hairdos, hamburgers, and Cokes.

"He makes me laugh," Carolyn recalled, smiling about those early days. "We laughed all the time. I never had so many laughs." She said Leslie liked to play records and dance naked around the apartment chanting praise for Buddha. He charged her imagination with tall tales of the Big Apple and they talked about moving to New York, but Carolyn wanted to finish beauty school first. Because she spent so much time goofing off with Leslie, she was hopelessly behind in her lessons. Carolyn did not graduate on schedule in November and could not go to the state capital in

Austin with the rest of her class for a two-day licensing test.

Sylvia was jealous of Carolyn. She was devastated by the way Carolyn monopolized her son. "I tried to talk to him several times about her, but he refused to listen to me," Sylvia said. "I could never talk to him about her when she was around." That meant Sylvia could hardly talk to him at all. "She was always with Douglas, always with Douglas," Sylvia repeated. "They reminded me of Siamese twins."

Their love life worked in the bedroom, but they also got along well because their precocious sexual appetites included prostitution. Leslie already knew the ropes about street hooking; Carolyn was a quick study, a lot quicker than she had been in school or beauty college. She began working bus stops a few blocks from the Truxillo apartment. San Jacinto High was right around the corner and adventurous boys started coming by the apartment after school. She tacked notes for them on the front door when she wasn't home. "Waiting for the bus on Main Street." They could not pay much, "different prices," Carolyn said. Five dollars was the boys' limit, so she and Leslie started marketing volume.

Leslie dressed in drag and they both peddled French dates. Leslie took on as many boys as he could so Carolyn could avoid dealing with them until she mastered her craft. The silver brace anchoring her false tooth slowed her down. The boys might show up wanting Carolyn, but after Leslie brought them off with his assembly-line technique they weren't so demanding. The high school boys had no idea they were saving their lunch money to have a man go down on them.

It could have been early in the month or closer to the middle. It might have been after Christmas, neither Leslie nor Carolyn could remember the exact day in December. At the time, the date did not seem important. Carolyn recalled that it was morning, just before noon at the latest. A Saturday or Sunday, she wasn't sure. She was wearing "slim jims," tight slacks also known as toreador pants. Leslie was still in his pajamas when Carolyn took a small red throw rug out to the front porch. They were chatting through the living room window while she shook dirt and crumbs from the rug. A white Lincoln sedan lumbered up Truxillo on the opposite side of the narrow street. When the driver saw the shapely teenager, he hit his brakes and threw the big car into reverse.

Leslie believed Carolyn knew the score from the start. "He stopped the car, and she said, there's a trick there. . . . He was motioning for her to come to the car."

Carolyn put down the red rug and walked to the street. She chatted with the driver, then she stepped around the huge Lincoln and climbed into the passenger seat. The driver told her that he was a real estate agent "hunting for property," Carolyn said. "He was going to talk to some man about property," but he was ready for a break. "He asked me if I would get some coffee with him and he wanted to discuss business with me." Her business, not his. They did not go far, just a few blocks to a drive-in restaurant where carhops could wait on them. "We got a cup of coffee and we went by some park." She let him take the lead. "We were discussing business and he wanted to come back to the apartment."

Leslie expected them, although he didn't change out of his pajamas. "I was watching for them every few minutes at the front door and I saw them when they drove up." He retreated farther into the apartment when Carolyn brought her trick inside, less than half an hour after they met. Leslie hovered in the shadows and exchanged a glance with Carolyn. They were both positive the trick never saw him. Carolyn completed what she called her "professional date." She said she let the trick set the price. The big Lincoln impressed her and she did not want to sell herself short by underbidding the going rate with rich men. The trick paid her twenty-five dollars, "voluntarily," she claimed.

"He gave me his card and he said when I wanted to meet him again to call him." Her new customer was satisfied, but he wasn't taking any chances. "He told me when I called, if his wife answered the phone to play like I was asking about property and not tell her no names."

As soon as the trick split, Leslie said he and Carolyn hopped in the sack with each other. Oral sex was their favorite passion.

Fred A. Tones was a little man with a big car. Just five feet four inches tall, he weighed less than 150 pounds and dyed his thinning hair dark. He would celebrate his forty-fifth birthday next April 27, four months after his first date with Carolyn. Tones ran his own real estate agency, a one-man operation, strictly small-time. He roamed around looking for homes to represent, and he kept the trunk of his Lincoln stuffed with cardboard filing boxes and Tones Realty lawn signs. His green plastic briefcase was crammed with paperwork. One of his competitors called him "a good real estate salesman of the high pressure type."

The area where he worked was criss-crossed by sprawling diagonal road—Telephone Road, Mykawa Road, Old Spanish Trail (usually shortened to O.S.T.). Griggs Road intersected them all at random angles, and residential neighborhoods were tucked into triangles and diamonds carved by the diagonal roads. The tract homes in these subdivisions were built for the salt of the earth, foremen and service managers, teachers and clerical employees, workers on the cusp between blue-collar and lower management whose wages were rising with the international economy's reliance on oil. Many of them could buy their homes with VA loans. One neighborhood had streets named for memorable battles from both World Wars—Iwo Jima, Guadalcanal, Ardennes, as well as for military heroes like Doolittle, Pershing, and Eisenhower.

Tones was a veteran too. After his army discharge, he went to work in a factory in New Britain, "the hardware city," in central Connecticut. He did not stay there long before he moved his wife and baby son to Chicago. They soon returned to Connecticut, then bounced back to Chicago again, where the itch to push on for a fresh start in unfamiliar geography overwhelmed him after four years. Fred A. Tones could not stay in one place very long.

By the time Tones migrated south in 1952, he and his wife, Dorothy, had three children. The oldest, a boy, had started school; their younger son was in his terrible twos; and they had an infant girl. The move would not be easy. Tones had just turned thirty-six by his own count, but like millions of men in the early 1950s when everything seemed possible, he wanted more.

He spent the next five years in Pasadena, Texas, the aromatic ship channel suburb with a skyline of petrochemical refineries. A realtor named George Billingsley put him to work in 1957, just a few months after Tones moved his family into Houston, but the new salesman on the staff was a restless scrambler. Tones left Billingsley and Company once, then returned briefly before quitting for good. After seven years in Texas, he was ready to be his own boss. Like a lot of salesmen, he put more confidence in himself than he deserved.

Tones hung out his shingle in 1959 at an office near the strategic spot where Griggs and O.S.T. ran together. He hired a salesman and a full-time secretary, but his wife hedged their big gamble. Although Dorothy Tones held a real estate license, she kept her secure job with an insurance agency downtown. Her income would be the family cushion if her husband's master plan went sour. Within six months, Tones Realty had to scale back. Both employees moved on, and the business relocated to less expensive space in half of a converted cottage on an anonymous strip facing Griggs Road. Tones kept a separate telephone line with his realty number that rang at his home, which was just two blocks away from his office. That explains why he wanted Carolyn to say she was calling about real estate in case his wife or one of the kids answered. He didn't need any headaches from teenage prostitutes.

Tones put a premium on his respectable front. He was a devout Catholic, a pillar of the parish at St. Peter the Apostle Church. He loved the camaraderie and the costumes of the Knights of Columbus. He even wore a gold ring that showed off his status in that religious fraternity, but a tattoo etched into his right forearm, of a crab reaching for three stars between its claws, seemed to clash with his pious facade. In fact, his entire personality was riddled with contradictions. When he met Carolyn Lima, Fred A. Tones was struggling to stay afloat while he maintained a wheeler-dealer's flashy appearance. After he sublet an office in his half of the duplex, the landlady, who lived in the other half, began to keep closer tabs on him. "We were not very busy," Madeline Harlan said.

Despite his cash-flow problems, Tones used his credit to splurge—his 1960 Lincoln Premiere was fresh off the dealer's lot when he met Carolyn. The sparkling white four-door sedan had power steering, power brakes, air-conditioning, and thick, white carpets covered with ebony mats to match the rest of the interior, which was done in sharply contrasting black and white.

Jim Vickery ran his own real estate company on Griggs Road just a block from Tones's office. Their paths crossed that December. "I asked him how he was doing. He said, 'Very good. I sold thirty-one houses over the last month.' That was very good. That would've amounted to around six or seven thousand dollars in commissions." Vickery was suspicious, "I wondered at that. My business was way down and the real estate business in this section of town was getting awful slow." The neighborhood was about to be integrated. "I'd have been happy if I could've sold thirty-one houses in six months, so would anybody else out here, but he'd bought that big white Lincoln and they don't give those things away."

Fred A. Tones played a good game. He knew appearances could be deceiving.

A couple of days after their first encounter, Carolyn dialed the office number on the business card Tones had given her. Her new trick came right over and Carolyn made a quick twenty-five dollars without telling Leslie.

The first time Tones met Leslie was part farce, part yawn. Tones swung by their apartment unannounced, around 8:30 or 9:00 at night. Leslie answered the door in drag, Carolyn wasn't home. "I was on the bus stop," she recalled. Tones knew nothing about Carolyn's roommate. "He didn't come there to see me," Leslie remembered. Tones had a friend with him, "a business acquaintance," Leslie guessed.

Leslie told them where to find Carolyn. Tones did not waste any time getting her, the bus stop was around the corner, but Leslie was wrong about Tones's lack of interest in him. The real estate salesman needed a girl for his pal. Five minutes after Tones left to pick up Carolyn, the big Lincoln returned to the apartment. Carolyn went in alone to talk Leslie into joining a double date. He left Truxillo in his full regalia—a tight black sweater, leopard-skin pedal pushers, and a dark brown wig. Carolyn rode beside Tones, Leslie got in the backseat with the "business acquaintance."

Carolyn could not recall if she introduced Leslie as her sister. She thought she described him as her girlfriend. She called him Rose, the name of Leslie's ex-wife. "Carolyn couldn't think of the name Renée," Leslie explained. "She would come up with the name of Myrtle or something." Better Rose than Myrtle. Tones's friend thought Rose "had a deep voice for a woman," according to Carolyn. Leslie was not impressed with his match either, "He was a Texan, wore boots, and looked real country." Tones's friend was drunk and Leslie did not bother to remember his name.

Tones and his pal broke out a fifth of whiskey when they pulled into a drive-in restaurant not far from the Truxillo apartment. Leslie helped them with the booze, but Carolyn did not drink. The Heights, where she grew up, was a "dry" neighborhood, liquor was not sold there. Although she was wild and promiscuous, Carolyn never developed a taste for alcohol. The double date disintegrated into hours of apathy as they moved from drive-in to drive-in while Carolyn nodded off in the front seat and Leslie fended off his date's clumsy advances.

Around 2:00 A.M., maybe later, the Lincoln rumbled to a stop in front of the Truxillo apartment. Leslie's date had passed out. Despite her exhaustion, Carolyn let Tones come into the apartment alcove with her for about ten minutes. Carolyn claimed she did not have sex with him and no money changed hands. Leslie did not make a fuss, he was glad to finally crawl out of the backseat where he had been trapped with the unconscious drunk.

The stupefying date was a night to forget, but Tones became a steady customer. "I seen him a lot," Carolyn said. He even asked her to be his secretary, but she couldn't stand being cooped up from nine to five so she turned him down. They got together more often than Leslie realized. Carolyn counted five dates with Tones during December. Leslie only knew about three: the morning he stayed in the shadows when Carolyn met Tones, the marathon double date in drag, and the night he came home and discovered Tones inside the Truxillo apartment with Carolyn.

Leslie made his presence known "about five minutes after we got through," Carolyn recalled. Leslie wore men's clothes, but he and Carolyn were prepared, they had standard introductions for each of his identities. Carolyn told Tones what Leslie told their landlady—that they were brother and sister. She only called him Cookie in private; for tonight, with Tones, he was Douglas.

Tones did not hurry home to his wife and kids. Sex made him thirsty, so they all piled into the Lincoln and hit another drive-in, the Pig Stand, part of a regional chain out of Dallas that specialized in barbecued pork sandwiches. Maybe Tones had become comfortable with Carolyn, perhaps Leslie's company made him feel like taking a risk. He parked his Lincoln and they walked inside together. It was the first time that he had let himself be seen out of his car with either of them. They could have sat at the counter, but they chose a booth instead.

Neither Carolyn nor Leslie knew when Tones guessed Douglas

and Rose were the same person. He was not as easy to fool as high school boys who paid chump change for French dates. When the moment of revelation came, Tones was not repelled. He was aroused.

5

Leslie and Carolyn rang in 1961 by adding a hungry mouth to the menagerie of four cats and tropical fish they kept in their apartment. They claimed that they found the silver French poodle in a supermarket parking lot during the first week of the new year. The dog obviously had an owner because, as Carolyn said, it was "trimmed down" and wearing a collar studded with colored glass. "We couldn't see who it belonged to so we just took it with us," Carolyn had shrugged when she recounted finding the new pet. "We looked in the paper too." They named the poodle Fifi.

Leslie turned twenty-three on January 3, 1961. The year was off to a good start. "We had loads of fun," Leslie remembered. But their life was not completely carefree. Carolyn needed to take the cosmetology licensing test in Austin during February. Mae Lima had sacrificed to pay her daughter's beauty school tuition, and Carolyn had already missed the exam once; she had to try the test, no matter how slim her chance to pass, to avoid disappointing her mother.

Around the middle of January, the beauty school began to make registration arrangements. Thirteen girls were on the roster. Carolyn Lima was number twelve, but the way her luck was about to turn she should have been number thirteen.

For Tones Realty, 1961 began dismally. James Vickery, the realtor with an office a block up Griggs Road, heard rumors that Tones quit selling homes to concentrate on vacant property in January. He believed the speculation when Tones called for information about a plot of undeveloped property near the end of the

month. Vickery's company owned a "block book," a collection of
tract maps detailing the layout of every lot in the city. Tones
apparently bought himself a luxury Lincoln and paid for sex with a
teenage prostitute instead of investing in the maps that were a
basic tool of his trade.

When a FOR RENT sign appeared outside of his office at Mrs.
Harlan's duplex, it became obvious that his business was in trouble. Tones and Carolyn saw less of each other in January, "about
twice every two weeks," according to her. His financial problems
forced him to cut back on their trysts, but he always played the
big shot and took Leslie and Carolyn on tours of drive-in restaurants during his weekly trips to Truxillo. No matter where else
they went, the Pig Stand remained their final destination. "Every
time she had a date with him we went up there," Leslie
remarked. The Pig Stand was the only place Tones would be seen
with them.

Spending time with Carolyn and Douglas, as he came to know
Leslie, gave Tones an idea. "He asked me sometime if me and
Douglas and him could have a three way date," Carolyn said. "He
asked me to ask Douglas." She continued, "He said he used to go
with a young boy and they really enjoyed it." Carolyn said Tones
told her exactly what he wanted from Leslie. "In the rear," she
bluntly stated. Tones had tried to talk Carolyn into anal intercourse, but he did not persuade her, and she did not expect Leslie
would do it either. "I told him I didn't think Douglas liked that,
but I would ask him."

She was right, but Leslie was always interested in making more
money. He and Carolyn were turning tricks with adults and keeping up the afternoon assembly line of French dates with the high
school kids. They augmented their income with handouts from
their families and by hocking photo equipment at pawnshops.
"Probably stolen from me," Ted Kipperman grumbled. Security at
his camera shop was lax.

On January 31, with money in their pockets, Leslie and Carolyn
went to a used car lot within walking distance from their apartment. A four-door 1953 Packard Clipper impressed them. It was a
transitional model, heavy and square like a sober postwar tank,
with an awkward, unconvincing lurch toward the snazzy stylings
that came along in the late 1950s. The paint had faded so badly
that no one agreed on the color. Some said gray, others said blue.

The finish was dull, but there was plenty of chrome. A lightning bolt of silver trim ran from the front fender to the tail lights; chrome tips created an early hint of the exaggerated tail fins that were still on Detroit drawing boards in 1953. The cash price was $260. Taxes and finance charges increased the total to $323.25. Leslie paid $120 down and signed his full name to the contract. He turned the keys over to Carolyn, "She always drove." Carolyn said they cruised in the Packard "all the time." Leslie agreed, "while it was working we did."

The car was a lemon and broke down shortly after they bought it, stopping while they were idling in traffic. "It just went dead while we were sitting there," Carolyn complained.

The Packard stopped again a few days later and stranded Leslie miles from home. He offered to barter the $5.50 towing fee for hauling the car to the Truxillo apartment. "He said, 'Just a minute, if you want to come in I have a nice young lady inside,' " the tow truck driver recalled. "I'm a married man." The driver did not yield to temptation. "I don't go for that stuff, and he went back inside and came back with the money."

Trouble with the Packard was not their worst problem. Near the end of January, their teenage customers turned hostile. Leslie and Carolyn each put their own slant on the reason for the conflict. Leslie said a few of the boys saw him bleaching his hair; they suddenly realized they had been getting head from a man. "That's how it was, that started the whole thing," Leslie moaned.

Carolyn told a different version. She was the center of her story, "They wanted about four of them to come in at one time and I didn't want that." She preferred to run an orderly business. "I just wanted one coming in at a time because I didn't want no trouble." Instead of going along with her, the boys showed up in bigger groups, fifteen and twenty at a time. They parked in front of the Truxillo apartment every night while they hooted and hollered on the sidewalk.

Whether their motive was to bash Leslie or gangbang Carolyn, the teenagers' rage erupted on Friday, February 3. Carolyn came home about six that evening and found a note from Tones asking her to call him. She left to use a pay phone because she and Leslie had never had their own telephone installed at the Truxillo apartment. When she did not reach Tones, she decided to stay out for awhile, but she was home by 11:30 or midnight. An angry mob of teenagers arrived shortly after she returned. "There was about four cars of boys, must have been about twenty or thirty of them," Leslie counted. "They tried to get inside and beat the hell out of me."

Leslie and Carolyn bolted themselves behind locked doors. The boys pelted the apartment with rocks. A front window shattered and a bottle landed on the porch.

Eventually, the boys stopped and drove away, but a smaller group came back and tried to force their way into the apartment. Two boys got inside and ransacked the kitsch decor after Leslie and Carolyn escaped. Carolyn ran to a telephone and dialed the police. Leslie made himself scarce while two squad cars responded. Four police officers inspected the broken window, the debris on the porch, and the vandalized apartment. After listening to Carolyn's account of the break-in, she said one of the cops gave her some old-fashioned Texas advice, "He told me I ought to keep a gun in the house."

Leslie and Carolyn put that suggestion at the top of their Saturday morning agenda. They did not even bother to clean up the mess on the front porch. For once, the Packard cranked right up and they drove downtown to the bad end of Main Street, where pawn shops and peep shows prevailed. They went into a combination jewelry store and hock shop. Gold plated rings and flawed gems, hot cameras and cheap guns shared the display cases.

The owner waited on them. "They didn't mention a police officer," Samuel Shainock recalled, "but they did say some teenagers were throwing rocks at their home and they wanted it for protection." He recommended a German-made Eig pistol, a .22 caliber revolver. The barrel was only two inches long. "It was a small one, blue steel and had a white handle," Shainock said. "It was a six-shooter." He filled in two blank spaces on a standard form he used for gun transactions. It was labeled RENTAL AGREEMENT:

Received of PUBLIC JEWELRY COMPANY
22 Eig   Revolver No. 4045 48   for which I have this day deposited with said PUBLIC JEWELRY COMPANY, as security for the rental and safe return of the above article, the sum of $12.95.

"Rental agreements" for pistols were printed in bulk, like telephone message pads. They satisfied Texas gun laws and let pawnbrokers sell Saturday night specials to teenage girls wearing braces without requiring accurate identification. Shainock could not remember who paid, but Carolyn signed the receipt as Carolyn Ashley.

The proud possessors of a new German pistol wheeled the Packard to their favorite drugstore soda fountain. They bumped into Vernon Lowrey, who carried a fancy title as executive director of the Houston Humane Society. Leslie had been getting animals from Lowrey for years; he considered Leslie "a good dog man," although he almost did not recognize the familiar face at Walgreen's because Leslie's hair was "a gosh-awful shade of pink . . . peach pink."

Carolyn remembered a German shepherd, a perfect guard dog to complement her pistol, that Lowrey had saved from being gassed at the city pound because it had heartworms. Lowrey had dubbed the dog Big Gray and he believed three weeks of medication had begun to show positive results, "I thought he was in pretty good shape." Leslie and Carolyn went to the animal shelter, which was just beyond the edge of the city airport's runways.

While airplanes roared overhead and they waited for Big Gray's paperwork to be finished, someone called about bringing a French poodle to the shelter. Leslie and Carolyn decided Fifi might like a companion her own size. They left a five-dollar deposit and arranged to return after the poodle arrived. They loaded Big Gray into the Packard and again the car started without a problem. At Truxillo, the landlady was supervising repairs on the window smashed the night before, but Leslie and Carolyn did not want to listen to her lecture them, so they went shopping.

Leslie was a regular in department 31 at the W.T. Grant store downtown. The inventory combined two of his favorite items, plants and small pets. The manager knew him well. "He admired tropical fish and so on," Mrs. Violantha Opersall said. That Saturday, he wanted to buy a potted plant, a philodendron climbing around a three-foot pole. Leslie was always looking for a discount, and he convinced Mrs. Opersall to knock a dollar off the price. "He wanted the plant very bad and sometimes we do make arrangements." He gave her a sob story about losing his receipt for a Christmas layaway, so she sold him the plant for $3.98.

Leslie and Carolyn asked Mrs. Opersall to hold the plant for a few hours. They also left behind some mollies and angel fish they bought for their aquariums, as well as a fresh supply of kitty litter ("cat sand" to Leslie) for their Truxillo menagerie. With a woman around the house, the cats had learned to use a box.

They returned to the animal shelter after the stop at Grant's. "I saw them in the yard," Vernon Lowrey said. "I understood from the kennel boy they came back to see if the poodle had come in." Since the dog had not arrived, they left empty-handed and drove to a remote stretch of Almeda-Genoa Road, two lanes of surveyor-straight concrete lined with thorny wild rose thickets. Carolyn nosed the Packard off the pavement onto the soft gravel shoulder and got out of the car with her Saturday night special in her hand.

"The policeman told me to make sure I could fire it because a person that don't know how to shoot a gun won't do any good," she explained.

Richard Stroud lived in a lonesome shack set back about a hundred feet from the road. When he heard shots, he stepped to his door. "The girl was standing on the rear end side of the car, right near the door, shooting a pistol into the ditch." He said the gun was a .22, although he had never owned one. "I know what a .22 sounds like and it was a .22."

Stroud watched the girl plink at bottles and rusty cans that littered the roadside. He kept his distance and later refused to say for certain that Carolyn was the girl he saw, but he came close. "It could be her twin sister if she had one." She wasn't alone. "Two men were sitting in the car," Stroud said. "As long as I observed them, they stayed in the car." Stroud did not move nearer. One of the men "turned around and looked at me and I went back into the house," he said.

The Packard died after Leslie and Carolyn returned to the Truxillo apartment, but the anonymous third person stayed with them to retrieve the fish, kitty litter, and potted plant from Grant's. Two employees saw Leslie with his friend. A clerk in the pet and plant department believed the stranger hefted the tall climbing ivy. Mrs. Opersall, the manager, contradicted her, "I believe it was Mr. Ashley." She was positive about an accessory Leslie had added to his peach pink hair job. "He had a hat on. He had a little hat on the back of his head."

Leslie and his anonymous friend rejoined Carolyn, who said she waited outside. The trio shared the big load as they walked to

Simpson's Dining Car, an all-night short-order restaurant that shared an intersection with Kipperman's Camera Shop. Different kinds of people came to eat or sober up at Simpson's. The Pink Elephant, a drag bar, was around the corner. For gays in Texas in 1961, Simpson's was an isolated public oasis.

Leslie and his friend went inside and found a booth with enough room for the philodendron. Carolyn stopped to use a pay telephone because she wanted to answer a message from Tones. "He left me a note the night before and he asked me to call him so I called him," Carolyn said. "He didn't know if he could get away or not because his wife was with him, but he said he would try to be over at Simpson's in about fifteen minutes."

Carolyn hung up, then plopped into a booth with Leslie and his friend. "They had ordered me a Coke when I was phoning and I went in and drank it." Leslie yakked with a waitress who was fascinated by his potted plant. The cashier left her post behind the cash register to gape at the philodendron too. "It was a huge plant," Claudine Lambert recalled. She thought it might be fake. "I told him I wanted to feel of the plant and see if it was real because he wouldn't tell me." Mrs. Lambert always got a kick out of joking with Leslie, but it was a busy evening at Simpson's so she went back to work.

According to Carolyn, their friend noticed Tones first, but it was not the trick who caused the comment. "Robert said, 'Isn't that a gorgeous car out there?' " Carolyn remembered. "Everybody turned around and looked and it was Mr. Tones parked out there." Leslie and Carolyn understood Tones well enough to know he wouldn't come inside. "Me and Douglas walked out," Carolyn said. They left their friend "Robert" alone in the booth. His identity and the story told by a man who claimed to be "Robert" would become a crucial bend on the path to death row.

Leslie climbed into the backseat of the Lincoln with the plant and all the other merchandise he had bought during the day. He requested a stop to buy dog food and Tones obliged. Carolyn still referred to Leslie as her brother, Douglas, when they were with Tones. "I asked him if I could drop Douglas off at the Pig Stand and to take me back to the house to have sexual relations and then drop me back off at the Pig Stand." The trick agreed again. When Leslie got out, he left everything in the Lincoln—the philodendron, the dog and cat food, the kitty litter, and the tropical fish, "I even left my hat."

Leslie waited at the Pig Stand while Carolyn had sex with Tones at the apartment. "It seemed to me about five minutes, maybe it was a period of thirty minutes" before he saw the Lincoln return. Tones did not stop for a postcoital chat. He and his wife were due for a Saturday night out. "Carolyn came in and had my hat," Leslie recalled. They were twenty-five dollars richer, and Carolyn told Leslie that Tones was pushing for a three-way date again. "This time it was stronger," Leslie said. He and Carolyn sipped Cokes at the Pig Stand and discussed sex "in the rear."

Leslie perched his cap on his peach pink hair. Carolyn wore the bridge for her false front tooth anchored by the metal brace that looked like a typical teenager's retainer. They could have been a couple of crazy kids at their first stop on a Saturday night date, but they were debating anal intercourse with a high-strung, middle-aged man leading a double life.

By the time they finished their Cokes, Carolyn said Leslie was leaning toward the date despite his distaste for penetration. "He said he didn't like it," Carolyn remembered, but Leslie believed in his powers of persuasion. "Maybe he could talk him out of it and give him a French job," Carolyn said. Leslie made a career out of deception. He wore drag to entice customers, then convinced them to settle for blow jobs instead of intercourse. He envied female prostitutes' advantage with straight tricks. "They're selling the real thing," Leslie said.

He postponed the final decision for a three-way date with Tones. Leslie was more interested in his hair. On Saturday nights, Carolyn tried her beautician skills on him. She needed to practice before her licensing exam began on Tuesday, and Leslie wanted to change his shocking peach pink tint for a more subtle shade. They had bought a conventional brown dye when they dropped off some film at Walgreen's that afternoon. "It didn't take," Leslie grumbled. The color came out much lighter than he expected.

While Leslie sulked over his botched dye job, Carolyn went to work at the bus stop. Around midnight, she ran into the teenagers again. The boys surrounded her on the sidewalk, a short run from her apartment. Leslie heard the squabble and scuffled with them, but they chased him inside. According to one of the teenagers, a man charged out of a back room while they were slapping Leslie around. The stranger held a gun to the boy's head and promised to kill him unless he left Leslie alone. The threat worked. As the frightened kids scattered, someone fired at them; Leslie took credit for the warning shot. His mysterious rescuer vanished before police responded to the disturbance call, and Leslie told them he fired into the air to scare off his tormentors.

The midnight skirmish caused Carolyn to make a lethal decision. She saw that the cheap .22 was an effective weapon. Since she could not predict when the teenagers might ambush her again, she put the pistol in her purse and packed it wherever she went.

A week of winter sunshine ended with rain on Sunday. Leslie and Carolyn needed their Packard more than ever in wet weather. They could have pushed it back to the used car lot and demanded repairs or a refund, but they had skipped a twenty-dollar payment due the previous Friday, so it was cheaper to bypass the dealer and buy a new battery themselves.

A Gulf station pump jockey named Robert Wallace Clifford took a quick look under the hood, "The wires around the starter were rusted and we couldn't guarantee the battery on account of the defective wires. More than likely it would run the battery down." The mechanic at the Gulf station told them to touch the wires with a screwdriver to start the car whenever it died. They had to rely on this crude method while the mechanic ordered a new starter, which could take a day or two since it was Sunday. The Packard left the Gulf station running on borrowed time. Once the faulty wiring drained the charge from the battery, a screwdriver would not help.

The dreary afternoon ticked along. "We just rode around town," Carolyn said. They decided to go to her mother's house. "Carolyn came by Sunday all excited about taking the exam," according to Mae. "She came in the house by herself, but there were two other people in the car." As usual, her supposed son-in-law shied away from Mae, who didn't recognize the third person in the Packard. Again, a conflicting version of the entire day would come back to haunt Leslie and Carolyn when the mysterious friend turned into their worst enemy.

"She had to have permanent waving rods and combs and things of that sort," Mae said. The licensing test in Austin was just two days away. "We checked everything she had to take with her. She wanted to pick up a red wig I had there to practice on at the last minute." Mae handed her daughter a bon voyage present—ten dollars. She thought the visit ended around 3:30 or 4:00, but she could not place the exact time. Carolyn was wearing the red wig over her black hair as the Packard drove off into the storm.

Sometime during that dark Sunday, after their anonymous friend left, Leslie and Carolyn dropped in on Sylvia. She had planned to visit her grandchild, who celebrated his first birthday at the beginning of the year, but Leslie was not interested in seeing his baby, and he said the bad weather convinced Sylvia to stay home too. The downpour gradually stopped as the sun went down. Leslie and Carolyn went back to their apartment, but they left right away for more nervous wandering.

They made their usual circuit of drive-ins and drugstores with two new reasons to be restless. The uproar on Saturday was the last straw for the landlady at Truxillo. On Sunday, Madge Duncan Staples had marched across her "estate" and ordered her troublesome tenants to move out. Besides being evicted, they had to think about another note from Fred A. Tones. "It might have been there Saturday evening," Leslie said. The skirmish with the teenagers distracted them. "We might not have seen it. It was under the door."

Leslie and Carolyn had too much on their minds to call Tones Sunday night. They had been discussing his three-way proposition on and off all day, but Leslie was waffling. He still wasn't ready to give the trick an answer.

If Carolyn planned to commit a crime with her gun, she did not bother to conceal the possession of a weapon from a vice cop. Lieutenant W. B. Higgins saw her working a bus stop over the weekend. Carolyn was a familiar face on his beat and he knew where she lived. Before his shift ended, he drove by the Truxillo apartment. Higgins had not heard about the trouble with the teenagers, and he came to warn Carolyn about working the bus stop.

Carolyn was alone when he arrived and they talked about her battles with the high school boys. The vice lieutenant remembered that Leslie showed up before she finished bragging about her brand new security system. "She told me they purchased a small pistol for $13.95 or a price very close to that range."

6

On Monday morning, February 6, the temperature was not quite freezing and the drizzle was not quite rain. Dorothy Tones, a petite woman, had her hands full getting three kids ready for school before she went off to work herself. Her two youngest, Christopher and Susan Elizabeth, were still in elementary school; Michael was a student at Mount Carmel, a Catholic high school. She always left the house with Michael at 7:30. On his way to school, he dropped his mother at a bus stop on Griggs Road where she began her long, slow ride to her job at a downtown insurance agency.

Fred A. Tones was still at home when his wife and eldest child left that gloomy morning. He put on a pair of navy blue slacks, custom-cut to fit his squat physique. His powder blue shirt was off the rack, bought for him by his wife. He fastened the French cuffs with square black-and-gold cuff links embossed with musical notes. He had his Knights of Columbus ring on his right hand and he wore a gold Elgin wristwatch with large numerals on the dial, a gift from a company that made "advertising novelties," pens and pencils and matchbooks printed with business names.

He slid his feet into blue stretch socks and laced up a pair of black Nunn-Bush shoes that were a little scuffed. There was no point buffing a high gloss on shoes in wet weather. He would be splashing through puddles and tiptoeing across mud as soon as he went outside. Dorothy Tones could not recall which tie her husband was wearing that morning, but she remembered that he topped his natty ensemble with a jacket she described as "gray shadow plaid," a sensible purchase from Sears. She said his health and spirits were excellent, despite the foul weather and the shaky status of his real estate business.

His wife made her tedious commute downtown by bus; Tones only had to grab his hat and swing his Lincoln two blocks to his office in the half of the duplex he rented from Madeline Harlan. He was at work by nine when she came over to answer the phone for him. They swapped hollow good mornings, then Tones left.

Leslie and Carolyn were night owls and did not stir until the middle of the morning. "It was early," Leslie said, "about ten-thirty."

Carolyn thought she woke up even earlier, around ten, because she was nervous. Her beauty exam was only a day away, and she was not any better prepared for this one than she had been for all the tests and quizzes she had flunked in school. They puttered around the apartment for awhile, then headed over to Walgreen's for lunch.

"We always went together," Leslie said.

Dorothy Tones had a telephone conversation with her husband around noon. She did not know where he was, but he was not at his office. Madeline Harlan did not see him from the time he left at nine that morning until he returned at about 2:00 or 2:30. "He came in with some man," she recalled. She didn't keep a telephone log, and she only remembered fielding two calls while Tones was out.

A freelance bookkeeper, Betty Gutierrez, had phoned to confirm she would come by to pick up some financial records and take the office inventory to get a jump on Tones's income tax return. The second call came from Leslie and Carolyn.

That morning, they ate and goofed around Walgreen's for a couple of hours. The subject of the three-way date kept cropping up. They couldn't turn their backs on fifty dollars. His experience hustling in drag made Leslie feel confident he could talk Tones into a French job. When he and Carolyn dialed Tones from Walgreen's, Leslie was in a decisive mood. He took control of the call "so it wouldn't be a woman's voice." He phoned Tones around two o'clock. "I'm the one who asked for him," Leslie recalled, but Mrs. Harlan said Tones was out.

They had worked up their courage for nothing, now they had too much stray energy to sit around Walgreen's. "We went to

Penney's, Grant's, Woolworth's and back to Walgreen's again," Leslie said. It was their usual routine of aimless dime-store browsing.

According to Mae Lima, who received a worried call from her daughter, Carolyn could not shake her anxiety about the beautician's test. "She said she didn't have a model to work on in Austin and wanted to know what she should do about it." Leslie did not qualify; models had to be female. Mae told Carolyn to demonstrate her skills on one of the other students, "Whoever is in your class, you're supposed to work on them." If Carolyn couldn't find a volunteer, she could hire a willing victim. "If you don't have someone to work on, it used to be five dollars to rent a model," Mae said. Carolyn wasn't pacified, but her mother had to get back to work, "I didn't have time to talk then. I had a patron."

Mae remembered that Carolyn called a second time about an hour later. "It was the same thing about the model." Mae could not calm her daughter's jitters this time either. Not long after they hung up, Mae tried to reach Carolyn again. "I called the drugstore and asked them to page her." Mae knew Walgreen's was Carolyn's home away from home. "I thought she might be there. . . . They said they paged her and she didn't answer." Mae might have had a mother's premonition that something horrible was about to happen. She called Kipperman's Camera Shop, but Sylvia was on a coffee break. Mae waited a few minutes and called again. Sylvia was back, but no one at the store had seen Leslie or Carolyn all day.

Leslie dialed Tones's number and gave the receiver to Carolyn when a male voice answered. "He told me to come up to his office, me and Douglas, to come at five o'clock because nobody would be there and his bookkeeper would be gone."

Although the rain had ended, the streets were slick. Rush hour made the five-mile ride a thirty-minute battle. As usual, Carolyn drove. She turned off the wide, divided avenue and steered the Packard onto a narrow block of pavement that paralleled Griggs Road. Locals call these service roads beside freeways and busy commercial strips "feeders." Tones's office and the other buildings along this block had Griggs Road addresses, but they actually fronted onto the feeder that let cars pull in and out of driveways without fighting heavy traffic. Carolyn was lucky to be in a ready-made breakdown lane when she pulled over near Tones's driveway.

"We stopped the car," Leslie said. "She tried to start it again because we were a little bit in the driveway and because we saw another car in the driveway." The Packard was blocking a dark blue 1960 Ford parked beside the front door of Tones's office.

Carolyn tried to move her car, but it was too late. "As soon as I turned it off, it went dead." She cranked the ignition, but the engine would not turn over. The Ford would have to squeeze around it. "I don't know how they got out," Leslie commented.

Leslie and Carolyn went into the realty office together. "We didn't figure no secretary was there," Leslie said. "I remember just walking in." Carolyn thought they rang a doorbell.

According to Betty Gutierrez, they did ring the bell. "I opened the door and said, 'Hello, won't you come in? Mr. Tones is on the phone, have a seat.' " Mrs. Gutierrez had spent an hour and a half listing Tones's furniture, right down to the wastebaskets, for his income tax return; she also wanted to bring his books up to date, but his January bank statement was still in the mail, so she resigned herself to returning later in the week. She expected to be gone before five, but she was in no hurry to brave the wet streets during rush hour.

Leslie recalled the bookkeeper was "a little blonde." He said, "She was getting ready to leave. She was a little shocked or something to see us." He struck Mrs. Gutierrez as a female impersonator from the moment he walked in the door. His profile made him look like a girl to her. "Dishwater brown," she called his do-it-yourself dye job. "Very bushy in front and a little long on the neck, not like he needed a haircut, but it was full." Carolyn was a symphony in black; her sweater and pedal pushers matched. "The young woman was wearing a scarf on her hair," the bookkeeper observed.

Leslie and Carolyn sat on a white vinyl divan jammed under a window. Beyond the glass, the gloomy day faded without a sunset. Mrs. Gutierrez left them alone in the front office, "I went to Mr. Tones's private office and started closing up the books. . . . He was sitting at his desk in his private office talking on the telephone." She didn't interrupt him. "I put on my coat and I was ready to leave, but I waited for him to finish his telephone conversation. I waited in the hall between the two offices."

Leslie and Carolyn fidgeted on the divan. Hanging on the wall over the second-hand furniture and dog-eared catalogues of real estate listings, they could see a framed drawing of John F. Kennedy. Camelot was less than three weeks old. The portrait floated above them, beaming a charismatic smile upon Tones's wilting enterprise. The first Roman Catholic president was a talismanic presence for a dedicated Knight of Columbus.

When she heard Tones finish his call, Mrs. Gutierrez stepped into the private office. She said he did not seem to be expecting anyone. "He was putting on a topcoat, an overcoat." The heavy fabric was a checkered charcoal pattern. "I told Mr. Tones he had a young couple waiting for him and he told me to send them on back." She returned to the front office and relayed the message, along with a question for the visitors. "I asked them if it was still raining outside, and the young girl said no."

The rain had stopped, but the damp evening chill dropped the temperature near freezing. Leslie and Carolyn stepped down the heated hallway to the converted bedroom where Fred A. Tones waited for them. "I never knew any of this was going to happen," Leslie said, "I only went over there to make some money and have some fun."

Outside, Mrs. Gutierrez had a problem. Her dark blue Ford was parked in the driveway beside Tones's huge white Lincoln; the Packard on the feeder partially blocked her vehicle. If she had been a worse driver or a chronic complainer or the helpless type, she might have walked back into the office and asked to have the Packard moved out of her way, but Mrs. Gutierrez didn't need any help. She squeezed her car past the obstacle and drove away.

Clinton McDaniel, the pharmacy student living next door to the realty office, was exhausted. His grueling classload and drugstore job drained him. His classmate left after they snickered about the strange-looking couple they saw get out of the Packard, then McDaniel ate an early supper and curled up for a nap on the living-room couch.

"I faintly recall hearing some noise that I presumed to be a backfire from an automobile, which we hear quite often," he said. McDaniel had learned to roll over and snooze through the racket on Griggs Road. He never suspected the sound was a gunshot.

Mrs. Harlan did not notice if her tenant's big Lincoln was still in the driveway when she returned from an early-bird dinner with a friend. "I didn't pay any attention to when he would go home.

He would go in and out." Her living room shared a common wall with Tones's office, but noise was not a problem. "Not very often," she said. Except that night. "I wasn't at home an hour when I heard a noise over there," she remembered. "I heard a noise like somebody hitting on something. It was an unusual noise and I looked out the window and saw a light in his office." The sound might have been hammering. "I thought he might be working over there, but I didn't know."

A precaution caused her to step away from the window. "I heard the sound and I went back to the bedroom." The noise in the next apartment did not stop. "I heard it first and then went back and heard some more. . . . All I can remember is that slapping noise." The memory made her ramble. "I just heard it and looked out because it was unusual, and I saw a light and I went back and my telephone rang, and I went back and started to talk over the telephone." Perhaps an instinct chained her to the receiver. "I was talking by telephone and wasn't paying no attention to what was going on over there."

Three people fought for their lives on the other side of her living-room wall. "I never did go back," she mumbled. "I did hear a car start off while I was talking on the telephone."

She missed the getaway, and the call that kept her away from the window saved Leslie and Carolyn from being captured before they got too far from Griggs Road. But the phone call that seemed to be a blessing was actually a curse. Leslie and Carolyn would have been better off if they had been spotted right away. When the last breath rattled from Tones' lungs, they were propelled on a corkscrew path veering between slapstick and the macabre. The aftermath of the shooting transformed them from misfits into pariahs, and the different versions of the disaster inside the duplex that surfaced later turned the truth into a kaleidoscopic ruin.

"The only people who know what happened in that room are the ones who were there," Leslie said, frowning.

Gaps and contradictions, laughing in terror, and skin-saving lies under oath in courtrooms would echo long after the sound from six gunshots. Leslie and Carolyn would tell their tale many times, seldom the same way twice. Deciding whom to believe would become a dangerous game of musical chairs where the losers are led to a seat called Old Sparky.

7

A shivering image emerged from the gunsmoke. "I asked her if he was dead. I was afraid he would get up again," Leslie said.

Carolyn was nude from the waist down, wearing nothing but her black sweater. "Douglas was in a panic . . . worse than I was." She stooped beside Tones, "I reached for his pulse to see if the man was dead." Carolyn felt nothing. Leslie said, "She took a mirror and did something with a mirror." Leslie still had all of his clothes on. "I don't know what she did with the mirror."

Carolyn searched for any sign of breath from Tones's lips or nostrils. The mirror stayed clear, no mist appeared. The short, deadly party had moved to the front office. The smiling face of John F. Kennedy loomed on the wall. Tones's body was bleeding on the floor in front of the vinyl divan. Except for his blue stretch socks and a white T-shirt, he was naked. His eyes were open, but his corpse was riddled with bullets from the Saturday night special.

"I was all choked up," Leslie recalled. His lip was cut and the left side of his face was swollen from punches. He quickly began to wipe off everything in the office. Carolyn had been drinking a Coca-Cola that she never finished; Leslie rubbed the bottle clean. He soaked up a puddle of blood on the floor. "I was doing that while she was seeing if he was dead or alive or what was wrong with him." Carolyn hovered over Tones's body, but she couldn't bring him back to life. A cold fact hit her, "He was a businessman and we were there for an immoral purpose." She knew what the world would see—a whore and a queer had emptied a pistol into

47

a religious family man.

They decided to run, but the Packard delayed their getaway. "It was dead," Carolyn said, "so we took his car." The keys were in a brown leather case. Carolyn rushed outside, but she was so frantic she flooded the carburetor. Leslie jumped behind the wheel and got the powerful engine started. "I went out there and backed it up," he said. He slowly maneuvered the rear of the big car close to the front door of the realty office. They didn't want to leave Tones's corpse behind. Leslie and Carolyn believed they could buy time for their escape if Tones simply disappeared.

Panic made simple jobs impossible. "We couldn't get the trunk open," Leslie said. Since the Lincoln was a four-door, they decided to hide the body on the backseat floorboard. "We dragged him out," Carolyn recalled. "Head first." She thought his skull might have smacked against a concrete step. Leslie disagreed, "His head didn't bump." He claimed they carried the body. They brought his clothes too. Carolyn remembered to grab his shoes. Leslie spotted something worth taking—the dead man's portable television. "For money, trying to get money, the only reason we took it," Leslie admitted. "It was on and I thought about it as we were going out the door."

Although Tones was only five feet four inches tall, they couldn't shove his inert weight over the driveshaft hump. The Lincoln's door would not close. When they slammed it shut, Carolyn thought she heard Tones's neck snap. She ran to the Packard. Leslie drove the Lincoln behind her, pushing the stalled car up the feeder street until the engine turned over and they drove off in tandem.

Leslie's family had finished dinner when he and Carolyn burst into the bungalow on Wentworth. Ted Kipperman was in the living room reading his evening newspaper. Jim Ayres was relaxing with him. The visitors didn't slow down to say hello. Carolyn ran into the bathroom while Leslie zoomed into the kitchen, where his mother was washing dishes.

"His face was swollen and cut, he had a cut lip," Sylvia remembered. Leslie rinsed his wound in the kitchen sink. "I said 'Douglas, what in the world has happened to you?' He said something about he'd been in a fight and don't worry about it, he'd been in a fight." He refused to say more as he daubed his injured mouth with a wash rag.

Ted Kipperman put down his newspaper. "I went into the kitchen for a glass of water and I looked at Douglas and his face was red and swollen up, and his lip was cut." Uncle Ted tried to get an explanation too, "I asked him what happened to his face and he said he'd been in a fight. He didn't elaborate, but it was pretty obvious he'd been in some sort of fight."

Jim Ayres was curious too. "I went into the kitchen and examined his face. He was putting water on his face. It appeared to be swollen, kind of red and looked like he had a little cut on his lip, in the corner of his mouth. . . . My recollection is one side, his left side. . . . I asked him what happened to his face. He said he'd been in a fight, somebody had hit him. I tried to pursue it, but he didn't want to talk about it."

"I couldn't get any sense out of Douglas about the fight and he kept telling me not to worry about it," Sylvia complained. She left the crowded kitchen and went after Carolyn, who was still in the bathroom with the door unlocked. "Carolyn had her pedal pushers down and her legs apart," Sylvia said. "She had black and red spots all over her legs. That's how she was, and I said 'Carolyn, what's happened to you?' " Carolyn did not mention the throbbing pain in her vagina, she just pulled up her pedal pushers and darted into the kitchen. "She kept hurrying and saying 'We gotta go, we gotta go,' " Sylvia remembered.

Carolyn could not pry Leslie from his mother, so she retreated to the living room with Ted Kipperman. "She looked very pale and very nervous and she didn't have anything to say," Ted recalled. No small talk about a corpse in a stolen car parked outside. "She was just sitting there . . . waiting."

Leslie gave his mother a key to the Truxillo apartment. Sylvia said he was jabbering a mile a minute. "He was moving, planning on going somewhere with her to take a beauty test and he wanted me to move his things for him." Sylvia knew the drill. "I had moved them a dozen times because he always had animals and cats and I always had to move them."

Jim Ayres eavesdropped on the kitchen conversation. "He said he had some difficulty with some teenage boys," Jim explained. "They had broken the window and he said he was going to Austin with Carolyn for her beautician's license and the landlady had asked them to move." Leslie was worried about his plants and statues. "He didn't want to leave his things because the boys might break in and steal everything."

Leslie lied to his mother to create a smokescreen for his get-away, "I told her the trouble we'd been having over there . . . so she wouldn't think nothing else. . . . I told her not to worry about it. It wasn't nothing serious." He did not mention the shooting.

"Certain things he didn't want to tell me about," Sylvia said. "He didn't want to worry me."

Leslie and Carolyn only stayed a few minutes before they left the house on Wentworth. "I was in the Lincoln and she was in the Packard," Leslie said. He did not have to push Carolyn to start the Packard. "We never turned it off, we left it running," Leslie remembered.

He was still nursing his lip with the wash rag from his mother's kitchen as they drove toward Truxillo. Leslie stopped a couple of blocks short, "I didn't want anybody to see his Lincoln." Carolyn drove all the way to the apartment by herself and stripped a bed-spread off the mattress. "I left the car running," she said, "because I knew if I cut it off I couldn't get it started again."

Leaving the apartment, she got another scare, "I seen them boys and I took off." Although she sped away from the teenagers, the close encounter shook her up and she could not keep the Packard running. The engine died twice, but stopping traffic was part of her profession. "The first time a colored man pushed me and the second time another man," she said.

With the corpse lying behind him, Leslie was too frightened to be patient while he waited for Carolyn to show up where he was parked. He put the big Lincoln in motion and drove in circles, then returned to their rendezvous spot before she arrived. This time, he stayed until Carolyn delivered the shroud. She and Les-lie covered Tones's dead body with the bedspread, but a new problem lurked on the dashboard. "The car had been running," Leslie meant the Lincoln, not the Packard. "I had never turned the motor off and the gas showed empty."

The tank was low when they stole the car; now they needed fuel, but they couldn't pull into a gas station with a body on the floorboard. Self-serve was not an option in 1961. They knew about a twenty-four-hour operation near Sylvia's home on Wentworth, only a block from the Gulf station where the new battery had been installed in the Packard the day before. Leslie stopped the Lincoln across the street, just a few feet away from the station. The corpse gave him the creeps. He slid out of the front seat and made a feeble attempt to hide behind the big car while Carolyn pulled the Packard up to a pump.

Ralph Lee Mizzell was on duty. He was a skinny Alabaman with big ears and a pompadour. Mizzell had never seen Carolyn before, but he approved of her outfit, "She had on black toreador pants, the type ladies wear, and a kind of sweater like, a black sweater." Carolyn chain-smoked. "She seemed nervous and a little worried." Mizzell said Carolyn told him she needed gas "for a friend whose car ran dry down the street." He thought she turned off the Packard's engine, but he wasn't sure. "I told her we had five-gallon cans and had a three-dollar deposit on it." He filled a red metal can with regular octane gas, "At that time it was $1.19." Total, not per gallon. "There was a gas war on." The competitive battle had shaved a nickel off normal prices, dropping the price below a quarter a gallon.

"She handed me five dollars and asked me for a package of cigarettes," Mizzell said. "I gave the money to her and then told her it was three dollars deposit on the can." Carolyn was so agitated that she did not understand the transaction. Although Mizzell charged her for the gas and cigarettes, she still owed the deposit. She was in no condition to count her change. "I thought he took it out of the money."

Five dollars would have covered everything, and Mizzell was unable to explain why he did not subtract the deposit. "I just didn't." But he believed Carolyn knew she was stealing the can. "After she pulled out she said, 'I'll bring it back.'" Mizzell grabbed a pencil and quickly scribbled a description of the car: "LIGHT GRAY 4 DOOR-PACKARD #SK 7185." He added RED 5 GAL. GAS CAN, drew a box around the word *red*, and finished with MONDAY NIGHT FEB. 6. He underlined *Monday*.

Carolyn followed Leslie to the next corner, where he stopped the Lincoln again. She pulled the Packard behind him and Leslie took the red can, but he could not keep the nozzle in the tank. "I was spilling gasoline and I was nervous. I got about half of it in and I was wasting it." They had to dispose of Tones's body and an idea flashed "right then when we filled the Lincoln with gas," Carolyn said. Maybe it was the danger of the gasoline splashing so close to the cigarettes they were chain-smoking. Desperate with panic, they came up with a solution to get rid of the corpse.

Leslie thought he knew the perfect spot, a few blocks from the shack where his ex-in laws lived. He took the lead in the Lincoln, but Carolyn could not let him get too far ahead. "I had to stay beside him because the Packard was going dead." She did not want to lose sight of Leslie in case the Packard conked out while she followed him to the far edge of the East End, to the very last block of Avenue I between Seventy-eighth Street and Navigation Boulevard.

"We just drove to a little section where there wasn't nothing," Leslie said. He pulled off the asphalt, no curbs or sidewalks separated the pavement from the weeds. Carolyn stopped the Packard in front of the Lincoln because they did not want anyone to hear their engines idling. "After I cut off the motor he would have to push it," she said.

They both got out of their cars, but Leslie wrestled with the corpse. "I took him out by myself. He was stiff. He came out much lighter than he went in." Carolyn remembered that Leslie dragged Tones from the Lincoln head first. He only carried the body a few feet into the vacant lot while she checked the gas in the five-gallon can. "There wasn't very much," Carolyn recalled. "There was a little left." Enough to get the job done.

"We both smoke, but I didn't have a match," Leslie said. "Carolyn did. Book matches . . . I don't remember. . . . " The truth flickers in the firelight. Who poured the gas? Who lit the match? The possibilities will cover almost every combination in the years ahead as the facts go up in flames.

"It was the only way we could think of to get rid of it," Leslie pleaded. "We didn't stay to see the fire." He didn't look back, but Carolyn paused to capture the demise of her dead trick. "He lit up like a Christmas tree," she said.

Around 9:00 P.M. and a little over two miles away, an unidentified male left the apartment of Mrs. Margaret Hines. Her address was on a quiet residential block of a street called Clay, named after Senator Henry Clay, the Great Compromiser in the era before the Civil War. Mrs. Hines's apartment was behind the main house, halfway to the next parallel street, Polk; commemorating President James K. Polk, who occupied the White House when Texas entered the Union in 1845.

This part of Polk was only two lanes wide, but the traffic lights were spread out so the road was a well-traveled path from the center of downtown out to the East End. The roots of Howard Hughes's empire remained headquartered on this part of Polk. The drill bits the reclusive billionaire's father helped to invent were on the business end of oil wells all over the world, but they were manufactured at the plant on Polk, across from Margaret Hines's apartment.

When her gentleman caller left, he found a pair of navy blue trousers rumpled on the hood of his car. He pitched them into the gutter before he drove off.

B. A. Cook showed up on Avenue I at about 9:00 P.M. He worked for the Houston Fire Department and his specialty was arson. He ordered an ambulance driver to remove a sheet covering the charred body, then he squatted in the weeds next to what remained of Fred A. Tones. The burns were more severe on the left side of the corpse, from the shoulder past the waist line, and down the left leg. The head was badly burned; the face was damaged too.

B. A. Cook had seen plenty of incinerated bodies in his years as an arson investigator. "It was my opinion the body was saturated with some type of flammable liquid," he concluded. "The flammable liquid was gasoline." He didn't have to be a genius to reach his conclusion, "We found a can a few feet away from the deceased body." He knew what gasoline could do to human flesh. "The burns were of the type which is indicative of the flammable liquid being used, that is, where bodies are concerned."

Cecil Mills was a mechanic in the automotive department of a Sears store in the East End. His home was about five blocks off Polk, near a newer section of the street than the narrow road that separated Hughes Tool from Margaret Hines's apartment. At one time, Polk had ended at the tool plant, but an extension was built to connect with major roads leading to the ship channel. The addition was wider, two lanes in each direction split by an "esplanade," the local term used to describe a broad, raised divider between opposing flows of traffic.

Mills saw a bundle along the curb on the inbound side of the esplanade. He drove home, but the mysterious pile of rags stuck in his mind. An undiscovered treasure might be lying on the roadside. The mechanic drove back and unrolled the bundle. "I found a shirt, a man's shirt, and a man's pair of shorts." The shirt was light blue; the underwear was white. "I took them home and showed them to my wife." Tones was small but he was thicker in the middle than Mills. "They were too large for me so I said, 'Well, wash them and clean them up and give them to my brother-in-law.' "

Officer Newelton Free rode in a patrol car with his partner, C. J. Lofland, on February 6. "I received the call at approximately 9:04 P.M." Free had a knack for appearing to be meticulous without pinning himself down too precisely.

As soon as he got to Avenue I, Free began noting data that everyone else had overlooked. The red metal of the gasoline can was galvanized; the color was scorched dark on one side; the top was missing. Free said he broke out his camera and started snapping pictures. He aimed his lens at the charred corpse, which had been moved to a stretcher. His partner printed the address and date, then added his initials, CL, onto a small chalkboard mounted on a flat stand. Lofland wrote two more words much larger than the rest: DEAD MAN. The sign was placed in the vacant lot next to the burned grass where the corpse was found and more flashbulbs lit up the cold darkness.

Conway Brock hauled explosive chemicals for a living. He was turning into the terminal for Robertson Tank Lines when he saw something in the street in front of his big truck. "It was laying somewhere about the center of that left-turn lane." He climbed down from the cab of his truck to get the black laced shoe for a man's right foot, size 9C. The shoe wasn't new, a scuff mark blemished the leather above a worn heel.

"I took it into the dispatch office of the company terminal," Brock said. "I thought it dropped out of one of the other rigs, belonged to one of the other drivers."

By 10:00 P.M., the police activity on Avenue I had subsided. Two homicide detectives prowled the vacant lot for evidence. One of them, J.W. Kindred, noticed the body had moved while it was blazing. He didn't realize a fireman had flipped the corpse over before drenching the flames. Kindred thought the movement could mean the victim was burned alive, but an autopsy would tell him one way or the other.

8

While the police scratched their heads and cleaned mud from the vacant lot off their shoes, Leslie Douglas Ashley and Carolyn Lima raced into the next phase of their cockeyed getaway plan. They drove both cars back to Sylvia's house and tried to switch the license plates from their Packard onto the big Lincoln. Leslie was hopeless with tools and he could not unscrew the plates from Tones's car, so Carolyn took over. "We got our license plate on the Lincoln, on the front part, and couldn't get the back one on," she said.

While Carolyn struggled with the rear plate, Leslie gave up and went inside. He talked to his stepfather about the Packard. Jim Ayres remembered, "Douglas told me he was having trouble with his car and he was going to leave it in front of the house." Jim had never seen the Packard before that night, but he wasn't surprised by its dilapidated condition. His stepson was always buying lemons that broke down.

Leslie led his mother to believe someone was giving him and Carolyn a ride to Austin for the beauticians exam that began the next morning. "They never told me who," she said, sighing. Before he left, Leslie asked his uncle for road money. "I loaned him either fifteen or twenty dollars," Ted Kipperman said. Ted often gave cash to his kinfolk. Leslie might be an embarrassment to the family, but Ted could not play Scrooge with his big sister's only child. Besides, he believed a little well-placed currency could smooth out the rough spots and buy some peace and quiet from the turmoil constantly swirling around his transvestite nephew.

Leslie took the loan and hurried outside. Carolyn had not made any progress screwing the Packard's plate onto the rear of the Lincoln, so she brought all three loose license plates with her as she hopped into the Lincoln with Leslie. She knew the night man at a gas station across the street from a bus stop she worked. Leslie thought he was one of her tricks. His name was Colvin Lester Wilder, but everyone called him Red.

Red Wilder said Leslie pulled the Lincoln into the service station between 10:30 and 11:00 that night. "I gassed it up," Wilder recalled. "We fill 'em till it comes out the neck," he said. "I know exactly how much they bought." Wilder believed the pump read $5.95. They paid cash, "all in ones," he remembered. He chatted with Carolyn who sat in the passenger seat, but another customer interrupted them so she and Leslie waited until he finished the sale before they asked him for a favor.

"I put on the rear license plate," Wilder said. "Miss Carolyn gave it to me." He didn't bother with washers and screws, he rigged his own solution. "I put it on with wire." Red Wilder did not know SK 7185 was registered to an eight-year-old Packard Clipper abandoned in front of a red-brick bungalow.

With license plates that linked them to a murder on the Lincoln, Leslie and Carolyn drove to Truxillo for some extra clothes. Carolyn could not find her key to the apartment so they had to double back to the house on Wentworth. They both went in to get the key they had left with Sylvia, and she asked them to come back for a final farewell before they left for Austin. She was terrified of highway driving after dark. Leslie promised he would return to say goodbye, but he was just pacifying her.

They stopped to buy ice that Leslie pressed against his cut lip and the swelling on his face. Everything was quiet at Truxillo; the teenage boys were not around. Leslie and Carolyn quickly let themselves in the back door. Inside, they saw the key lying on the floor. Carolyn must have dropped it during her frantic trip to grab the bedspread they used to cover Tones's body. This trip, she and Leslie snatched armloads of clothes, especially Leslie's favorite drag gowns that he refused to leave behind. They herded Fifi the toy poodle and Big Gray the German shepherd with heartworms into the Lincoln. There wasn't enough room for plants and cats and fish. "I didn't want to leave them there," Leslie moped.

They still could not get the Lincoln's trunk open, so they piled everything in the backseat. Big Gray jumped in too; they kept Fifi up front. Leslie drove the big Lincoln onto the Gulf Freeway, heading south. "We first was going to Galveston," he recalled. "That was the freeway we were going on."

Galveston was a dead end, a sandbar island only fifty miles away, a summer beach resort empty and windswept in February. Then, an inspiration struck Leslie. He pulled off the freeway and turned around, "We decided to give it up and head for New Orleans." The drive would take all night, but the big engine destroyed the miles. They roared east in the stolen Lincoln, tearing over the flat coastal prairie and into the Cajun swamps. They tossed Tones's wallet from the car. His cash was in their pockets and his ID's had been flushed down the toilet at Sylvia's bungalow on Wentworth.

Leslie kept his homemade ice pack on his cut lip. He covered the swelling on his face with cosmetics. He and Carolyn stayed awake as the moonlight relfected through the Spanish moss in alligator territory. They did not slow down until the sun rose over the twisting current between the wide banks of the Mississippi River.

Dorothy Tones did not sleep either. Her husband had not come home or called all night. She climbed in and out of bed for hours. She gave up on getting any sleep and got up for good at about five o'clock. It was still too dark outside to see the frost on the grass in her front lawn.

The sun was barely coming up an hour and a half later when Mrs. Betty Wiederhold left her home on Clay. She lived in the house in front of Margaret Hines's apartment, where the gentleman caller had tossed the pants that he found on his car into the gutter.

Mrs. Wiederhold had a southern way with verbs. "I carried my husband to work at the Hughes Tool Company and it was dark," she remembered. The Hughes plant was practically across the street, but the weather was too cold to walk the short distance. Mrs. Wiederhold saw a strange shape lying next to the curb, "I thought it was a black dog." She did not realize the lump was a pair of pants until daylight. "I picked them up by the belt and I saw a name in the trousers." Fred A. Tones meant nothing to her.

Mrs. Wiederhold did the same thing with the pants that Cecil Mills did with the shirt and undershorts he found. "I threw them on the washing machine," she said. "I didn't do anything with them that day. I forgot them."

The house on Wentworth came alive when the telephone rang. "I had a call real early in the morning," Sylvia said. Leslie was on the line. "He said, 'Well, we got here all right.' " She thought her son was in Austin. "It was early and it didn't dawn on me until much later where it was coming from. I didn't realize where the call was coming from."

New Orleans was the perfect place for two fugitives from a murder rap. The entire city was in disguise and running wild for the final week of the Mardi Gras celebration.

9

Carnival comes from the Medieval Latin words *carne vale*, meaning farewell to meat, which refers to the Catholic vow to give up the finer things of life during Lent. New Orleans celebrates the days before Ash Wednesday with a bash of hedonistic excess.

Three hundred and fifty miles west, in Houston, Tuesday morning, February 7, began at the Harris County morgue with the autopsy of a charred corpse. A woman who heard the broadcast description of a crab tattoo on the victim's right forearm came to the morgue. Although the face was badly burned, she determined the remains did not belong to the man who was missing from her life. When the coroner began the autopsy, he was dissecting a John Doe.

Dr. Joseph Jachimczyk became an institution in Houston. He came to town in 1957, rising to chief medical examiner three years later. His tenure in the top job spanned four decades, but on this winter morning in 1961, Doctor Joe, as everyone called him, was still building the foundations of his reputation. He got underway at about 8:00 A.M. The body was sixty-four inches long and weighed 145 pounds. "The eyes were brown and there were two dentures in place. There were no scars I could see," he reported. "The external genitilia were those of an adult male, circumcised."

Dr. Jachimczyk did not discover any obvious evidence of drugs or alcohol. With a visual inspection, he estimated two-thirds of the body was charred. "Much of his hair was burned away and singed." There was enough left to expose the dead man's vanity. "The hair was dark, but was gray at the very roots." Tones had a recent dye job. The coroner did not find a Knights of Columbus ring on the brittle fingers, but the right forearm was one of the few places on the body that was not scorched. There he measured the crab tattoo, "four by two and one-half inches in area." Both feet were intact. "The feet, from the socks level, were not burned," Doctor Joe observed. "There was a clear line of demarcation." Tones's synthetic stretch socks had retarded the flames.

The autopsy determined the burns were postmortem. "There was no evidence of any soot or carbon particles anywhere in the respiratory tract. The individual was not breathing during the time the fire was raging." Further examination revealed more negative findings. "There was no carbon monoxide in the blood. If a person were alive, you would expect to find some . . . and the margin of the areas not burned did not show any evidence of vital reaction. In other words, there was no evidence there was circulating blood present at the time the tissues were being burned."

Doctor Jachimczyk had to search further for the cause of death. "Externally, in the charred remains, it was not possible to visualize or recognize any injury because the holes were burned." He opened the body and located three areas of internal damage, probably from a small-caliber firearm. Two of the gunshots were potentially fatal—one in the head and one in the left chest. The coroner could not find any exit wounds so he probed for the bullets.

One path began at the tip of the victim's right ear, puncturing the skull. Doctor Joe dug through the right temporal lobe and followed the damage across the center of the dead man's brain. The bullet tore a hole a half-inch wide through the dense tissue. The coroner confirmed his suspicions about the size of the gun when he pried a .22 shell from the left temporal lobe.

The autopsy turned up another potentially fatal wound near Tones's heart. This bullet entered the left side of the chest. Doctor Jachimczyk used anatomical language to describe precisely the point where the bullet's path started, "one inch below the suprasternal notch, which is the notch called the breast bone . . . four inches to the left of the midline." The slug traveled downward diagonally, roughly thirty degrees, causing the coroner to conclude the short-statured victim was upright when this shot hit him. The bullet ripped through Tones's left lung and perforated his aorta to cause a deadly hemorrhage. The left chest cavity contained one quart of type A blood. "Normally, there is no free blood in the left chest cavity," Dr. Jachimczyk explained.

A third wound entered an inch below and behind the tip of the left ear, then plowed through the sternocleidomastoid muscle, the neck muscle attached to the skull directly behind the ear. Doctor Joe said the bullet "bounced off the left mastoid bone, which is the bone protruding behind the ear." The ricochet sent the bullet veering beneath the skin and muscles on the left side of Tones's face. The coroner found the bullet resting against the left mandible, or lower jaw.

Doctor Jachimczyk took a full X ray of the corpse, routine procedure with decomposed or severely damaged bodies, "to be sure that something isn't overlooked," he explained. The coroner did not know what else might be lost inside the charred flesh, but the autopsy had already turned up enough evidence to keep the police busy. The coroner gave the bullets he found in the victim to a homicide detective waiting at the morgue. The victim's right fingers were so badly burned that fingerprints could not be taken, but the fingertips on the other hand were not completely destroyed. They required sensitive treatment by an identification expert, so Doctor Joe severed the dead man's left hand and gave it to the homicide detective.

The movement J. W. Kindred had detected in the scorched grass was not caused by a man writhing in flames. The autopsy proved the victim was not burned alive. Kindred was part of the first wave of homicide detectives who came to the office on Griggs Road looking for more answers. He saw blood stains on the sidewalk outside the duplex; inside, he noticed a mop propped against a wall near the front door. Mrs. Harlan admitted that she had cleaned blood from the office floor. She also told him about the previous evening. "She heard several loud bumping noises," Kindred said. "She did not go over."

Kindred noticed the long military bayonet on top of a filing cabinet in Tones's private office. Like the other cops, he believed the bayonet was not important. "I didn't touch it," he said, shrugging. Kindred was more interested in the open safe in the private office. Mrs. Tones did not think her husband kept money in the safe. Neither did Richard Grant, who sublet a spare room in the realty office, but Grant did not say what might have been in the safe. And, he did not mention that he had arrived at Griggs

Road before the police. He was with Mrs. Harlan when Dorothy Tones reached the duplex, but he was gone when the first patrolman responded to her call. Richard Grant did not reveal he was at the duplex early that morning, nor if he had opened the safe and left before returning. He faded into the woodwork and evaporated from the case.

Before noon, Mrs. Tones's worst fear came true. The identification of the torch murder victim was upgraded from tentative to positive. Her husband would never come home. Captain Weldon Waycott, the ranking officer at the scene, took on a tough job. He drove to Mount Carmel High to break the bad news to Michael Tones, the oldest child in the family. His father's death was going to be all over the newspapers and the publicity would make the grief in his home even harder to bear.

Media coverage was already reporting the victim's fingerprints were matched with a two-year old arrest record in police files. The reason for the arrest was not disclosed, neither was a dual identity on the rap sheet. The name was unusual in this part of the world. Only his family and the police were aware that Fred A. Tones had once been been known as Salvadore Pasquale.

Dr. Joseph Jachimczyk spent his afternoon digging through the charred cadaver. X rays of the remains exposed three more wounds. "A fourth bullet entered the left [side of the] neck and went in behind the other [bullet]," he reported. The first neck wound struck bone and deflected down the jaw line; this fourth bullet traveled straight through the muscles in the back of the victim's neck and almost exited on the right side. A fifth shot hit an inch below Tones's left shoulder, shattering the bone in his arm before lodging in the muscles of his armpit. X rays showed the coroner that he had one more bullet to remove. This shot entered the left shoulder also. It missed the bone and lodged in the victim's back.

Dr. Jachimczyk summed up his findings, "There were a total of six entrance wounds, one on the right and five on the left: two fatal and four not fatal." The lethal shot to the head was the only bullet that entered on the right; all the others came from the left. The wounds in the body were a quarter of an inch in diameter; the track through the brain tissue was wider, about one half inch. Although he recovered all six .22 caliber bullets, the coroner could not determine the sequence of the shots.

The quart of hemorrhaged blood in the chest cavity allowed him to conclude no more than "several minutes" had elapsed between the first shot and the last. Given that time frame, Dr. Jachimczyk was certain the dead man was alive when all six shots were fired.

The lucky impulse that brought Leslie Douglas Ashley and Carolyn Lima to New Orleans during the Mardi Gras buildup also brought them to the Golden Age Mansion, where an unexpected vacancy made a room available. Leslie had covered the swelling on his face with cosmetics. "Just plain liquid make-up," Carolyn said. He was an expert at hiding his acne scars, so the red blotch on his face was easy to conceal. "You couldn't tell," Carolyn remembered.

During their stay, Leslie went through his pockets. He discovered black-and-gold cuff links decorated with musical notes. "I don't even remember taking them," he said. "I probably stuck them in my pocket without realizing what I was doing." He left the cuff links on top of a dresser.

Hortense Cooke overheard her young guests laughing and giggling inside their room Tuesday afternoon. Around 6:30, they left with a man she didn't recognize. "I don't know how he got in," Mrs. Cooke said. "He was dark and hid his face from me." She wanted a word with her guests. "I called to the boy. . . . He was so nice." Carolyn was curt. "I called as they were leaving. . . . They acted peculiar. The woman said they were in a hurry." The honeymooners climbed into the front seat of the Lincoln; the stranger sat in back. Carolyn later said this man was a trick. They dropped him off and came back to the Golden Age Mansion by themselves.

Mrs. Cooke saw Leslie alone after they returned. "He was downstairs at the Coke machine. He said he lost four nickels in it." She still wanted to show off her rich young Texan. "I really wanted my husband to meet him, so I called out." Leslie pouted about his twenty cents. "The boy acted funny and resentful until my husband opened up the machine, returned the money he lost, and gave him the Cokes, then he burst into a big smile." Mrs. Cooke was enchanted by his sparkling grin.

Leslie would not have been smiling if he had known how fast the law was closing in on him and Carolyn. When the pharmacy student living next door to the Tones Realty office told police about the film Leslie had left at Walgreen's over the weekend, they followed a trail to the developing lab. The photos not only included snapshots of Leslie in drag, they also listed Sylvia's number as the place to reach him since he did not have his own telephone.

Jim Ayres said the homicide detectives came to the house on Wentworth after dinner. He knew a few cops from his days as a freelance stringer shooting news film. He recognized John Thornton, who was in charge of the case, but he had never met Detective Kindred. They asked him about the Packard parked along the curb. "They called me outside and said, 'Do you know the car doesn't have a license plate on it?' And I said no. I hadn't paid any attention when I left in the morning."

The detectives guessed the missing plates were on the stolen Lincoln. They quickly ran down the tag number registered to the Packard and added SK 7185 to their all-points bulletin.

On Wednesday, Mrs. Cooke did not see her rich Texans until early in the afternoon. They were both standing near the stolen Lincoln. "The man was fooling around with the back right tire. It wasn't flat, so I don't know what he was doing." Carolyn baffled her too. "She seemed to be taking off the heels of her shoes."

Around 2:30, Mrs. Cooke was outside the slave quarters, "I heard them giggling, both of them, in their room." She didn't see them leave to look for a telephone about an hour later when Carolyn called her mother. The collect call came on the pay phone in the beauty parlor, but Mae wanted privacy so she moved to the extension inside her home for the conversation with her daughter. "She wanted money," Mae remembered. "I was so surprised and excited that I didn't ask where she was or who was with her. I guess I didn't ask a lot of things I should have. I guess I was just stupid." The homicide detectives suspected she was hiding details she heard from her daughter.

Mae did not ask questions, instead she gave advice. "What I did was tell her that she was in trouble." The torch murder was already front-page news in Houston. "Her picture was in the paper here. I told her, 'If you're mixed up in this thing . . . if you're guilty of anything . . . you should go straight to the nearest police station. And if you're not guilty of anything, that's all the more reason to go to the police.'" Her mother's naïveté did not convince Carolyn. "She didn't say anything about that," Mae said. "She just hung up." Carolyn never called again.

Leslie dialed a long distance operator too. "I made a phone call to my mother afterwards because I didn't know if they were sure about us." He called collect. "They wouldn't accept the charges." His family was not shunning him. As soon as she had found out her son was a murder suspect, Sylvia had consulted the family lawyer. Jack Knight had handled Leslie's divorce, as well as his vice arrests. Leslie's family wanted him to receive legal advice, so they gave the long distance operator Jack Knight's number. "That's when I really got scared," Leslie recalled.

Instead of phoning the lawyer, Leslie and Carolyn rushed back to their room. Boarders at the Golden Age Mansion saw them for the last time shortly before 4:30. "Charley Adam" and his bride were in too much of a hurry to check out. They quickly decided which clothes to pack. Most of the fancy drag gowns were expendable. "We were scared and we didn't have time to get all of them up," Carolyn said.

They planned to head northwest. "We started to go to Oklahoma City," Leslie remembered. He used a map he found in the Lincoln's glove compartment. "On the map I was looking at, to get to Oklahoma City you had to go through Texas." They wanted to stay away from Texas. "Tones had marked a route to New York," Leslie said, "so we stayed on that highway."

They hugged the Gulf Coast of Mississippi and stopped for gas in Biloxi before turning north. "He would drive in the daytime and I would drive at night," Carolyn said. They were hundreds of miles away when their pictures appeared in New Orleans newspapers on Thursday morning after Mae Lima informed Houston police about her daughter's call.

In the lingo of the Houston police department progress reports, New Orleans detectives were "checking all known 'Q' joints there." They rousted the My-O-My Club, a drag bar beyond the city limits, as well as transvestite hangouts in the French Quarter, but the big break did not come from hassling snitches and crossdressers. When the telephone trace confirmed that Carolyn's call came from a public pay phone in New Orleans, the FBI was brought into the case. Leslie and Carolyn were charged with violating the Dyer Act, a federal law against transporting a stolen vehicle across state lines.

Mae was bewildered by the turmoil surrounding her daughter, "She was too pushed." The pressure of beauty school and living on her own had led Carolyn astray. "It was just too much, she must have flipped," Mae said.

10

The dead man was remembered in rosary vigils on Thursday night. Hours after the last Hail Mary was said, a ferocious storm battered Houston. The wind and thunder rolled in at about 3:30 Friday morning. Violent rain slammed into the city; lightning lit up the sky. A jagged bolt hit an oak tree growing in front of a home just west of downtown. The trunk splintered and the force of the explosion blew out windows on both sides of the street. A curtain caught fire as power along the block shut down.

The storm passed before dawn. By 9:00 A.M., the weather was clear and pleasant, a perfect morning, freshly washed. Fred A. Tones's funeral was a closed-casket ceremony. There was not much a mortician could do with the dead man's charred remains. Mourners gathered at Saint Peter the Apostle Church for a full-dress Knights of Columbus burial. The pallbearers wore somber suits, but the Order of Alhambra honor guard decked themselves out in top hats, white ties, and tails. They could have been Social Register blue bloods presenting their daughters at a debutante ball instead of middle-class members of a religious fraternity laying one of their own to rest. When the mass ended and the casket was wheeled from the church, the honor guard lining the sidewalk whipped out their ceremonial swords and crossed them over the coffin of their fallen comrade.

Mrs. Tones could not hide her sorrow in seclusion after the funeral ended. She went to police headquarters to identify the slacks, the scuffed 9C shoe, and the size 16–32 light blue Van Heusen shirt homicide detectives had collected. She also recognized a pair of men's cotton underwear. Although she did not yet realize that her husband stripped off these shorts to romp with a teenager and a female impersonator, Mrs. Tones might have suspected sex was involved. The cops not only asked her for a hair sample from her head, they also needed a pubic hair specimen to compare it with evidence found inside her husband's office at the duplex on Griggs Road.

The widow signed a written statement giving her husband's original name as Salvadore Pasquale. She said he was born in Italy. She admitted the name on their marriage license was Tones, although the paperwork to make her husband's public identity official was filed less than five years before he died. The obituary printed in the *Houston Post*, the city's morning newspaper, listed the victim's name as Fred Arthur Tones, Jr.; the WANTED posters for Leslie and Carolyn said he was Fred Anthony Tones. Neither was correct. When Salvadore Pasquale legally adopted his new identity on September 6, 1956, the middle initial on the document registered at the Harris County courthouse did not stand for anything. He could change his middle name to suit his mood or add "junior" to make himself seem more authentic.

Mrs. Hortense Cooke finally caught up with Thursday editions of the New Orleans newspapers on Friday night. She saw the pictures of her rich Texas newlyweds and realized her delightful guests were wanted for torching a real estate man in Houston. Mrs. Cooke had no idea that Leslie and Carolyn had been gone more than forty-eight hours when she called the police at about 9:00 P.M. Two New Orleans officers arrived at the Golden Age Mansion within twenty minutes.

"The police and I broke in," Mrs. Cooke said. "The couple had taken the master key."

Mrs. Cooke's rendition of reality was a bit more dramatic than the truth. Although Leslie and Carolyn left with the key that opened the outside door to their room in the slave quarters, the police said Mrs. Cooke was able to use a pass key that unlocked another door she could reach from inside her guest home.

"I heard this terrible racket in the bathroom," she recalled. Something alive was trapped inside. "We opened the door and the big dog lunged at me and just sort of threw me into the hall."

Leslie and Carolyn had taken the poodle with them, but had shut Big Gray in the bathroom. "I was scared, very scared, but I later found out he was gentle as a lamb," Mrs. Cooke said. "He must have been tired of staying in that room. He'd torn the bathroom to ribbons. The drapes, the woodwork, the linoleum, everything was in shreds." Two days in a tiny bathroom had made Big Gray claustrophobic, but he was not hungry. "We found a fifty-pound bag of dog food in there too. The police loved the dog. They fed it, walked it around the block, and took it with them. I think they're going to use him in their canine corps," Mrs. Cooke said at the time

Mrs. Cooke conjured up a valiant destiny for Big Gray as the New Orleans cops went through the mess in room 8. "There was quite a bit of men's and women's clothing," Patrolman Edward Hyde remembered. Garments were thrown across the bed and dumped on the floor, stuffed inside a dresser, and left hanging in a "chifferobe," the Southern term for an armoire lined with drawers.

The cops found gowns, two pairs of high-heeled shoes, and a woman's short coat made of synthetic wool. They discovered cuff links decorated with musical notes and an empty brown leather key case on top of the dresser. They gathered several sales slips, as well as a receipt for a long brown wig rented under a false name from a costume company in Houston. Officer Hyde said they also picked up a pair of blue jeans smeared with blood. In the ashtray, mixed with crushed cigarette butts and burned matches, Sgt. Cornelius "Connie" Drumm collected six brass .22 hulls from the bullets that killed Fred A. Tones.

Mrs. Cooke was devastated, "They seemed so polite." She had misjudged her rich Texas honeymooners. "I just hope my other guests don't get upset and leave," she fretted to reporters covering the case.

11

Leslie and Carolyn unloaded the Lincoln at 424 West 57th, between Ninth and Tenth Avenues on the edge of Hell's Kitchen. Room 34 was on the fourth floor of a walk-up at the rear of the brownstone tenement. A half-dozen rooms shared a bathroom and one kitchen on the floor. A fortune teller, who had posted a KEEP OUT! sign on the door, had lived in room 34. When Leslie and Carolyn moved in, the door was decorated with a crayon drawing of the well-known cartoon poltergeist labeled "Casper the Ghost." A refrigerator was the only amenity inside their Manhattan hideout. The rent was $12.50 per week.

The management did not bother with written receipts, but the superintendent believed the new tenants were Mr. and Mrs. Charles Scott. A neighbor described Carolyn as "attractive, but coarse"; so tight-lipped that she seemed rude. Carolyn asked where she could find a convenient market that sold food at reasonable prices and the neighbor told her about a store around the corner. After that, Carolyn kept quiet. She brushed by people in the hall or on the stairs without speaking. Leslie made a better impression. He always said hello and he could not resist exchanging quips with the other tenants. If they ever saw him in drag, they did not recognize him.

The neighbors thought Leslie and Carolyn rarely left their room because they never cooked in the community kitchen, but "Mr. and Mrs. Charles Scott" were not quivering in their hideout. They went unseen on West 57th because they seldom stayed there. They rented another place on West 80th Street, in Leslie's favorite stomping grounds on the Upper West Side under the alias Mr. and Mrs. Ted Kipperman, the name of Leslie's bachelor uncle. The vibes were bad on West 80th, they could feel suspicious eyes staring at them, so they moved to an apartment even farther uptown at 155 West 95th Street.

Leslie rented this place in drag. He and Carolyn posed as sisters, Rose and Joan Goldberg. They could afford the extra expense because they were both working the winter streets. They left some clothes in Hell's Kitchen, mostly the spare men's wardrobe Leslie had brought from Texas, but they moved most of their contraband possessions to West 95th. They plugged in the portable television they did not have to sell because their trip was financed by hustling and money taken from Tones after he died. They also hung on to his gold Elgin wristwatch. "I didn't find that until we was in New York," Carolyn said.

Down south, two Houston cops arrived in New Orleans. Detective J. W. Kindred and Tom Metz, an HPD chemist, looked over evidence retrieved from the Golden Age Mansion—a pair of bloody Levi's, six empty .22 shells, and gowns "the wrong size to be worn by the Lima girl," the detective concluded. "We have no reason to believe they've left New Orleans," Kindred said at the time. He had confidence in his mistake, "On the contrary, we have some reason to believe they're still in this area."

Leslie's attorney, Jack Knight, concurred, "It would be more dangerous for him to leave than stay there." The carnival revelry was peaking. Hundreds of thousands of drunk, masquerading tourists clogged the city. Knight placed a message in the personal section of the classified ads in the *New Orleans Times-Picayune*. The plea for Leslie to call him collect appeared on February 14, not only Valentine's Day, but also Fat Tuesday, the climax of Mardi Gras in 1961.

"I hope to God he'll see the ad, that someone else will see it and show it to him," Sylvia said that morning. She was desperate for contact with her son. "Where are they? God, where are they? . . . I can't sleep. This thing is wrecking all of us," she sobbed. "Who was this Fred Tones? What was his connection with these two kids?"

Jack Knight's phone rang constantly, but most of the calls were from pranksters. "Cranks and crackpots," he complained. The voice he wanted to hear never called.

The love that had held Leslie and Carolyn together chilled in New York. Leslie's exciting tales of bright lights and high times in the Big Apple were not panning out for Carolyn. The big Lincoln that cut such a wide path in Houston and chewed the miles on the highway north was an albatross in Manhattan traffic. Their minds were so tangled they did not realize the left rear tire was flat until bystanders told them. Leslie and Carolyn rolled up the windows, locked the doors and abandoned the car across the street from their Hell's Kitchen hideout.

The gun that had killed Fred A. Tones vanished. "A boy stole it from me," Carolyn said, claiming the anonymous thief unzipped her purse and snuck off with the pistol at a restaurant. Leslie denied her version. He said a trick swiped the .22 revolver from her at the Hell's Kitchen hideout. Carolyn described herself as "a real mean little bebopster . . . hell on wheels" in Houston, but the gray, callous metropolis up north left her homesick and terrified, shivering and wanted for murder, while Leslie was in his element. If his mother had not exerted such a hold over him, he might have stayed in New York turning tricks in drag from the time he was a teenager.

Carolyn's depression deepened. She and Leslie fought and even separated, spending time apart in their different hideouts. Carolyn composed a despondent letter of pure teenage pain. She wrote "I love you, Cookie" on the envelope she left for him:

> I miss you very much. . . . I love you with all my heart. . . . I can't keep you out of my mind. . . . I guess I fell in love with the wrong boy again. One day I'll find one who loves me as much as I love him. I'd hoped it would be you. Well, tears won't help now.
>
> > Love & kisses,
> > Carolyn

She scrawled "I love you very, very, very much" in the margin. Carolyn's broken heart got through to Leslie. They had no one but each other and loneliness reunited them. They had been talking about going home to surrender from the time they arrived in New York. Confused and miserable, they were frozen at a crossroads. Whenever Leslie's thoughts became pure static, he turned to his mother.

Sylvia did most of the talking during the telephone call. "I didn't want to know where he was staying." She could not give the police information she did not have. "I wanted him to come back. . . . I wanted him to surrender. That's what I wanted him to do, that's what I wanted him to do," she repeated. "I didn't want the law to take him. 'Armed and dangerous,' that's what they said in the papers." Her wish failed to persuade him. Leslie and Carolyn stayed in New York.

Gradually, the HPD realized Leslie and Carolyn were no longer in New Orleans. The Houston homicide detectives still could not come up with a motive for the killing. They had not turned up a link between the dead man and the fugitives.

New Orleans police did not enlist Big Gray in their canine corps. They put the German shepherd on a train and consigned him to the Houston Humane Society, where the sick dog with heartworms was returned to the kennel he had come from. Big Gray's story had a happy ending, though. Front-page publicity attracted a farmer who owned a small spread beyond the city limits, midway to Galveston. He and his wife adopted the convalescing dog to roam acres of flat, salt-grass prairie.

Walking his beat on West 57th, an NYPD patrolman from the Eighteenth Precinct noticed an abandoned car. The white Lincoln was locked and dusty, the left rear tire was flat, and the hubcaps were missing. The Texas license plates made him suspicious.

On Wednesday evening, February 22, the patrolman called Detective Raymond Manners, who came over from the precinct station. Manners gave the Lincoln a once-over, noting the Texas tags read SK 7185. He jimmied a door and opened the glove compartment. Inside, he found a map with a route marked from Alabama to New York, as well as a $5.82 receipt for gas and oil at Chet's Esso station in Elkton, Maryland. Under the passenger seat, Manners discovered two more Texas license plates sharing a different number from the tags that were on the car. He figured the Lincoln might have been used for something worse than a fifteen-hundred-mile joyride.

An NYPD lab technician named Ed Meagher, an Irishman who

pronounced his last name "mar," arrived around 8:30 that night. Detective Manners was already gone. Meagher's primary job was looking for latent fingerprints. "Latent means they're not usually seen by the eye," he explained. He dusted the car's interior and lifted some prints from the rearview mirror. Before he took the impressions back to the lab, Meagher checked the Lincoln for bloodstains. The seats and floorboards seemed to be clean, except for crumpled cookie and snack wrappers, so he did not give the car a complete examination. He could not get into the trunk, but there was no urgency because he saw no indications of violence. Meagher stayed with the Lincoln to make sure microscopic evidence was not disturbed before he turned the car over to an NYPD tow truck.

Watching from up the street, Leslie and Carolyn saw the police activity around the stolen car, but they brushed off this fresh worry.

Carolyn turned eighteen on Thursday and they had a soda fountain celebration. "Leslie bought me a big piece of cake with a lot of candles on it." They were glad to be a step ahead of the law. "We lit the candles and he sang 'Happy Birthday.' I think everybody in the store thought we were crazy," she laughed.

There was no party for Carolyn at her mother's home. "We thought she'd be a successful hairstylist by the time she was eighteen." Mae Lima refused to see her daughter as a murder suspect, "All they want her for is questioning. That's all it will amount to when this thing is straightened out."

Carolyn said Leslie did not buy her a gift to unwrap, but Detective Raymond Manners found something to open on her birthday. He popped the Lincoln's trunk with a crowbar at the Eighteenth Precinct on Thursday. Under the lid, he found a toolbox, a spare tire, several portable cardboard files filled with real estate records, and two FOR SALE yard signs from Tones Realty. The NYPD reported a description of the Lincoln, plus the numbers on both sets of Texas license plates to the FBI. Before Carolyn's birthday ended, the FBI contacted the police in Houston. Detective John Thornton and HPD chemist Tom Metz, as well as an investigator from the district attorney's office, booked a private plane to New York, but a winter storm delayed them overnight in Washington, D.C.

They reached New York Friday morning and enlisted Detective

Manners as their guide on a search for signs of Leslie and Carolyn through "drag spots . . . homo hangouts . . . hotels (homo)," in the jargon of the HPD progress report. At 1 A.M. on their first night in New York, they surprised "a known Houston homosexual" living on the Upper West Side. But the late-night knock on the door led nowhere. The man said he had not seen the suspects.

While the Texans were exploring the Big Apple, two of New York's finest frisked Leslie. He was in drag with Carolyn in a penny arcade when a pair of patrolmen hauled him outside. Carolyn quietly drifted away as the cops spread Leslie against their squad car. As soon as Carolyn thought she was safe, she bolted to a pay phone and dialed Sylvia collect. Carolyn was petrified. Sylvia became hysterical so Jim Ayres grabbed the phone. Carolyn was too rattled to give him any details, but she told him Leslie was in custody and she was on her own.

Instead of running a check on Leslie, the cops shook him down for the cash they found on him, about $150, and told him to get lost. Leslie did not waste any time finding a phone, and Sylvia did not know whether to thank God for a false alarm or be frightened when she learned he was free again. Her son was considered a killer. Sylvia was terrified that he might be hurt if he did not turn himself in voluntarily. She wanted him to be aware of his legal rights. The first time Leslie called to test the water about returning to Houston, Sylvia had put him in touch with Jack Knight. She had Leslie speak with Knight again on Friday after the shakedown, and Knight agreed to go to the house on Wentworth for another call from New York on Saturday so Sylvia could join the conversation.

Leslie and Carolyn found each other before that Saturday call, and Knight convinced Leslie not to be afraid of a bug on the phone. "I told him tapped or not tapped, I damn well had to have their story before the New York police got hold of them." Knight learned why Leslie and Carolyn were at Tones's office. "You might call it business and social," he explained. He also heard about the getaway and the encounter with the corrupt NYPD cops. "Apparently they didn't know what they had." Knight advised his clients to give themselves up. "But Ashley told me he preferred not to do that." Knight warned Leslie about his rights, especially his right to remain silent, but he did not relay the same information to Carolyn.

The next day, just before five o'clock on Sunday afternoon, not quite three weeks after the shooting, Carolyn dialed the superintendent at the tenement on West 57th. Although she and Leslie knew Hell's Kitchen was dangerous for them, most of Leslie's male wardrobe was stashed at the apartment on West 57th. Without those clothes he had to spend almost all of his time in drag. They took a risk by phoning ahead, but Carolyn thought she could outfox the cops; she told the super that she would bring the back rent they owed during the next afternoon. If the super relayed the lie, Carolyn believed the cops would not swarm the tenement until Monday.

A cab pulled in front of the rundown five-story brownstone about 5:15 on Sunday evening. Leslie waited, holding Fifi the toy poodle in his lap, while Carolyn got out alone with a scarf tied around her head. She would not be gone long, just the time she needed to run up to the fourth floor, snatch Leslie's clothes, and carry them down, but Carolyn never made it to room 34. The super was not fooled by the call from Mrs. Charles Scott, and neither was the FBI. Agent Alex Winterson was waiting two flights up the stairs. Carolyn could not turn around and race away because another FBI man had followed her into the building. Agent Leo Reuther III was standing a few steps below. "She was detained by myself and Agent Alex Winterson," Reuther said dryly. "She identified herself as Carolyn Lima."

Carolyn did not resist. "We knew they would catch us, we were tired of running," she said. "We were ready to give up."

She was arrested on the Dyer Act charge: transporting a stolen car across state lines. Reuther informed Carolyn of her rights, "I personally advised her that she did not have to make any statement, and that any statement she did make could be used against her in a court of law, and that she was entitled to consult an attorney before making any statement."

Leslie was still in the backseat of the cab with Fifi when the FBI agents brought Carolyn outside. The taxi driver tried to make a U-turn; Leslie claimed he told the cabbie to drive up and down the block because he wanted to be arrested. A third agent on the stakeout sprang from his post across the street to help Reuther and Winterson stop the taxi. "I asked the occupant to please remove himself from the cab," Reuther said. Leslie did not comply. "The occupant was removed," the agent deadpanned.

"Yanked out" was Leslie's description. Apparently his desire to be caught was not overwhelming because Leslie tried to hide his identity by telling the FBI men that he and Carolyn were Rose and Joan Goldberg.

"He was dressed in female attire," according to Reuther. "He was wearing a long overcoat and long silk or rayon gloves, and a white kerchief around his head." Leslie was ahead of the fashion curve in "a black button-up sweater over a black dress and long black stockings and moccasins." Reuther left out a few of the details. Leslie's gloves were black too, his hose were ribbed and the hard-soled Indian-style moccasins were decorated with beads. Leslie was also wearing lightly smoked dark glasses.

He and Carolyn were searched for weapons, but they were clean. Leslie gripped a large handbag, almost the size of carry-on flight luggage. Carolyn had the same zippered purse that she had brought to the three-way date with Fred A. Tones. They had made a rapid financial rebound since the $150 shakedown on Friday. Between them, Leslie and Carolyn had sixty-eight dollars when they were arrested on Sunday. The suspects were booked, fingerprinted, and photographed. Leslie was still in drag for his mug shots. He was not the glamorous, effervescent Renée "Cookie" LaMonte, instead he resembled a worn-out frump exhausted from a marathon battle for discounts in a bargain basement.

"I looked terrible," Leslie groaned. "I didn't normally go around that way." He was wearing lipstick, mascara, and heavy powder, but Agent Winterson did not see any marks beneath the makeup that photos might not have revealed.

Carolyn was examined by an FBI nurse named Esther Corbett, "I was looking for concealed weapons and any body marks." Carolyn cooperated. "She completely disrobed." Corbett could not find any evidence of serious physical injury. "Just one scratch on her right thigh, on the outside of the upper thigh," the FBI nurse reported. "It was about two inches long."

Carolyn had a couple of specific complaints. "She had a slight scratch on her finger," the FBI nurse said. "She also called my attention to a slight infection on one of her toes, which I dressed for her." Carolyn did not report any pain or problems with her vagina, and the nurse did not observe anything unusual. From start to finish, the exam lasted about twenty minutes.

Leslie refused to make a statement about the shooting, but he cooperated when the agents found some keys in his purse. He not only told them the keys unlocked doors in Hell's Kitchen and on the Upper West Side, he signed written consent forms that let the FBI search the hideouts. Agent Leo Reuther returned to 424 West 57th Street. The room behind the door decorated with the crayon drawing of Casper the Friendly Ghost was a mess. Dirty sheets were rumpled on a sagging double bed. Fruit juice cans and chocolate milk cartons, aluminum pie tins, and rotting apple cores had been swept into a pile in the closet.

Clothes and bare wire hangers hung from the tenement's corroded sprinkler-system ceiling pipes. Mouth wash, a bottle of cheap perfume, and a squeezed-out tube of toothpaste were on a beat-up dresser; half-empty cans of beer had been left on top of the refrigerator. Reuther also found loose keys that would unlock doors at Tones Realty and at the dead man's home in Houston.

An agent named Thomas Duffy went uptown to apartment 1 at 155 West 95th Street. He retrieved more of Tones's property— the portable TV stolen from the Griggs Road office and the Elgin watch stripped off the dead man's wrist before his body was torched. Duffy also brought back a fifty-round box of .22 caliber bullets. Only thirty-eight remained. The *Houston Press*, one of the city's afternoon newspapers, guessed six of the missing shots were fired into Fred A. Tones, and the other six were used to reload the revolver that vanished. The math worked out, but neither Leslie nor Carolyn ever accounted for the missing bullets. (The daily *Press* stopped publishing in 1964; a weekly *Houston Press* with no connection to the original paper began appearing about twenty-five years later.)

The suspects had vacated their West 80th Street apartment, but the FBI rounded up an assortment of appliances and paraphernalia from the other two locations. Besides the bullets, keys, and stolen property, they also found business cards from tricks that Leslie and Carolyn had serviced. The agents boxed up the banal debris of life on the run: a coffee urn; a combination cooker and fryer that was really a glorified hot plate; plastic dinner dishes and genuine crystal tumblers; an electric razor; a camera; a dog leash.

They tagged the transvestite equipment that Leslie always left in his wake: an array of lipsticks and mascaras; four wigs—red, black, platinum, and brunette with a long silver streak like a skunk's pelt. The FBI discreetely catalogued "ladies' undergarments," including padded bras, as well as two evening gowns and several pairs of pedal pushers. One pair was leopard skin, Leslie's favorite. In his fear, he had apparently fallen back on his religious roots for comfort. The FBI catalogued four pieces of costume jewelry in the shape of a Star of David. A fifth six-pointed star was made of cultured pearls. Leslie also kept an Old Testament with a sterling silver Star of David on the cover.

He was allowed to call home about three hours after he was picked up. Sylvia answered the phone around seven o'clock, Houston time, and her relief collided with anguish. She began to get overexcited as she spoke to Leslie, then Carolyn, jabbering instructions to follow Jack Knight's advice and say nothing to the FBI. Sylvia was hysterical when Jim Ayres drove up the driveway during the call. He knew something was wrong the instant he walked into the house. "My wife said, 'They've apprehended them! They caught them in New York!' " Then she fainted.

Jim kept his cool, "I picked her up, then picked up the phone and talked to Douglas." Jim called his stepson by his middle name. "I asked him if Carolyn would call her mother." The FBI did not separate the suspects during the phone call. "Douglas asked Carolyn and she said no, so I talked to her. All she said was 'Will the lawyer take care of me too?' I told her he would." When the called ended, Jim dialed a doctor who made a house call and put Sylvia under sedation.

Because Carolyn refused to call her mother, Mae learned of her daughter's arrest from a man who identified himself as "Mrs. Lima's brother." He spoke to a reporter from the city's larger afternoon newspaper, the *Houston Chronicle*. "I first saw it on television when she was out of the room, and I told her." He said Mae hid behind her shell. "She didn't react at all." Mae told the *Press* that she had not contacted a lawyer. She had no plans to fly to New York, "I can't afford the trip." Asked if she was worried, Mae replied, "I guess so." The man who spoke to the *Chronicle* said she had slept without medication.

After the FBI agents took the suspects into separate interrogation rooms, Carolyn's purse was emptied onto a desk. She had a datebook listing the names and numbers of a few regular tricks, but the agents did not care about her current clientele. They were looking for links to a former customer buried in Houston's soft gumbo soil. They asked her to sort through keys she kept on different rings. One set was more important than the others. "She identified the keys, saying they were the keys to Fred Tones's automobile," Reuther recalled.

When Carolyn confessed the keys belonged to the stolen Lincoln she did much more than set herself up for a Dyer Act conviction. Under most circumstances, oral confessions were not admissible in Texas courts, but the keys gave Reuther a wedge that might let him testify about everything he claimed Carolyn told him. Carolyn did not tell him everything, but she told him too much.

In 1961, the FBI agents were not required to inform Carolyn Lima that she had the right to remain silent, merely that she did not have to make a statement if she did not want to talk to them. A teenager with a 72 IQ needed simple, specific language; the Supreme Court recognized the necessity by writing the explicit language for police warnings in the *Miranda* decision five years later. And, Carolyn's right to have an attorney present, although she could not afford to hire a lawyer, did not exist in 1961. That landmark decision, *Gideon v. Wainwright*, was two years away.

Carolyn spent hours talking with Agent Reuther, then he wanted to get her incriminating words on paper so he asked if she would sign a written confession. "She said she would not," Reuther remembered. He put her to bed in New York's House of Detention for Women around eleven o'clock on Sunday night. The Houston officers missed the excitement because they were touring Times Square. The HPD men heard Leslie and Carolyn were behind bars when they strolled into the Eighteenth Precinct after an evening spent searching for them in various dives and dumps.

Monday morning, Leslie Douglas Ashley and Carolyn Lima were scheduled to be arraigned on the Dyer Act charge. The key to the stolen car, found in Carolyn's purse, implicated her, and some of the fingerprints the NYPD lifted from the Lincoln's rearview mirror belonged to Leslie. The arraignment was a formality and, like most formalities in the judicial system, it was postponed. The procedure was rescheduled for after lunch, so the FBI let the HPD's Detective Thornton talk to the suspects at the federal courthouse.

Leslie was still wearing his beaded moccasins, but his black dress had been swapped for a khaki jail uniform. Traces of lipstick and mascara were still on his face. He was cryptic with Thornton. He told the homicide detective that he and Carolyn knew Tones from the real estate man's visits to their Truxillo apartment. Leslie called the bisexual Tones "a three-way man." He said the shooting on Griggs Road was self-defense, and that statutory rape was involved since Carolyn was underage when Tones was her trick.

"The whole thing was a panic from start to finish," Leslie told Thornton. But he would not provide any details. "Everything will come out when we get home." He began to giggle. "All the officers here think we're a couple of criminals." His weird snickering convinced them.

In Thornton's session with Carolyn, she refused to answer direct questions about who pulled the trigger, but she was easy to manipulate. "There were six shots fired," she recounted, then blurted, "I don't know where I hit him." The impact of that sentence suddenly struck her and she tried to retract her words. A reporter the *Houston Chronicle* sent to New York could see that Carolyn was about to break. Her weight was twenty pounds below the 125 pounds listed on her WANTED poster. Carolyn tried to keep her composure, but Leslie's nervous giggle was contagious. When she allowed her emotions to show, they revealed themselves as laughter.

At the arraignment, Leslie and Carolyn were represented by O. John Rogge, a New York attorney who had handled the out-of-state procedures for another notorious Houston murder case. Howard Stickney was charged with killing a married couple on a remote beach on Galveston Island. Stickney dumped the husband's remains in a vacant lot; he drove the wife's corpse home and had sex with the dead body until he decided to run. The Royal Canadian Mounted Police caught him in New Brunswick before he could hop a ship to England.

Rogge was Stickney's lawyer during the formalities that led to his extradition. In February, 1961, Howard Stickney was sitting on a death sentence. Leslie Douglas Ashley and Carolyn Lima were following in his footsteps when they stood beside O. John Rogge at their Dyer Act arraignment. Although the Texas murder warrants had not arrived, the U.S. commissioner (a title that has since been changed to federal magistrate) was satisfied when he was told they were on an airplane en route from Texas. Leslie's constant giggling irritated the commissioner's sense of decorum. He doubled the standard Dyer Act bail to fifty-thousand dollars for each of them.

"We will not oppose the government's move to send them back," Rogge announced. Jack Knight wanted his clients in Houston as soon as possible. He was confident a preliminary hearing would produce a charge less than murder with malice. He never expected the Harris County district attorney to get a quick indictment from a grand jury that made a preliminary hearing unnecessary. The D.A. had more traps that would catch Jack Knight by surprise.

From the reports she read, or saw on TV, Mae Lima began to realize that her daughter needed her own attorney, but Mae did not know any lawyers to call. Her only legal experience had been in divorce court. She told an interviewer at the time, "We've never had anything bad like this happen in our family before. I just don't know how it happened or what to do." Mae distracted herself with steady hours at her beauty salon. "I have standing appointments to keep," she said. "I've kept working since this thing started, trying to get my mind off it, but it hasn't helped much." She also relied on her faith. "I don't know what to do but pray. That's all I've done is pray. I hope it helps Carolyn."

Her daughter would need all the help she could get because District Attorney Frank Briscoe announced he would seek the death penalty for both defendants. He was not constrained by Carolyn's age. If she had been arrested before her Manhattan soda-fountain birthday party, she would have been turned over to juvenile authorities, but that would have been a temporary haven. In Texas, boys became adults at seventeen, girls at eighteen, but the age of a defendant at the time of the indictment, not the offense, determined whether the trial fell under juvenile or adult courts.

The statutes regarding capital punishment were less clear. Article 31 of the Texas Penal Code read: "A person for an offense committed before he arrived at the age of seventeen shall in no case be punished by death." The pronoun in Article 31 was masculine and boys became adults in the Texas legal system at seventeen, so the wording obviously applied to them, but the awkward clause was interpreted to imply that no one could be executed for an offense committed as a juvenile. Females were juveniles until they turned eighteen, and custom kept girls immune from death sentences for crimes committed before that age, but the Harris County D.A. used his own definition to expand the meaning of Article 31.

"The word 'person' in this case refers to both sexes," the D.A. said. Just like a boy, a seventeen-year-old girl could be tried for her life. Almost one hundred years had passed since a woman of any age had been executed in Texas. Death sentences for teenage girls were so far beyond judicial reality that the penal code did not explicitly address the subject, but Carolyn Lima would have an equal opportunity to ride the lightning in the electric chair.

Jack Knight cringed when he learned that Carolyn had admitted firing shots that hit the victim. "I wish she hadn't said that," her lawyer groaned.

After Leslie discovered Carolyn was talking, he decided to speak for himself. At the beginning of an interrogation the day after the arraignment, Detective Thornton claimed Leslie suddenly said, "I might as well tell you the truth." Thornton censored Leslie's version with a printable euphemism, "Tones made an unusual request of the girl. . . . A scuffle developed between Tones and Miss Lima."

In Leslie's version, the fight quickly turned into a B-movie climax. He leaped into the battle, Tones knocked him down. Leslie saw Carolyn's purse. "I just got so excited," he told Thornton. Leslie whipped the pistol from the purse and fired a shot that staggered Tones, but the wounded man wrestled with him. The gun fell out of Leslie's hand. Carolyn grabbed the pistol from the floor and emptied five more bullets into the berserk trick. Leslie rattled on about the aftermath—hiding the body in Tones's white Lincoln, driving to Sylvia's house on Wentworth, torching the dead man in the vacant lot. Thornton said Leslie confessed to pouring the gas, striking the match, and lighting the corpse.

The homicide detective dismissed most of the scenario, "Just a load of hogwash." Thornton said Leslie kept changing the sequence of the aftermath, juggling the order of visits to his mother's house between torching the corpse and packing up the Lincoln for the getaway.

"He smirks and giggles most of the time, and he dodges many questions with beatnik talk," Thornton said after the session. "When he can't think of a good answer, he falls back on saying, 'It was a panic, man, it was a panic.' " Thornton developed his own theory, "I'm convinced Tones's attention was on the girl, but he happened to see Ashley going through the pockets of his clothing." The homicide detective did not believe Leslie's story about the NYPD shakedown outside a penny arcade either. "Just more hogwash," he scoffed.

HPD chemist Tom Metz studied the Lincoln at the Eighteenth Precinct. He collected hair samples and spotted dark stains on a rear floor mat. Metz felt certain the stains were blood, but he did not criticize the NYPD for missing them. The stains were so small he was not sure he could scrape off enough flakes to determine the type or even if the blood was human.

After he finished collecting specimens, the chemist had to get the big Lincoln ready for the long drive to Houston. He and Thornton planned to make the trip together, along with five cartons of evidence from the suspects' hideaways. Metz had some repairs to make. The huge Lincoln had not been started for three weeks. The battery was dead and he received permission to replace it, but the HPD saved Houston taxpayers a few dollars by having him swap the spare tire in the trunk for the flat tire that had caused Leslie and Carolyn to abandon the Lincoln on West 57th Street.

Before they left New York, Thornton and Metz observed the extradition hearings to be sure the procedures started smoothly. The removal process was a two-step ritual. The defendants would appear before a U.S. commissioner, where their local lawyer would agree to waive any fight against extradition. Then, the commissioner would turn over the case to a federal judge with a recommendation to send Leslie and Carolyn to Texas. The judge would grant the order and a federal marshal would escort them south.

The Wednesday appearance before the U.S. commissioner was a perfunctory affair, a formality lasting a few minutes. Leslie wore his jailhouse khakis, Carolyn wet a fingertip and smoothed one of his eyebrows as the hearing began. Their lawyer, O. John Rogge, warned them to be quiet, but they could not stifle their snickering when he announced they were not opposing extradition. They kept giggling as the U.S. commissioner recommended a federal judge order their return to Texas. To Leslie and Carolyn, the whole procedure was a pompous charade. They were still chuckling and making monkeyshines at each other when they were taken back to their cells. In Houston, the *Press* headlined ASHLEY AND GIRL LAUGH AT TROUBLE.

Away from Leslie, Carolyn was serious when Detective Thornton saw her in jail Wednesday. He questioned her again about the date that went bad. "She stated Tones wanted to eat her," Thornton typed in his report, "and at the same time wanted Ashley to commit oral sodomy on him, and wanted Carolyn to commit sodomy on Ashley (among queers known as a Daisey Chain)." Thornton was paid to solve murders, not spell the names of flowers correctly.

Carolyn said she refused to join a circle of sex, but she agreed to go for a sixty-nine with Tones. His technique got too rough for her and Leslie tried to stop him, but Tones turned on Leslie. "Carolyn stated that Ashley was sitting near her purse and he reached in and got the gun and shot Tones one time in the right ear. Tones fell to the floor in front of the couch and Leslie laid down the gun." Thornton's report continued, "Carolyn stated that she picked up the gun when Tones got up from the floor and she started shooting and shot at Tones until the gun was empty."

Carolyn was not sure about the sequence of the aftermath. She was too scared to recall the order of their stops at Sylvia's house and the Truxillo apartment, but her memories of the trip to Avenue I were vivid. "When they arrived there, Cookie told her to stay in the car." She was using Leslie's nickname in her confession. "He put Tones's body in the ditch and he poured the gas over it and he lit the fire." Thornton said Carolyn lifted all the blame for torching the corpse off herself, "She believes it was Cookie's idea."

Leslie and Carolyn were brought back to the federal courthouse for the second step of the extradition ritual on Thursday morning. The day before, Leslie's jailhouse khakis had been neatly pressed, fitting tightly, the way he liked to wear male clothes. This morning, they were wrinkled and baggy. Carolyn was not laughing anymore.

They stood side by side, both in a daze, while the extradition proceeding began. They were grim and numb as the U.S. attorney explained the legal situation, "These defendants have waived removal to Texas and the commissioner has recommended their removal. . . ."

The judge realized Leslie and Carolyn were not listening. He barked at them, "Do you two know what the government just said?" Both defendants jerked, bobbing their heads up and down. The judge aimed his glare at Carolyn. "All right," he asked, "what did the attorney just say in your presence?"

Her face dropped and she mumbled something, but her voice was so low no one understood her. "Pay close attention," the judge scolded them. "I want you to know exactly what your rights are and what's going on here."

The hearing resumed. As the U.S. attorney addressed the judge, Leslie suddenly blurted, "When will we get to Texas?" He was ready to go home.

TWO

Be Not Deceived...

12

Detective John Thornton and Tom Metz, the HPD chemist, pulled the Lincoln into Houston just before midnight on Sunday, March 5, 1961. They were both worn out from four days on the highway. "That's a long drive to take without a spare tire," Metz said. "We held our breath all the way." They used the same key the FBI had found in Carolyn's purse to start the engine during their trip. Besides the crates of evidence, the officers brought along a mascot for good luck. Before they began their journey, they rescued Fifi the toy poodle from her cage at the New York Humane Society.

TRAVELER RETURNS, read the caption below the photo on the front page of the *Houston Press*. The paper called the toy poodle "the last of the fugitives" in the Tones case, and the picture reunited Fifi with her owners, a couple who owned a gas station near the supermarket where Leslie and Carolyn said they found Fifi. The original owners took the dog home, according to the HPD file, "with the understanding the poodle be available for court."

U.S. Marshal Thomas Lunney removed Leslie and Carolyn from their New York cells on Friday morning, March 10. Leslie found something to like while he was in jail in Manhattan. "Nice food," he remembered. "Beets, other vegetables, roast beef, food like that." Four walls and steady nourishment made him think. "I wish I could cry," he admitted. "I did cry a little once when I wrote my mother." Thoughts of his father stopped his tears. "My real dad, he's in Hot Springs, a bus driver." Leslie had no fond feelings for his father, "I couldn't cry for him."

91

The marshal handcuffed his prisoners for the ride to the airport; JFK was still called Idlewild in 1961. Carolyn had polished her fingernails. A religious medallion hung from a chain around her neck; the inscription said, "May the good Lord bless and keep you." A gift from Leslie. He wore his khaki slacks, and he had put on a clean pink shirt topped by a lightweight blue windbreaker despite the chilly, winter weather. He completed his back-to-school look with bright yellow socks inside his dark, beaded moccasins, which were identical to the shoes Carolyn had on her feet.

Reporters and photographers were waiting at Idlewild. "Oh my goodness," Leslie shrieked in a theatrical falsetto. "We're getting famous. I can hardly wait to get back to Houston." He primped his long curls and camped like a movie star. Carolyn played coy as she posed. "I'm not going to say a word, not a single word." She did not know how much damage her talking had already done.

Lunney removed their handcuffs while they waited to board the plane. The marshal refused to let reporters ask his prisoners any questions. He did not want to encourage their antics. Lunney told the press, "They've been acting like that ever since we started from the detention house. They don't seem to have a care in the world. They laugh and joke all the time."

The marshal held four tickets for an American Airlines flight departing at 9:15 A.M. His wife had been sworn in as a special deputy for the trip south; they could use a weekend together in warmer weather. Lunney waited until the other passengers were on the plane before he and his wife led the prisoners to the gate. They stopped and turned toward photographers for a picture at the airplane's door. Carolyn squinted and tried to look tough, she raised her left hand to display a wedding band. Leslie smiled, but he did not wear any makeup to hide the deep bags beneath his eyes.

The flight left a New York winter and landed in an early Texas spring. The temperature in Houston was perfect, seventy-two degrees—ideal weather for a media circus. The crush at the airport was the first real measure of the local frenzy stirred up by the torch-murder case. Two hundred people gawked at the killer queer and the teenage whore. Reporters peppered both defendants with questions that Leslie and Carolyn were not allowed to answer. Carolyn just showed off her wedding band as the Lunneys swept them to a federal lockup downtown.

The media motorcade raced along, and the speed was not wasted. The marshals in Houston were a husband and wife team also. Kathryn Matthews was the chief deputy marshal; her husband, Neil, was her assistant. They gave the press more leeway than their colleagues from New York had. Once Leslie and Carolyn were processed into her custody, Kathryn Matthews let reporters interview them in her office. Leslie rolled his eyes as Neil Matthews struggled to remove the handcuffs.

"I hope they're not stuck," he quipped. "It's wonderful to be home." He smiled as the cuffs unlocked. Leslie rubbed the circulation back into his wrists, then ran his hands through his curls. "A New York beautician did my hair for six-fifty, isn't it pretty?" He suddenly seemed to realize his high spirits were having the wrong effect. He could not stop laughing. "I can't help it. You all think me and Carolyn keep giggling because it's funny. Well, it ain't. We just can't help it. It's a nervous thing with both of us. We aren't making jokes about this like all you paper people say. You're making fun of us and it isn't very nice."

He tried to explain his condition. "I giggle all the time. I went to a doctor and he gave me some tranquilizer pills, but I quit taking them. I haven't seen him in two years." The reporters wanted to know if he and Carolyn were married, but Leslie kept babbling about his anonymous doctor. "He told me I should never get married. He advised me strongly against marriage."

Leslie claimed he had ignored that advice. "Me and Carolyn are married. We were married last October." The reporters tried to pin him down because there was no marriage license on file in Harris County. "Where? We're not saying. It was about thirty miles from here." He sidestepped them by praising Carolyn, "She's the most wonderful girl I've ever met. . . . we're closer now than we've ever been," he chattered. "We'd be thrilled to take a lie detector test," Leslie boasted. "We'll prove our story and get out." He only proved that he did not know anything about the judicial system. "We're not going to have anything like an open court. We're going to have our trial in private. We can't have all this made public."

Carolyn agreed, "I won't tell what happened in an open court. It's all too terrible. I'd be too ashamed to say all that in front of a lot of people."

She chewed the corners of her murder indictment as Leslie

reversed the grisly finale of their previous story. "She lit a match," he said. "She had poured the gasoline on him." Carolyn nodded. "She threw the match," Leslie contended, and Carolyn did not correct him.

A reporter quizzed her, "Do you have any remorse?"

"Any what?" she replied.

Showing weakness was not part of Carolyn's vocabulary either. "I don't want to sit around crying and all that. It's better to smile." She had built an iron wall against her mother. "I don't want to see her," Carolyn told reporters, "I love Ashley's mother better."

Mae Lima was stung. She had not met her daughter's plane at the airport and she tried to rectify her absence by bringing some clothes to the federal lockup. "They wouldn't let me in," she sighed. Mae was battered by the lurid headlines and revelations of her daughter's prostitution. "I just don't believe it," she said. "This just doesn't sound like my girl," Mae shook her head. "I can't believe it." Mae clung to denial, "All this just isn't like her."

The next day, March 11, the prisoners were transferred from federal custody to the Harris County jail. Carolyn spotted a familiar face while she was being booked. "He took me to my first prom," Carolyn said as she waved to an eighteen-year-old inmate. "I remember I wore a red corsage. It was the sixth-grade prom at Cooley Elementary School." Her puppy-love boyfriend was doing two years on a child molestation conviction.

Being close to home gradually melted Carolyn's hostility toward Mae. She agreed to see her mother when Mae came for a visit on Saturday morning. Mae brought along her Church of Christ pastor. Carolyn showed that she was ready for a reconciliation by wearing one of the dresses Mae had left behind on her thwarted visit to the federal lockup Friday night. Mae was shocked at the change in Carolyn's appearance, "She was tired and awful thin. She's lost a lot of weight," Mae told the ever-present reporters. Mother and daughter began to bawl as soon as they saw each other in a sheriff's office at the jail. "We both nearly washed out the office with our tears," Mae said.

"I thought Mama was mad at me," Carolyn sobbed. "Now I know she's not. I love her and she loves me. She's going to stick by me through this thing." They prayed with the pastor. "I got a lot off my chest," Carolyn said. "I feel like I'm square with God now, and I know I'm square with my mother. All I need is to be square with the law." Carolyn may have found religion, but she was not too pious to fudge the truth. "I never missed a Sunday, even the Sunday before this awful thing happened." She wanted to worship in the jail chapel. "I'm going to church tomorrow, wherever you go in here."

Carolyn wiped away the tears after her visitors left. She started laughing when Leslie was brought into the office for a conference with Jack Knight. "We're just happy when we're together," she said, grinning. She admitted they weren't really married, "We loved each other and wanted to get married, but we never had the chance."

The meeting with their lawyer lasted over two hours. "They were just leisurely discussions," Knight said. "I didn't go the whole way with them." Before the meeting, Knight hinted that self-defense would be his courtroom approach. After the long session with his clients, another strategy occurred to him: He wanted them to have mental examinations. "I'm not saying that insanity will be a defense. I just feel it's a precaution due them." And due himself as well, "An attorney should know the mental state of the people he represents."

Jack Knight was not alone in rethinking options on that Saturday afternoon. After she made up with Carolyn, Mae Lima went back to her small home in the Heights. The tears, the reality of jail, the weight Carolyn had lost, all pressed on Mae's mind. Prayers alone would not get the job done, and relying on legal advice from an attorney hired by someone else was not what a good mother should do, but the case was moving faster than she could act.

On Monday afternoon, March 13, Leslie Douglas Ashley and Carolyn Ann Lima were brought into court to respond to their indictments for murder with malice. Mae Lima attended the session in Criminal District Court Number 3, where Judge Miron Love presided. He ran down a standard list of questions, which included asking Carolyn for the name of her attorney.

"Mr. Jack Knight," she responded, but her mother did not consider this answer final.

"I don't know what I'll do," Mae said after the hearing. "My daughter is in trouble because of Ashley." She became more and more certain that Carolyn's defense was not Jack Knight's top priority. "I don't want Ashley to sacrifice my daughter for his freedom."

13

Although Jack Knight announced his intention to have his clients examined by private psychiatrists, the district attorney was ahead of him. As a routine measure, the prosecution had all defendants evaluated to anticipate insanity pleas.

On Monday, before the indictment hearing, the D.A. sent his own psychiatrist to the Harris County jail. Dr. Benjamin Sher spent over an hour on the exam and said Leslie cooperated completely with him. "I love attention," Leslie told him. Dr. Sher reported, "We went over many details and events preceding the actual occurrence of what brought the defendant to jail. Some of his past history, something about his marriage, his child, his relationship to his girlfriend." Chain-smoking, Leslie claimed he and Carolyn took the fatal trip to Griggs Road because Tones wanted to give her a television for her birthday.

The evaluation began to echo the diagnosis of the general practitioner who examined Leslie as a teenager. "My basic impression was not so much an emotional disturbance, but immaturity, rather childlike behavior," Dr. Sher said. The psychiatrist noted Leslie's effeminate mannerisms, "and sexual deviation in the form of homosexuality and transvestism." As a normal procedure, Dr. Sher ordered a full battery of clinical psychology tests, although he did not need to wait on a psychologist to help him reach a conclusion. He had already made up his mind about Leslie.

Mental competency in the Texas judicial system was based on the M'Naghton Rule, a standard with a strange spelling widely incorporated in legal codes throughout the United States. (The M'Naghton Rule was established in British common law in 1843 from a case involving the murder of the prime minister's private secretary.) Under the M'Naghton Rule, defendants are not legally responsible if they do not know "the nature and quality" of their acts because of a defect of reason—"disease of the mind" in the original case language from England. The M'Naghton Rule includes the mainstream conception of legal insanity—defendants are not responsible if they do not understand the difference between right and wrong.

After his visit with Leslie, Dr. Sher reported, "His thinking was clear and well oriented." The doctor rendered his opinion to the district attorney immediately, "It was my opinion he was of sound mind at the time."

As soon as he finished with Leslie, Dr. Sher spoke with Carolyn. She told him that her mother remarried about a year after her family splintered. The man she knew as her stepfather hung around for "several years," but she did not explain why Mae did not take his name. Carolyn also told Dr. Sher that she was raped when she was ten years old. After that traumatic experience, Carolyn said Leslie was her next sexual partner. Her past was sad, but the future made her cry. Her eyes filled with tears when she worried about the years ahead.

"Her emotional response was appropriate," Dr. Sher remarked. "She gave a picture of an individual who had difficulty in finding acceptance." Carolyn was not out of touch with reality. "She is of sound mind," Dr. Sher concluded.

The defense faced a steep hill when Dr. Neil Burch examined Leslie two days later, Wednesday, the Ides of March. Dr. Burch was a private psychiatrist sent by Jack Knight. He spent about an hour and fifteen minutes with Leslie. "The thing that struck me most was his description of how inadequate he felt in men's clothing. I noted at the time, his comment that as he walked down the street he would look around and he could see men punching each other and perhaps snickering."

Dr. Burch pondered the obvious psychiatric reflex, "This might be construed as a paranoid component, which may be part of the psychotic picture." He rejected that conclusion. The hostility Leslie felt was based on reality, "if one would consider his effeminate pose and the way he moved his shoulders and head, and the way he relates to people, and his comment that if he walks through a room or down the street, men would punch each other and snicker and say, 'Look at the oddball.' "

The psychiatrist picked up Leslie's lingo, "His reponse to this behavior was that he felt safe in drag." Dr. Burch repeated what Leslie had told him, "He said the old heads would go back and he would feel as good as anyone, he could go down the street and feel safe and secure." Burch emphasized, "When he dressed as a woman he felt he had power, and dressed as a woman, he could pass as a female. He felt protected, comfortable, and secure."

Jail stripped away Leslie's protective camouflage, according to Dr. Burch. "He said, 'I don't think the jailers like me.'" Again, Burch did not consider this feeling an unfounded persecution complex. "I thought that was probably true, because of his homosexual behavior, which is not the ideal image of the American male. . . . He strikes out against it." Leslie was not fantasizing the hatred around him. "I recall on the first interview as he came through the sheriff's office, these tall men, Texans, in these hats and badges, the way they looked at him as he pranced through the room."

Burch empathized with the deputies. "I'm a Texan myself and the feeling I got was they would tear him apart if they could." The psychiatrist did not hide his disapproval behind clinical language and he assumed most people agreed with him, "When you see an individual who flaunts his homosexuality, then I don't like it and you don't like it."

Burch rendered his diagnosis, "It was my feeling that the need to wear female clothing was actually the most important thing to him. . . . I felt that was the primary symptom and homosexuality was secondary." He believed Leslie had "a very poor prognosis," but that was not enough to prevent him from being prosecuted for murder. "I felt that he knew right from wrong, and the nature and extent of the act which he was alleged to have committed." Burch labeled Leslie a sociopath, but he concluded, "I felt he was not psychotic." He reached the same diagnosis for Carolyn. She indulged in "amoral behavior which repudiates and rejects the value systems and codes of her social group and society in general," but she was not legally insane.

Dr. Burch qualified his report with routine advice that his conclusions be supplemented with a battery of tests by a clinical psychologist and full case histories of both defendants, as well as of their families, but the preliminary findings discouraged Jack

Knight. Two psychiatrists had now said his clients were legally sane. He could not see stretching the finances of their parents by ordering psychologists to question Leslie and Carolyn about ink blots or climb their family trees. Knight never ordered the supplementary testing and he dropped his plan to have a third psychiatrist examine his clients. His notion for an insanity defense had hit a dead end.

Mae Lima acted on her fear that Jack Knight made Leslie his priority and neglected her daughter's defense. She asked Richard "Racehorse" Haynes to visit Carolyn in jail. Haynes was at the start of a career that would take him to the peak of his profession, putting him in the middle of high-dollar, high-profile cases. Later, he represented Dr. John Hill, the plastic surgeon accused of poisoning his socialite wife in the *Blood and Money* case. Haynes was also hired by Fort Worth multimillionaire T. Cullen Davis, "the richest man ever tried for murder," according to *Blood Will Tell*, the book that chronicled Davis's legal troubles after his estranged wife was seriously wounded, and her daughter and the wife's lover were both killed during a ferocious divorce.

In 1961, Racehorse Haynes was a young defense attorney just four years out of the University of Houston law school. He was a local boy from the wrong side of town. Like Carolyn, he had gone to Reagan High School, but Racehorse Haynes had graduated. He conferred with Carolyn in jail and agreed to represent her, "When I left her I understood I was her attorney." He believed Carolyn's best chance was a separate trial. Under the Texas Code of Criminal Procedure that governed the state's judicial system at the time (now changed), multiple defendants for the same offense were entitled to an automatic "severance." In other words, they had the right to separate trials, their lawyers only had to enter the motion.

"Leslie Douglas Ashley was making no bones about being gay and in my opinion a joint trial would have been detrimental to Carolyn," Haynes said. "Houston was still pretty 'western' at the time and it would have been hard to seat a jury that could see anything but Ashley's sexual preference." If a jury tilted toward a death sentence for Leslie, their momentum might give the chair to Carolyn as well. Jack Knight was hoping the tilt would work in his favor. According to Haynes, Knight "was of the opinion that he had a better chance of avoiding a death penalty for both or either of them if they were tried jointly." A jury might think twice about executing a teenage girl. If they backed off from one death sentence, they might have a harder time voting to condemn a second defendant, even a giggling transvestite, for the identical crime in the same trial.

The two lawyers clashed in the courthouse a few days after the indictment hearing. "Jack and I got into a serious difference of opinion 'discussion,' " Haynes said. "Jack refused to yield on his theory that a joint trial was best. I refused to yield on my opinion that a separate trial would be best for Carolyn."

Knight got angrier the next day when Carolyn told him Haynes had discussed his "separate trial" strategy with her. He fired off identical special delivery letters to Haynes's office and home. He wanted to be sure his message got through. "I consider this a very disturbing intrusion on my client in the state of her present trouble and certainly one of the basest acts of professional lack of ethics that I have ever encountered." He threatened to file misconduct charges with the Houston Bar Association. "If you make any further effort to talk with Miss Lima about this case it had better be by a court order and after due notice to me that you are seeking such an order."

Knight was the attorney of record. He had been practicing for more than twenty years; Haynes was just getting started. Later in his illustrious career, Racehorse Haynes might have been more stubborn, but he was not eager to fight a lawyer whose seniority outranked him in their profession and on the case. The impasse over strategies was impossible to break. "It was clear we could not work together under those circumstances," Haynes said, "so I withdrew." Carolyn lost a defense attorney who later became famous for his skillful ability to get his clients acquitted.

Jack Knight blasted an angry letter at Mae Lima too. "I think you have done quite enough harm along these lines," he wrote. "I need your cooperation, but if necessary I can do very well without it." He wanted Mae Lima to stick to her permanent rods and curlers. "I hope I make myself perfectly clear when I tell you that any further intrusion of this kind in this case will be met with steps that I deem best to protect your daughter's interests."

He enclosed a copy of a card he had asked Carolyn to sign:

Dear Mother,
I hereby request and instruct you not to talk with any attorney about my case except Mr. Knight. He is my permanent and only attorney in this case. I do not want Mr. Richard Haynes or any other attorney. Please drop the subject.

Her life was tied to Leslie and the joint defense Jack Knight could muster for them.

Jack Knight did not see any need for a third psychiatric interview, but the district attorney was a meticulous man. Frank Briscoe seldom left a hair out of place in his perfectly clipped brush cut and he finished what he started. The psychiatric opinions were two for two in his favor, but he could sense a hat trick on the horizon. His office got in touch with Dr. Howard Crow, who had a private practice. Dr. Crow did not do much work for the D.A., he guessed that he had examined inmates "four or five times" when he went to see Leslie and Carolyn on March 22.

The D.A.'s office had called him two days earlier, so Crow arranged to have a battery of psychological tests performed during his visit. He referred the tests to a Ph.D. in psychology named Jack Tracktir, who was with Leslie about an hour before Dr. Crow arrived. Leslie had spent a week and a half having his mind probed in the Harris County jail. He was a willing, helpful subject during his first session with Dr. Sher. Ten days later, Leslie's mood had changed.

"It was rather difficult to work with him," Tracktir said. "He was not overly cooperative. I wasn't able to get an intellectual showing. He was functioning below the normal level at the time." Exactly one week earlier, Dr. Burch had estimated Leslie's IQ at 100 to 105, in the upper half of the "normal" range.

The psychologist stayed for Dr. Crow's psychiatric exam, which lasted another two hours. "I found him somewhat breezy," Dr. Crow recalled. "I found him unable to logically tell me about his life and the present problem he was having." Leslie did not want to talk about the past either. "We attempted to go into his childhood and talk a little about his family. He was breezy, quite facetious, making jokes of things, continually making jokes. He would ask inappropriate questions and give inappropriate answers. He was a difficult man to tie down to a point and get a story related correctly."

Crow noticed what the other medical experts had noticed, "There was an implication of a feeling of being persecuted, being pushed around. The world is against you. People have bad feelings for you, they're twisted." The psychiatrist continued, "This is called a projection mechanism, blaming the other fellow. I got a feeling he felt this way and had a projection mechanism. . . . In this illness, people think people are going to do things to them . . . and they have magical powers to combat that." To Dr. Neil Burch, the power Leslie received from wigs and padded bras made him a sociopath. Dr. Crow read Leslie's compulsion to wear women's clothes as a supernatural transformation rooted in mental illness.

Dr. Crow and Jack Tracktir left together. Getting information from Leslie was not easy, but the psychologist had heard enough to reach a conclusion, "Under the material he did give me, I was able to get the opinion he was psychotic." The psychiatrist agreed. Dr. Crow fit Leslie's behavior into a more specific diagnostic framework, using Leslie's middle name, "After being with him approximately two hours, I felt Douglas Ashley represented the clinical evidence of a schizophrenic reaction." The psychiatrist went deeper, "I felt the schizophrenic reaction was paranoid and it was a chronic thing."

Dr. Crow listed the symptoms he observed: inappropriate emotions that did not fit the situation, ambivalence mixing contradictory feelings, illogical reasoning that garbled answers to specific questions. "You think how long it takes a person to get this way, and you have a profoundly sick person," Dr. Crow said. "I felt his behavior was a disabling disease, beginning way back in his childhood and had become almost a way of life with him."

Crow was aware of the consequences of his observations. He wanted to back up his impressions by seeing Leslie again, a week and a half after his initial interview. The psychiatrist said, "I found him again breezy, laughing, giggling, and making numerous mannerisms and postures." Leslie camped for over an hour. "Some people are silly sometimes and laugh and giggle at something we would take seriously. They laugh and giggle and can't control it, they have peculiar posturing. I found him this way, which was also observed on the original contact, but more so on the second date."

Dr. Crow made an effort to break through to Leslie, "I tried to get him to understand the terrible situation he was in. He took it very lightly, he laughed about it. I couldn't get him to be serious about it. He couldn't present it in a logical way. He did not seem to me to understand what might happen to him." Leslie said yes when he meant no. "Intellectually, he might say he did, but emotionally he did not. I did not feel he understood it. Again, I felt he exhibited schizophrenia and paranoia and giggling and so on. I felt it was chronic and I felt he was incompetent at that time. My understanding was that he was legally incompetent in accordance with my definition of the law as I understood it."

Dr. Crow said he notified the district attorney that he and Jack Tracktir believed both defendants were incompetent to stand trial. Crow went further with Leslie, advising treatment in a hospital. Crow did not receive any more instructions from Frank Briscoe. "I told him I thought the man was sick and incompetent, but I don't believe I'm in a position to tell Mr. Briscoe how to run his job." Dr. Crow was not a lawyer and forensic psychiatry was not his specialty. The D.A. decided the report should be kept secret. The defense was not informed of Dr. Crow's opinion.

14

His critics called Frank Briscoe a "hang 'em high" D.A. He was from an old guard family that had settled in Texas during the final year the land belonged to Mexico. The lore of his clan gave him a finely honed sense of the flimsy line between frontier chaos and the civilized restraint of decent folks. He was prone to under-stated patrician tailoring, button-down collars and wing-tipped shoes, more country club than rodeo, a stern southern aristocrat rather than a cowboy. He practiced his profession with a personal creed, "He who spares the guilty, punishes the innocent."

Frank Briscoe had joined the Harris County District Attorney's Office a week out of law school. He radiated the piercing light of moral certainty, and his cross-examinations were the sharp sword of retribution. He was born to be a prosecutor. At age thirty-three, he became the youngest candidate ever elected district attorney in Harris County. During his victorious campaign, he promised to take a hard line against every conceivable type of offender, from traffic violators caught behind the wheel without their driver's licenses to citizens who carried concealed firearms—"pistol toters," the newspapers called them.

Frank Briscoe summed up his attitude when he was sworn in on New Year's Day, 1961. "The greatest obstacle confronting the district attorney will be the tremendous public apathy that exists among the citizens here in Harris County regarding law enforce-ment." He made another promise that became prophecy, "I will not open my files to defendants. Open files can only lead to an open city for crime." Briscoe wanted discipline everywhere, and he installed a clock that timed the secretaries' coffee breaks in the

D.A.'s office. Fifteen minutes was their limit. The rule did not apply to the lawyers on his staff. "They're professional men," he huffed.

Instead, he imposed two rigid policy rules that limited the lawyers' initiative. First, no indictment for murder *with* malice could be plea-bargained down to murder *without* malice. The rule was a reaction to leniency in the antiquated Texas Penal Code. At the time, the *maximum* sentence for murder without malice was five years, exactly half the penalty for horse theft, too short for any homicide in Briscoe's view. He reinforced his rule against reduced pleas with another ironclad policy—prosecutors were not allowed to negotiate a penalty below fifteen years for any pretrial guilty plea to murder with malice.

The combination of these two policies meant prosecutors had to tell attorneys representing all murder with malice defendants that fifteen years in prison was their lowest offer under Briscoe's rules. Defense attorneys knew they could get a better deal from a jury, which set penalties in Texas trials at the time. "We got hung up trying the winners of knife fights when everybody knew the best you could hope for was a five-year suspended sentence," Neil McKay, an assistant D.A., remembered. He spoke from experience. "Sure enough, we'd try the whole thing and the jury would come back with five years suspended."

McKay specialized in capital murder cases. He knew when he had a shot at the electric chair or when he should dispose of a case over a couple of drinks. Being compelled to pursue stiffer penalties than he could win was McKay's only gripe about his boss. He and the district attorney saw eye to eye on capital punishment. McKay prosecuted Howard Stickney, the necrophiliac who made Houston headlines with a double murder and a cross-country manhunt. Stickney was waiting out the death sentence the assistant D.A. had hung on him when Briscoe tapped McKay to "sit behind him" as second chair for the Ashley–Lima trial.

McKay placed his faith in the ritual of trials, worthy opponents going head to head for the collective mind of a jury. "What the jury comes back with, that's justice," he believed. McKay thought appeals often twisted the truth on technicalities, and he could not stand lawyers who degraded trials by loading them with excuses for appeals. He reserved his respect for defense attorneys who dueled it out with him in front of the jury. McKay ranked Jack

Knight in that category. Knight might look like a portly, near-sighted gentleman esteemed for his impeccable manners who was being double-teamed by the D.A. and his courtroom ace, but McKay ran the jury selection for the prosecution and he thought Knight won the first move.

Justice worked fast in Texas in 1961. The trial was set for April 10, just a month after Leslie Douglas Ashley and Carolyn Ann Lima were extradited to Houston, but the court assigned to hear the case was tied up with a trial over a fatal barrio knife fight because of Briscoe's unyielding policies requiring trials for murder with malice indictments. Leslie and Carolyn did not have to wait long for a new trial date, however. Jury selection was re-scheduled for Monday, May 15.

Carolyn was sick of psychiatrists when she and Leslie met reporters the weekend before their lives went on the line. "I got tired of those dumb men pushing ink blotches and blocks at me so I acted crazy as a bug." She bragged that a frustrated psychiatrist lost his temper when she ricocheted questions at him that another psychiatrist had already asked her. Leslie was an unwilling subject too. He would not sit still for a battery of psychology tests and rocketed around the room until he threw open a door and escaped into an adjacent office. Leslie crossed his arms over his chest and refused to finish the session. "He behaved like a petulant child," the examiner said.

Leslie and Carolyn pledged their love for each other on the eve of jury selection. "We're as ready for the trial as we'll ever be," Leslie said. "We're going to face that jury together and take what-ever we get together." His brave front cracked and he began to giggle, "We would have been married here in jail, but they won't let us."

There was a reason for a wedding besides romance. Carolyn claimed she was four-months pregnant. She had a strong motive, "Would they let me have my baby before I go to prison if I have to go? Or before they put me in the electric chair?" She hoped a jury would not give a death sentence to a pregnant teenager.

Leslie tried to boost her confidence. "As a matter of fact, I don't think we'll get life or the chair." He started to crumble again and looked to her for reassurance, "Whatever we get we'll take it together, won't we?" Carolyn played with her package of cigarettes. Leslie wasn't much for silence, so he kept talking, "I never think about the outcome of the trial, especially the electric chair. I just put it out of my mind."

Facing execution cut through Carolyn's defenses, "I've thought about it plenty, too much, in fact."

Leslie refused to cave in, "Those people on the jury can't give us the electric chair. They just can't."

Carolyn was a pessimist, "You don't know what they'll do when that district attorney gets through." She dug at Leslie. "What's the matter? Don't you like the idea of them strapping those things on your arms?"

"Oh, how horrible," he moaned. He tried to look on the bright side, joking about the "terrible people they have me locked up with." Leslie giggled, "I'd even move to death row if they'd just get me out of that hospital tank." He didn't want to go alone. "If one of us gets the chair, the other will ask for it too."

Carolyn did not pick up her cue. She paused, "I don't know if I would or not."

Although it was only mid-May, the thermometer was expected to hit ninety so Carolyn wore a prim, lightweight summer dress checked with gray and purple for the first day of jury selection. The style fit tightly around her waist and reporters were unable to see any sign of the pregnancy she said was in the second trimester. Her shoes had modest heels; they were decorated with bows. Her nails were perfectly buffed and manicured, a testimonial to her beauty college training. Her black hair was freshly waved. Carolyn's most visible fashion accessory was a hardbound copy she carried of *The Greatest Story Ever Told,* a popular biography of Jesus Christ with the savior's portrait prominent on the cover.

Leslie looked like a bank teller in a gray-checked suit. His fashion sense did not include the proper fit for a man's suit; the jacket sleeves were cut a little short and the pants were much too long. A black necktie accented his dark hair, which was clipped short on the sides, but he had left enough on top to flip across his forehead. He kept from laughing by sealing a permanent frown on his lips.

Carolyn's father did not show up, but Leslie's did. Leslie Sherman Ashley made the trip from Arkansas with a female companion he called his "friend." He was working as a municipal bus driver now and his brief trouble with the law was twenty-five years behind him. The citizens of Hot Springs had elected him to be an alderman on their city council. Leslie Sherman Ashley came to the trial because he wanted to, neither side subpoenaed him as a witness. Before he took a seat in the courtroom gallery, he stopped outside the holdover cell where his son and Carolyn were. He peeked through the bars over a square hole cut into the solid metal door. "How are you, boy?" he asked in his Dixie drawl.

Leslie gave him a phony grin. "Oh, fine, fine." Leslie had never been able to tell his father the truth.

Bailiffs brought the defendants into Criminal District Court Number 3. A grumbling mob cramming the gallery was shooed out to make room for 350 jury candidates. The reason for calling so many people to fill twelve spots on the panel became obvious right away. Nearly 250 members of the jury pool lined up in front of the bench, stepping before Judge Miron Love to offer reasons why they could not serve. Carolyn fought back a smile as she listened to the upstanding citizens rattle off their excuses. She and Leslie exchanged a grin, but they cut their eye contact short to avoid a full-scale laughing fit. The real business of jury selection began with barely one hundred candidates left.

Trial lawyers accept the axiom that jury selection is the most important part of the case. Jack Knight was going for an all-male jury, and Neil McKay thought this move gave the defense an edge. "Men are hard on boys," the assistant D.A. believed. "Women are tough on girls." If the proceeding was going to pivot around Carolyn, her attorney did not want any self-righteous women to condemn her. The defense hoped an all-male jury would be unwilling to execute a teenage girl and their mercy might extend to Leslie as well.

Jack Knight began to play his hand with preemptive challenges against every woman the prosecution accepted, and he tried to determine if the men were biased against prostitutes. Carolyn rolled her eyes at references to her alleged profession, then buried her nose in *The Greatest Story Ever Told*, making sure the cover portrait of Jesus Christ was displayed to prospective jurors.

Knight used other questions to enlighten members of the jury pool on Texas statutes about justifiable homicide, especially self-defense. The law in Texas gave defendants a lot of leeway. Self-defense in most states relied on a doctrine from English common law known as "retreat to the wall" or "retreat to the ditch." The inability to escape allowed a response with deadly force. To prove self-defense in those states, anyone under scrutiny for homicide had to show that a reasonable person would *not* have been able to retreat from the conflict.

A Texan did not have to retreat. Until the penal code was revised in 1974, the Texas statute on self-defense clearly stated that a defendant had no burden to show that a reasonable person could not have backed away from the fight. The language was explicit to prevent the common-law doctrine from convicting a red-blooded man for doing what he had to do. That language also gave the statute its nickname—the stand and kill law. Simply put, if a hothead started a fight, lethal retaliation could finish it and leave the villain face down in the dirt.

There were drawbacks though. Courts restricted the introduction of detailed evidence about the deceased, plus Jack Knight would have to convince a jury that a law designed for macho straight-shooters also applied to a teenager who sold herself at a bus stop and a boy who wanted to be a girl.

More than twenty prospective jurors were questioned on Monday, only two were chosen—middle-aged men, a carpenter and a tree surgeon with a daughter the same age as Carolyn.

Frank Briscoe did not let Carolyn get much rest Monday night. She was using her self-proclaimed pregnancy to create sympathy, and the D.A. intended to prove she was lying, so he had her whisked from jail for a maternity test. The results were negative and Carolyn took the news hard.

"I am pregnant," she protested to reporters. "I should know."

She could not make the start of jury selection on Tuesday because she was throwing up. Morning sickness, she said. Judge Love agreed to a half-hour recess while a county doctor examined her. Thirty minutes stretched into an hour before Carolyn was well enough to come into the courtroom. The doctor said she suffered from cramps and nausea, probably due to nerves.

Carolyn showed the effects of her illness in the courtroom. Her pale, drawn complexion emphasized dark rings that had appeared beneath her eyes overnight. She tried to perk herself up with a new dress, the same lightweight summer style she had worn on Monday, but Tuesday's cream-colored material was a different print. Red and green spots replaced gray and purple checks. Carolyn began to wear the brighter dress more often, but she decided that reading *The Greatest Story Ever Told* was too obvious and she did not bring the book back to the courtroom on Tuesday or any other day. Leslie, however, tried to look pious. He carried a bible into court, although he left it in his lap or unopened on the defense table during most of the Tuesday session.

Carolyn spent the morning gulping frequently, queasy as if she was choking back the urge to vomit, so Judge Love called an early recess. Within a few minutes, Carolyn rallied and the session resumed. Because of the late start and the interruption, only two more jurors were chosen before noon. Both worked at oil refineries. The first was a young Southern Baptist with two small children. He hesitated, thinking deeply before he said that he could be impartial despite the defendants' "moral backgrounds." His own religious background made him a risk for the defense, but Jack Knight gambled that this juror's beliefs might compel him to think twice before casting the first stone.

The long break at noon gave everyone an energy boost. The lawyers made a breakthrough, six more jurors were chosen before Tuesday's session adjourned. All had salt-of-the-earth occupations: a retired steel foundry worker, a millwright for a paper company, another refinery hand. Two of the men picked on Tuesday afternoon worked at the post office substation in the Heights, the neighborhood where Carolyn grew up. One was a mail carrier, the other was a clerk. Another of the jurors was a self-employed estimator for electrical contracting projects, who drove around town with a clipboard and a pocketful of sharp pencils. The defense and the prosecution had found a common ground on which they were willing to fight, and that ground was the shared mentality of working-class men raising families or spoiling their grandchildren.

The lawyers expected to choose the final two jurors Wednesday morning, and then testimony could begin right away, so an even bigger crowd turned out. Eager beavers who did not want to miss a single witness stuffed themselves into every available seat. The crush in the corridor became frantic. Bailiffs had to push people away from the courtroom doors. Inside those doors, Carolyn wore the dress with red and green dots for the second day in a row.

Her perfect fingernails were polished scarlet to highlight the fabric of her outfit.

Leslie was in his bank teller's suit again. He had added a religious medal that he wore outside his shirt, next to his thin black tie. He had changed his hairstyle too; it was swept back instead of curled across his forehead. As the prospective jurors were questioned, he did not giggle, but he wasn't glum either. Leslie seemed to be lost in space, floating through infinite emptiness. Carolyn chewed her lips.

Against everyone's hopes, the momentum from Tuesday afternoon vanished on Wednesday. Progress snagged when the prosecution ran into a string of candidates opposed to capital punishment. Finally, an eleventh juror was selected, a rigger who climbed the catwalks at a petrochemical refinery. Exactly three minutes after noon, the panel was completed with a salesman for a battery and electric company. Jack Knight achieved his goal to seat an all-male jury. Testimony was scheduled to begin after a two-hour recess for lunch.

Courthouse insiders cut the tension in the cafeteria by spreading a wisecrack, "One's a prostitute and the other's a substitute." Because the gallery was emptied during the recess, veteran trial watchers without credentials brown-bagged their lunches so they could eat while they stood in line to regain their seats. Reporters taped handwritten signs on the benches to save space for themselves.

At two o'clock, when the doors reopened, so many spectators flooded into the courtroom and ignored those signs that bailiffs had to clear space for the press and interested attorneys who were curious to see the district attorney himself prosecute a capital case. Judge Love gaveled the trial to order. "Put down your newspapers," he ordered the gallery. The judge invoked "the Rule," a shorthand term for the procedure barring witnesses from the courtroom while testimony was heard. The Rule made it harder for witnesses to tailor their answers to what was said before they took the stand. The defendants' families, except for Leslie Sherman Ashley, who was not a witness, had to leave because of the Rule.

Both defendants entered not guilty pleas. Jack Knight did not hide his intentions in his opening statement—the killing was an act of self-defense. "The testimony will show that Tones was a Catholic and a member of the Knights of Columbus, that he was leading a double existence, sort of a Jekyll and Hyde life. He had his church life and his family on the one hand; on the other, he was out seeking young people for nefarious purposes."

In the prosecution's opening statement, Frank Briscoe declared the murder had resulted from a robbery gone sour, then he got down to business by emphasizing the family side of the victim's life with the trial's first witness. Michael Tones wore his hair in a teen-idol pompadour, about as long as the dress code at Mount Carmel High allowed. He was the kind of boy the men on the jury might have spawned themselves.

Carolyn riveted her eyes on Michael as he identifed his father's cuff links. The D.A. showed him a photo of the Lincoln, dusty from storage, missing the hubcaps stolen in New York. "They were all on there" the last time he saw the Lincoln, Michael recalled. "The car was in perfect condition." Briscoe moved quickly to defuse the victim's original identity. He could not let Jack Knight create the impression that Salvadore Pasquale was concealing dark secrets in a shady past. Michael Tones explained that his father did not change his name legally until 1956, but that he was known as Fred A. Tones "for as long as I can remember." The family had always gone by Tones; Michael had never been called anything else.

After opening with pathos, the prosecution switched to a detached documentation of horror. Robert Reyna recounted seeing "a big flash of fire" on Avenue I. In his testimony, fireman F. E. Blysard told the jury in his own peculiar grammar, "I taken my foot and put under the man and rolled him over." More cops and firemen followed. Knight did not ask many questions. To him, burning the body and the getaway were "window dressing," a clumsy choice of words for the gory scene on Avenue I. He announced that he would not cross-examine prosecution witnesses unless they testified about evidence from the shooting; his clients were not on trial for desecrating a corpse or for fleeing from the scene of a crime in the aftermath of the tragedy.

The tactic was a gambit to focus attention on the killing, not on the ghastly aftermath, but Knight's decision handicapped the defense. What he called "window dressing" was central to the prosecution's case. Frank Briscoe wanted to show that Leslie and

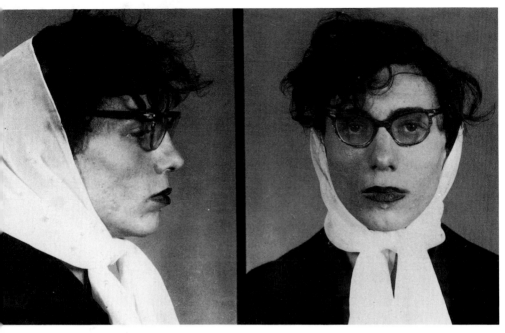

Leslie Douglas Ashley, aka "Rose Goldberg." (UPI/Bettman)

Carolyn Lima. (UPI/Bettmann)

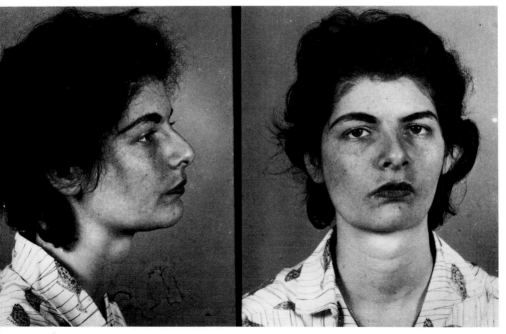

Leslie Douglas Ashley (second from left), dressed in feminine attire, and Carolyn Lima (third from right), flanked by FBI officers after their arrest in New York City, February 26, 1961. (UPI/Bettmann)

Leslie and Carolyn handcuffed and holding hands after their extradition by U.S Marshal Thomas C. Lunney (left) from New York on March 10, 1961. (*The Houston Post*)

Fred A. Tones, the man Leslie and Carolyn shot and burned after a three-way date went bad. Though they both testified that they killed Tones in self-defense, they were found guilty and received the highest penalty—death. (Houston Metropolitan Research Center, Houston Public Library)

The drainage ditch where Tones's torched body was found. (Photo courtesy Andrea Petor)

Carolyn and Leslie leaving the courtroom after hearing their sentence for the crime of murdering Fred A. Tones. (Houston Metropolitan Research Center, Houston Public Library)

Leslie reading his Bible on death row. (*The Houston Post*)

Sylvia Ayres, a Jewish mother, who would do anything to save her son from death. (*The Houston Post*)

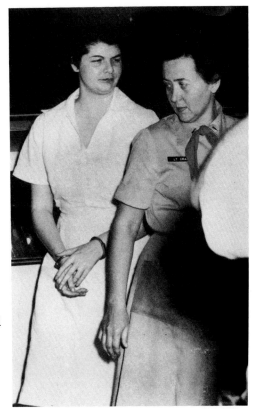

Carolyn (left) being led to "the Wall" for her execution. She would sit in the chair that would have electrocuted Leslie. (UPI/Bettmann)

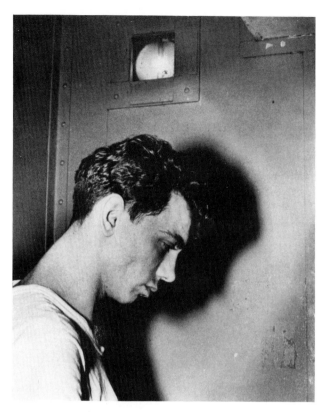

Leslie anticipating death that March evening in 1963. (*Houston Chronicle*)

Wanted poster the FBI issued after Leslie's escape from San Antonio Mental Hospital in 1965. (UPI/Bettmann)

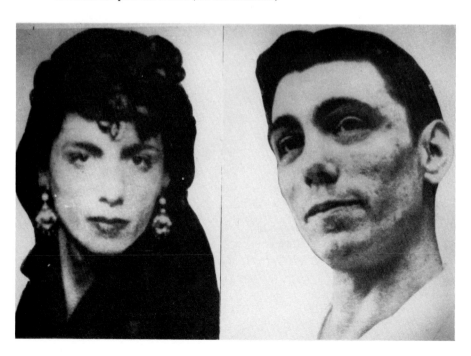

With the nightmare over, Leslie is able to start his new life.
(Houston Metropolitan Research Center, Houston Public Library)

True survivors, Leslie (right) and Sylvia at the Astrodome during the
1992 Republican National Convention. (Photo courtesy Andrea Petor)

Leslie at a Pro-Choice demonstration in downtown Houston, 1992.
(Photo courtesy Andrea Petor)

Carolyn behaved as though they were guilty—innocent people would not torch a dead body and then blast off for New Orleans. Knight's ploy left that contention unchallenged.

Knight was crafty during jury selection, but his concentration lapsed as soon as the testimony began. He let an opportunity slip when Newelton Free was on the stand. Free was the HPD investigator who took the photos at Avenue I that were entered as exhibits: tire tracks in the mud, the gasoline can floating in the drainage ditch, scorched grass where the body was burned. Free explained that he identified his photos by including the DEAD MAN chalkboard in the frame. "That's my sign on the picture. . . . My letters on the sign . . . I identify it by the letters on the signboard which is in the picture."

Jack Knight was scribbling notes to himself, but his mind must have been elsewhere. In the photos, the print on Free's chalkboard clearly read DEAD MAN 7800 AVE I 2-6-61, but the initials in the lower right-hand corner said CL. Free's partner was C.J. Lofland. His letters, not Free's, were on the sign.

It was a small inconsistency, a straw Knight failed to grasp. The discrepancy over initials on a chalkboard might seem petty, but Free was contradicting visible evidence. What else was incorrect about his testimony? Knight could have established that prosecution witnesses were not completely accurate. Their memories might be faulty, they could cut corners with their testimony, they were fallible. But Knight was not chipping away at their credibility. Undermining this foundation at every opportunity would have helped the defense when the going got rougher and Jack Knight had to challenge the prosecution's depiction of events.

If his attention had been wandering, Knight focused on the next witness. The coroner gave his full name, Joseph Alexander Jachimczyk, pronounced "ya-him-chick." The doctor was scholarly in horn-rimmed glasses and a bow tie. Doctor Jachimczyk brought along his autopsy records and double-checked his responses against his notes. He was precise and clinical, sprinkling his anatomical descriptions with language the laymen on the jury could understand.

The coroner boiled down the talk of temporal bones and the suprasternal notch, the sternocleidomastoid muscle and the acronion process to six gunshots wounds: two potentially fatal, four nonlethal. One mortal wound blew into the right side of the victim's skull, the second punctured the aorta on the left side of the dead man's chest. Four more slugs were dug from the left side of the victim's face and body. Toxicology tests turned up negative for the presence of drugs or alcohol.

Carolyn was impassive during the coroner's testimony, but the description of the autopsy clearly upset Leslie. His skin became pale and his eyes were wet and red as Doctor Jachimczyk recalled carving through bone and scorched flesh. Leslie recovered when Madeline Harlan took the stand. She was not used to reading floor plans, and a diagram of her duplex confused her, but she had no trouble remembering the blood she found on the office floor the morning after the shooting. "I mopped it up," she said.

Mrs. Harlan identified photographs of the Tones Realty office. The counters and desktops were cluttered, but there was no evidence of a struggle in any of the rooms. She denied that she had rearranged overturned furniture. She mopped blood, nothing more. Frank Briscoe avoided questions about the noises she heard on the night of the shooting. That was Jack Knight's job. Noises from a scuffle were not "window dressing," they were the heart of his case and he rose from his chair for his first serious cross-examination of the trial.

The morning after the shooting, Mrs. Harlan had described the sound as "thuds" or "hammering" or "slapping noises," sounds that implied she heard a fight. Knight wanted her to be more specific, but he did not want the answer he received.

"It seems like when I looked out the window I heard a shot."

Mrs. Harlan had never said the noise was gunfire before. Gunfire was the worst possible answer. Knight needed her to imply the sound was a noise that might have *caused* gunfire.

"You've heard Fourth of July firecrackers?" Of course, she had. "Did the noise you heard in that office sound like firecrackers?"

"No, sir."

"Did it sound like some kind of a scuffle?"

Briscoe leaped up to object. He claimed this was a leading question, but Judge Love overruled him.

Knight forged ahead. "Did it sound like firecrackers or like something striking something?"

"It sounded more like something striking something."

Knight was on the right track. "Would you say it was a heavy object, a hard object like two chairs striking together or two people striking each other?"

Briscoe objected. The question called for a conclusion. He was overruled again. The D.A. tried to argue, but the judge silenced him.

Knight repeated his question. "Did it sound like two hard objects, like two chairs hitting each other?"

"It sounded like somebody hitting each other."

"Were these metallic sounding objects or like wood hitting wood? A fist hitting something? Something like that?"

"It sounded to me like wood, I guess. It was an unusual sound is all I know."

"And that was the first noise you heard?"

Suddenly, he lost her. "I guess it was a shot I heard." She thought harder, "I'm sure it was." Knight battled to change her mind. "I don't recall," she answered. "All I can remember is that slapping noise."

The defense attorney saw a glimmer of light again. "Are you saying it was slapping you heard?"

"I imagine it was shots. I don't know."

"You think it could be shots, but you're not sure?"

"That's the only thing I know it could be."

Knight gave up without asking Mrs. Harlan when she decided the slapping noises were shots. He might have pressed her to admit that her conclusion came after she found out a pistol was emptied on the other side of her duplex, but he was too polite to badger a confused widow. His cross-examination petered out in Mrs. Harlan's memories of the victim's wardrobe on the day he died.

Judge Love recessed for the day. The general consensus gave the prosecution credit for an early blitz as the overflow throng left their litter in the courtroom and jammed into elevators. The crowd was excited, so their number was bound to get bigger. "I've never seen anything like it," a bailiff told a *Houston Press* reporter. People had been trying to sneak past him all day; a woman jumped into a stranger's lap when she could not find an empty seat. The bailiff became a bouncer, "I made her get out."

15

Early birds lined the sidewalk outside the courthouse on Thursday morning. The crime buffs had a new topic to gab about while they waited for the doors to be unlocked. Overnight, a patient in a local hospital went berserk with a pocketknife he had smuggled into the psychiatric ward. Charles White was lost in a spiritual crisis, unable to sleep since an encounter with evangelical missionaries made him feel like a sinner. "The veins were standing out on his head," his mother said. She wrapped cold towels around his brain, then called for help.

White had to be restrained before he was locked in a ward for violent patients. Although his clothes were confiscated, he managed to hang on to his knife. White erupted on an hour-long rampage singing "What A Friend We Have In Jesus," killing a nurse and an orderly, and slashing four more hospital employees before police shot the blade from his hand. He fell to the ground groaning, "Ashes to ashes, dust to dust." His own wounds were not serious; Charles White was expected to recover. The savvy crowd on the sidewalk knew homicides committed inside a psychiatric ward were perfect grounds for an insanity plea. The smart money said Charles White would never come to trial.

When the doors swung open at 7:00 A.M., the crowd forgot about White and charged into the courthouse. Four energetic women huffed and puffed up the stairs to the seventh floor to guarantee themselves front-row seats. Dozens of spectators, unwilling to make the climb, milled around the lobby for an hour, waiting to rush the courtroom when the elevators were turned on at eight. By the time the session began at nine o'clock, every seat was filled.

Because of the space reserved for the press and VIP insiders, there were less than 150 spots for the general public; one hundred more people waited outside. Gawkers pressed their faces against the glass in the courtroom's mahogany doors. They bumped and shoved, bickered and elbowed each other for the bailiff's nod to take a vacated seat. Mae Lima was barred from the courtroom by the Rule. She watched the hungry crowd from a bench in the hall. "What is it they want? Why are they here?" The crowd disgusted her. "Some of them even bring their babies. It makes me sick."

On Thursday, Carolyn arrived in high heels and matching gloves, plus a pair of dangling earrings. She had polished her nails again and changed out of the wrinkled dress she had worn for two straight days. She had adjusted to being on trial, and Leslie felt better too. He showed up on Thursday chewing gum. The defendants acted chipper, but Judge Love looked bad. During the morning testimony, he began to get ill. Barely an hour into the session, he needed a recess. A bailiff helped him to his chambers, while everyone waited for the judge to get a grip on his nausea. A doctor sent over medication and the session resumed when Judge Love's stomach calmed down.

Jack Knight cross-examined Officer David Hollub, the first cop to reach Griggs Road on the morning after the shooting. Hollub recounted Mrs. Harlan's description of the noise she heard the night before, "some thuds, like someone hit something," he said.

"Some thudding noise?" Knight repeated.

"Yes, sir." The landlady had never mentioned gunshots to the HPD patrolman.

Knight restored the impression that Mrs. Harlan heard a fight, so the prosecution came back hard, flaunting the victim's clothes that had been strewn along Polk. Cecil Mills, the mechanic who testified about finding the shirt and underwear, was served his subpoena while he was working the grease rack at Sears. The slacks almost backfired on the prosecution. Mrs. Betty Wiederhold swore the pants she was shown on the witness stand were not the pants she had found. "The pants I found weren't soiled, and these are black and not navy blue," she told the D.A.

Knight wanted her testimony stricken from the record and the dubious slacks removed from evidence. Briscoe countered that Mrs. Wiederhold's memory was wrong. The pants had a tailor's label marked with the name Fred A. Tones sewn into the waistband. The D.A. argued they were properly tagged by HPD Homicide Detective G.W. Gilbert, who took the stand and said the slacks were definitely the pants he received from Mrs. Wiederhold.

A homicide detective's testimony was enough to keep the pants in the record over Knight's objection. The defense attorney managed to make Gilbert admit that Mrs. Harlan told him about "several slapping sounds," not gunshots, but Gilbert stonewalled Knight's questions for details about the statement Mrs. Tones gave at HPD headquarters after her husband's funeral. He said his memory was foggy and he had neglected to bring his notes to court. It was an old trick. If law enforcement officers testified from interview notes or official reports, the defense was entitled to see the full text. Cops never brought their paperwork to court.

The thirty-minute recess Judge Love needed to settle his upset stomach had thrown the morning session behind schedule, so he decided to plow ahead without breaking for lunch, and the next prosecution witness destroyed Jack Knight's appetite. The defense was not ready for Richard Stroud, but Knight had no excuse for being unprepared. Stroud was not a surprise witness. Knight admitted that he knew Stroud was going to testify about watching Carolyn's target practice on the remote stretch of Almeda-Genoa Road. "Shooting at tin cans," in Knight's words. Stroud's account of seeing Carolyn with the gun in her hand two days before the alleged murder would be a disaster, as well as "irrelevant; immaterial and incompetent and highly prejudicial and inflammatory in every particular and remote and irrelevant to any issue in this case."

Knight was sputtering because he had not done his homework. He could not cite any precedents to keep Stroud off the witness stand. Judge Love offered the defense lawyer a fifteen-minute recess to research the case law that might reinforce his objection. Fifteen minutes was hardly enough time to duck into a law library, let alone turn up a relevant case. The recess was a token offer to avoid appearing prejudiced against the defense and giving Jack Knight grounds for appeal.

The defense attorney came back just before two o'clock with the fruits of his research, a murder conviction overturned, Knight argued, because improperly admitted evidence contributed to a fifteen-year sentence that was ruled too steep. The unorthodox argument Knight drew from the case that he cited emphasized the severity of the sentence, not the verdict itself. The slant he put on

the precedent provided a clue to his goal in the case that he was trying now—he was fighting harder against death sentences than guilty
verdicts.

Knight was vehement about Stroud's testimony, "It could only
leave the implication with the jury that she was out shooting, per-
fecting her aim to be good two nights later when she put this pistol
into practical application." Practical application was a euphemism
for shooting another human being, and Frank Briscoe said he could
link physical evidence from the "practical application" of the pistol
with evidence found at the target-practice site. He believed the
connection made Stroud's testimony admissible, and so did Judge
Love.

After the jury returned to the courtroom, Richard Stroud gave
the prosecution everything it wanted. He repeated that he saw a
woman who resembled Carolyn taking pot shots into the ditch near
his house. The woman was with two males he did not see clearly.
He recalled that a work crew was digging in the ditch about a
month later. Briscoe did not leave the jury wondering why the crew
was shoveling dirt and mud; a detective who sifted through the site
was waiting in the wings. J.W. Kindred said a handful of .22 shells
and slugs were found along Almeda-Genoa Road. He testified the
evidence was given to HPD experts for ballistic testing. That satisfied Briscoe. The bullets could wait; let them linger in the jury's
imagination. The D.A. preferred to save them for maximum
impact.

The long afternoon wore on with testimony from the pump jock-
eys who sold Carolyn the five-gallon can of gasoline and wired the
Packard's license plate to the rear of the Lincoln. Mrs. Hortense
Cooke brought her lyrical accent and poetic vision to the witness
stand. She scrutinized Leslie, "The boy has changed considerably.
His hair isn't the same color." Leslie was sporting his botched light-
brown dye job when he arrived at the Golden Age Mansion. "His
complexion isn't as smooth and nice," Mrs. Cooke said. "At that
time he was very friendly and laughing. They acted more like a
honeymoon couple, and his girl . . . "

Briscoe cut her off before she began her portrait of Carolyn. The
entire day had passed without a full-fledged break, everyone
needed a rest. Knight's policy of passing witnesses who only testified about the aftermath of the shooting might have hamstrung the
defense, but for now, it was a blessing. He had no questions for

Mrs. Cooke. Judge Love immediately called a short recess.

Mrs. Cooke was correct about Leslie. The wear and tear from the trial had taken a toll on him. Thursday morning, he entered the courtroom snapping gum. By the middle of the afternoon, he was nervous and brooding again. Carolyn was inscrutable behind a calm, straight face. Out in the hall, the crowd was taking on the flavor of a down-home revival meeting. An overweight sodbuster was wearing starched, striped overalls; a woman who was a courthouse regular accented her floral Sunday hat with a corsage.

The sheer speed of the trial made boredom impossible. The prosecution had already presented thirty-one witnesses, despite delays for illness and for Jack Knight's legal research, as well as an interruption to scold two spectators squabbling over a gallery seat and an interlude to question a woman caught taking notes of the testimony, then conferring with Sylvia in the hall.

Nothing about this trial was normal. After the recess Frank Briscoe startled the defense with a genuine surprise. James Edward Foraker was not on the subpoena roster. Knight swiveled to his clients when Foraker's name was called. Leslie drew a blank; Carolyn shook her head, stumped as Foraker took his oath. When he told the D.A. that he lived in Elkton, Maryland, Carolyn made the connection. "We bought gas there," she whispered. Frank Briscoe had secretly sent an investigator three thousand miles round-trip by car to prevent reporters from spotting the surprise witness at the airport, but Foraker's testimony was more flash than fury. He recalled gassing up the big Lincoln at Chet's Esso, a truck stop just off U.S. 40, about fifteen miles short of the Delaware line on the route to New York.

Foraker identified a receipt Leslie demanded for the cash purchase. He said that he was not sure Leslie was a male when the Lincoln pulled into Chet's Esso. The man riding shotgun had acted like a woman. Foraker recalled the transaction. "Not exactly a conversation, there was some wise remarks made." Carolyn was driving. "She said to fill her up the best I could. While I was filling it up, I was seeing what the gallonage was on it and I told him how much it was."

Foraker testified that Leslie could not see the price on the pump. "He said to her, 'It doesn't show how much there.' And I said, 'What do you want me to do, turn it around?' " Leslie could not resist popping off. "He said to her, 'Some things show up big and strong.' And I said, 'You're not in Texas now.' I had seen the license number, the Texas tags.' "

On the surface, Foraker's testimony looked like a lot of effort with slim results, but putting so much work into such a minor witness gave the defense fair warning that the prosecution was taking this case to the limit. It also demonstrated that the D.A. could blindside the defense with complete surprise, and the voltage in the next shock might have more juice.

The initial appearance by FBI Special Agent Leo Reuther III seemed harmless, almost comical. His concise, responsive answers collided with the ludicrous reality of capturing Leslie in drag with Fifi on his lap in Hell's Kitchen. Their rotund attorney sat between them, so Leslie and Carolyn leaned around him and grinned at each other. They began sending silent signals by lifting the religious medallions they wore around their necks. Their trial was perched on a dangerous cliff, divine intervention might be their only salvation.

Briscoe was curious about an item Reuther had found in Carolyn's purse. The D.A. produced a set of car keys marked State's Exhibit Number 42. He did not ask Reuther to say what make or model car these keys fit. Briscoe only wanted him to establish they were discovered inside Carolyn's purse. The keys were entered into evidence without objection from Knight, and Briscoe was careful not to attach any special significance to them.

While Leslie and Carolyn were settling into their cells after the grueling day, Frank Briscoe was dressing for an elegant soiree at the Bayou Club, an exclusive preserve for the cream of Houston society. The district attorney must have felt like a cat with feathers in his teeth—and the canaries did not even know they had been swallowed.

When Briscoe slipped State's Exhibit Number 42 into evidence, he took a giant leap toward total victory. With that set of keys, he planned to spring a trap that would destroy the defense Jack Knight had not yet begun to mount. Chatting poolside at the Bayou Club, surrounded by flowers and violins, Frank Briscoe felt he had this case by the short hairs, but the future could always take a nasty turn. Even here, beneath the pines in the perfect moonlight, fate could be cruel.

16

On Friday morning, the only obstacle to the prosecution buzzsaw was Judge Love's health. Although his stomach still bothered him, he managed to bang his court to order on time at nine o'clock. Thomas Metz, the HPD chemist, testified about blood he found at the Griggs Road office the morning after the shooting. The blood was type A, the same type found by the coroner at the victim's autopsy, and the same type as the blood caked on the Levi's that Leslie left in New Orleans. The blood could not have come from either defendant. According to tests Metz had performed at the HPD lab from samples drawn in jail, Leslie was type O and Carolyn was type B.

The trial moved into subjects Jack Knight was willing to challenge, and the defense attorney began to shake from his slumber. "Did you at any time in your investigation of this case see a large knife or dagger or bayonet or something that would fit that description?"

Metz remembered the bayonet in the office on Griggs Road. "I don't know if anybody had seen it prior to me or not." He did not know what had happened to the bayonet. It never turned up in his lab and he had not seen it in the HPD property room.

Knight stuck with Griggs Road. "Where was it in relationship to the blood spot on the floor you looked at, sir?"

"It was in the next room." Not very close.

Knight lost more ground. "Laying on the floor?"

"No, sir, behind the safe on a little shelf, on a little shelf beneath a window."

Knight backed off. He failed to establish a strong link between the front room where a fight allegedly occurred and the location of the bayonet, but at least he planted the weapon in the jurors' minds.

Briscoe rushed to erase the image of the long blade. HPD ID expert Kenneth Swatzel compared close-up photos of fingerprints on the Lincoln's rearview mirror with fingerprints taken from both defendants. Two of the prints from the stolen car were Leslie's; one print was made by Carolyn.

Then Briscoe lowered the boom. "I will ask you, Mr. Swatzel, if in your capacity with the police department you have had turned over to you any slugs or hulls of any kind in connection with this case?"

Swatzel handed the D.A. three slugs: the bullet dug from the victim's brain, the lethal chest-wound slug, and the bullet found along his jaw beneath burned skin. The missing bayonet faded like a mirage as Briscoe entered the deadly slugs as evidence, then mined more gold from Swatzel's mother lode of copper and lead. The ID expert gave the D.A. three more slugs found by X rays during the afternoon of the autopsy. He also had six cartridges and the ashtray from room 8 at the Golden Age Mansion. Swatzel did not reveal the origin of another batch he inventoried, "eight fired cartridge cases, one unfired round of ammunition, and two fired lead bullets."

All the slugs and hulls Swatzel examined were an identical type. "They were .22 caliber shorts . . . the smaller type of .22 bullet." His microscopic study made the match. "They were all fired by the same firearm." He could not be positive the bullets were shot from an Eig pistol. It was a possibility, but no gun had been given to him.

On cross-examination, Knight asked Swatzel if the bullets were the only weapons from the case that he had examined. "Yes, sir. That's the only evidence that has been submitted to me." Swatzel recalled seeing a large knife near a filing cabinet in the office on Griggs Road. He did not take it, and he did not know if anyone else had either. Knight was shadowboxing, working to build up suspense and expectations about the bayonet, while the bullets were doing real damage to the defense.

After a morning recess, the D.A. revealed where the mixed batch of eight shells, two slugs, and the single live round had been found. Briscoe returned Detective J. W. Kindred to the stand. Kindred said the entire exhibit was collected on Almeda-Genoa Road where Carolyn was seen plinking tin cans. "The fired hulls were recovered from the shoulder of the road right there. The slugs were found in the ground, they were dug up out of the earth at that location." Kindred's testimony proved Carolyn was practicing with the pistol two days before Fred A. Tones was killed. The D.A. gave the witness to the defense like a millionaire flipping a quarter to a bum.

Jack Knight sensed he was making headway with his questions about the bayonet. The first time Kindred testified, Knight had not even brought up the weapon. Today was different. Kindred said he saw it on top of a filing cabinet in Tones's private office, not the office where Mrs. Harlan mopped blood.

"She did tell you, as you described yesterday, she heard a fight in there the night before?"

"Yes, sir. That's correct."

"Didn't she further tell you she readied the office furniture in that place?"

"I don't recall that, sir."

"Didn't she tell you she picked up this bayonet and put it in the back office on a filing cabinet?"

"No, sir."

Knight did not care about Kindred's denial. He was creating possibilities.

"She didn't tell you that?"

"No, sir." A double denial emphasized the potential.

"Could she have told you that and you would've forgotten it?"

"I'm certain she didn't tell me that." Kindred was insulted. "I believe I would have remembered it, counsel."

Knight switched directions. He wanted Kindred to tell him about some business cards the FBI collected from the Manhattan hideouts.

"Have you seen those cards?"

"Yes, sir."

"Did you notice any of those being business cards of Fred A. Tones Realty Company?"

"I don't recall." Kindred was clamming up. "It's possible."

"Did you see, refreshing your memory further, a Tones Realty Company business card taken from these defendants on which, on the back was the notation 'call me' written in longhand?"

"I don't recall it."

"You do not?"

"No, sir."

Knight let Kindred step down. Despite the stonewalling tactics, the homicide detective had been Knight's best cross-examination yet. The defense attorney not only reinforced the existence of the bayonet, he also had the jury wondering if Mrs. Harlan straightened her tenant's furniture after she mopped up his blood. And, a "call me" message on a Tones Realty card could be sitting on a shelf with other evidence the D.A. did not want to present.

Briscoe refused to let Knight's flurry knock him off stride. He called John Thornton, the homicide detective in charge of the case. Thornton had twice as much seniority tracking killers as Kindred; he also had more experience on witness stands. The D.A. dangled a set of keys, State's Exhibit Number 42.

"Those are the keys to the 1960 Lincoln that belonged to Mr. Tones," Thornton said. "I used these keys in the ignition and drove back to Houston."

The time was not right for the D.A.'s trap, so he held up a second set of keys. Thornton knew where they belonged, and there was nothing high-tech about the method he had used to identify them. When he returned to Houston, the homicide detective spoke with Michael Tones, who recognized the keys and steered him to Griggs Road. "I went to the office and used those keys and entered it," Thornton said.

Jack Knight wanted to hear about the bayonet, not keys. No one steered Thornton to the weapon, he found it on his own.

"Did you just leave it there in that apartment?"

"Yes, sir, after I examined it, yes, sir."

"Did you yourself make any tests for fingerprints of any kind on that instrument?"

"Yes, sir. I examined it for possible fingerprints, and I also took it to Officer Swatzel, who at that time was lifting prints in Mr. Tones's office. I asked him to examine it for possible fingerprints."

Swatzel had testified he saw the bayonet lying behind a filing cabinet; he had not said Thornton brought the weapon to him. Knight missed this discrepancy, and that the ID expert had never spoken of a fingerprint test during his testimony, but Thornton's claim allowed the homicide detective to create the impression the

HPD had sufficient grounds for deciding the bayonet was not part of the case, even though a thorough lab exam was never conducted.

If Knight had not been working alone, a second defense attorney could have helped him keep track of inconsistencies by prosecution witnesses and exploit gaps between them. The wrong initials on the DEAD MAN chalkboard, the possibility that incorrect pants were offered as evidence, the contradiction between Thornton's claims and Swatzel's testimony about the bayonet; these were all examples of opportunities Knight missed because he was working alone. He overestimated himself and risked his clients' lives by trying the case without a partner. The D.A. had not made the same mistake. Neil McKay was there to make sure the prosecution team jumped on every defense mistake.

The D.A. seemed to be approaching the climax of his case, by calling his final witness, although he and his inner circle of confidants were the only people who knew it was a false climax, when Dorothy Tones took the stand. She was tiny and gaunt, weighing barely one hundred pounds, after coping with her tragedy for more than three months. In the courtroom, Mrs. Tones kept her eyes away from Leslie and Carolyn. When her testimony began, the widow spoke so quietly the district attorney urged her to raise her voice. He tried to get her through the ordeal quickly. She identified her husband's shoe and the blue shirt that she had bought for him. Frank Briscoe held up her husband's underwear.

"Yes, sir. I would say they are Fred's."

She hedged when Briscoe displayed the trousers.

"I would say that if they're not his, they are very similar to his trousers." Her answer seemed coached, carefully phrased.

Briscoe wanted to make the identification seem more positive than it actually was. He asked her about a tailor's band sewn into the waistband, "Did your husband purchase clothing from Jerome Tailors?"

"Yes, sir, he did. He had four pairs made there." The pants sailed through without being questioned. Knight had already lost his battle against them.

"At the time, Mrs. Tones, was your husband in good health and good spirits?" Briscoe asked.

"Excellent."

"You know, of course, that he is dead?"

"Yes, I do."

"Do you recall attending the funeral?"

"Yes, I do."

"Did you, perhaps, ever see Mr. Tones after death to identify him or anything?"

"No, I did not." Knights of Columbus spared her that horror and went to the morgue to confirm the name of their colleague, but Jack Knight was too wary of the widow to dispute the identification of her husband's body.

Her quiet testimony turned into indignation as soon as the defense took over. Mrs. Tones told Knight that she was familiar with her late husband's bayonet. "It was kind of a keepsake or something he had picked up someplace." The weapon was at her home.

"Could you bring it, please, to the court when we resume at two o'clock?"

"I wouldn't be able to get out to the house and get back in time, Mr. Knight," she answered.

"Well, on your next trip out there could you bring it into court?"

"I will be happy to." Her words hardly masked her animosity.

At last, Knight was going to get his hands on the bayonet. The D.A. did not seem disturbed. Just before noon on Friday, May 19, the prosecution rested. Since beginning his case after lunch on Wednesday, Frank Briscoe had called forty-two witnesses during the equivalent of just two days of testimony. Despite that formidable number, he was not guaranteed a pair of death sentences. With the bullets and the victim's clothes, the tidal wave of law enforcement experts and the secret trap he was waiting to spring, Briscoe had a lot going for him, but the defense had established that Mrs. Harlan thought she heard thumps or slaps, a scuffle instead of gunshots. The bayonet was real. Maybe the defendants actually were the winners of a knife fight who panicked in the aftermath. It was only a matter of time before the weapon surfaced in the courtroom.

Briscoe had other problems as well. Although he had thoroughly bashed the defense, he had not met the goal he set for himself. When the trial started, he had announced his intention to prove the shooting had resulted from a shakedown planned two days earlier—a robbery gone sour that exploded into murder. An evidence table piled high with items stolen from the victim buttressed the back half of that theory, but the D.A. still had a hole in the center of his scenario: none of the property taken from Tones had been pawned or sold.

People saw the defendants enter the victim's office, but none of the prosecution's witnesses said anything about a robbery. The word had not been mentioned since his opening statement; the district attorney had not established a motive. He had not even presented a reason for a link between the defendants and the victim, but he would not have to make that connection because Leslie and Carolyn were going to do it for him.

17

Court reconvened at 1:30, and Jack Knight began his defense by forgetting which witness he wanted to question. "We would like to call Mrs. Mae Lima. . . . " he boomed, then suddenly changed his mind. "No, excuse me. May we have Officer Higgins first?" It was an inauspicious start to a difficult job; confused lawyers dig holes for their clients with juries.

W.B. Higgins was the HPD vice and robbery lieutenant who had gone to the Truxillo apartment to scold Carolyn for working bus stops in her neighborhood. Knight used him to preempt the D.A.'s contention that Leslie and Carolyn were planning a robbery. Carolyn had bragged to Higgins about her new gun, and a thief would not boast to a cop about buying a weapon.

Mae Lima took the stand next. Her red hair was hidden under a white hat. She was so timid Knight had to ask her to speak up twice. Mae was unable to look at her daughter as she recalled how Carolyn had quit school and moved out of their house in the Heights to live with Leslie. Tears watered in Carolyn's eyes as her mother recalled helping her prepare the kit of curlers and beautician's paraphernalia for the licensing exam in Austin. Mrs. Lima said she always gave her daughter as much money as she could afford to spare. Her answers stressed Carolyn was planning a career, not a robbery, much less a murder. Carolyn could not stop crying.

Briscoe was stern when he took over. Mae Lima denied that she was unable to excercise parental supervision over Carolyn. When her youngest daughter left home, Mae believed she was married.

"Did you attend the wedding?"

Mae admitted she had not. Briscoe launched his "robbery gone sour" strategy, probing Mae's income to prove she was not able to provide Carolyn with much money. "However she supported herself, the funds didn't come from you, is that correct?"

Mae agreed. Carolyn was on the verge of falling apart completely when her mother stepped down and Leslie's mother took the witness stand. Sylvia's hat was a horror, a saucer covered with artificial flowers that ringed her head like a lair for squirrels. She zipped ahead of Knight as soon as he asked about Leslie's first visit to her house on the night of February 6.

"Jack, it was after we finished dinner . . . " Her familiarity seemed to startle him. She took control, "Let me tell you exactly what happened, may I?"

Knight did not want her running wild. "The district attorney may want you to answer some specific questions so let's narrow it down."

Briscoe spoke for himself. "The district attorney wants it done according to the rules of evidence."

Knight didn't appreciate the intrusion. "It will be done that way, counsel," he snapped.

Sylvia began to sob as she recalled her son's swollen face and the cut lip he rinsed in her kitchen sink. She cried harder when she described catching Carolyn in the bathroom with her pedal pushers around her ankles. At the defense table, Carolyn's weeping worsened; Leslie started crying too. The water was rising around Jack Knight.

Sylvia bawled, "I said, 'Carolyn, what happened to you? . . . ' "

Frank Briscoe broke into their wailing. He did not want Sylvia giving hearsay testimony about the other half of a two-way conversation. Judge Love sustained him. Knight was so intent on keeping an even keel in the flood of tears that he repeated his question about Sylvia's bathroom conversation with Carolyn, then turned to Judge Love and asked if an answer had already been ruled inadmissible. The judge realized the defense attorney had his hands full in the emotional chaos, so Knight was not lectured for his failure to heed a ruling from the bench.

Sylvia's mood shifted when Frank Briscoe began his cross-examination. Her tears dried up, she began to seethe, and Briscoe played to her anger. He wanted to know how much money she gave her son when he was out of work before the shooting. One hundred dollars? Two hundred dollars? One thousand dollars? Two thousand dollaers? Why hadn't she mentioned Leslie's cut lip to the police who came to her house on the freezing night of February 7?

"I certainly did."

"All right, what was the name of the officer?"

"I don't remember the name of the officer."

The D.A. did not ask about the night Sylvia let two police officers spend at her house less than a week after the shooting. He wasn't eager to show the jury that she had cooperated with the early stage of the HPD investigation. Throughout his questioning, Briscoe hammered at a contradiction: If Sylvia and Leslie were so close, why didn't Leslie tell her that he was in trouble when he rushed to her house after the shooting? It was a barb intended to upset her, and she did not have an answer.

Briscoe goaded her by waving Leslie's bloody Levi's. Sylvia parried with haughty antagonism, refusing to see them. Instead she described the jacket Leslie was wearing that night. "A little tan jacket, tan with white stripes." She despised Leslie's attempt to look tough, wearing the waist-length windbreaker with the collar flipped up hoodlum-style. The jacket had the opposite effect on her, "It made him look sickly, and I didn't like it. That's the reason I remember the jacket." The spectators chuckled at her disapproval, and the image of a female impersonator trying to come across like James Dean. Briscoe decided Sylvia's accidental ridicule was a good place to stop.

Knight was unable to get his redirect examination going before Sylvia's volatile mood tumbled. He never finished his first sentence, "Mr. Briscoe has indicated by his questions . . . "

Sylvia restrained her tears with belligerence when Briscoe was her adversary. With a friendly face smiling at her, she crumbled again. "I'm telling the truth," she pleaded. "That's how it happened. They make it sound like . . . "

Knight begged Sylvia to calm down, but her face melted and her body heaved with wild sobs. Somewhere in her mind, Sylvia saw the ghost of Fred A. Tones. She pointed her finger at a phantom. "That man is the one who killed them. . . . " Her shrieking stunned the courtroom.

"I'm sorry, judge," Sylvia wept. "I can't help it."

Judge Love called a twenty-minute breather. Some jurors watched solemnly as Sylvia stepped from the witness stand; others kept their chins in their hands and stared at the floor. A veteran trial fanatic, a retired scrubwoman who had been sitting in galleries for fifteen years, rendered an early verdict, "This is just about the best case I've ever heard." And, the defendants were waiting in the wings with X-rated testimony that would burn everyone's ears.

After the recess, Knight turned the clock back to Saturday, February 4, the day the prosecution said the robbery plot was hatched. A gun and a dog were the big-ticket items his clients purchased on their shopping spree, but Knight put all his chips on the potted plant Leslie bought at Grant's.

"The purpose of the philodendron is to identify Ashley as the young man seen with Mr. Tones later on Saturday," Knight proclaimed.

Knight's witnesses were women who worked for a living, and he was so polite that he tried to accommodate their schedules. Unfortunately, the sequence of the story was lost in the snarled order of the witnesses. Briscoe had unveiled his side of the case in a strict chronological order that was easy to follow; Knight played hopscotch, trusting the jury to leap backward and forward through the maze with him. Even worse, the waitress at Simpson's stymied his attempt to connect Leslie with Tones. The defense attorney thought the waitress had watched Leslie leave the diner.

"Did you see whether he walked up the street or whether he was picked up in an automobile?"

"No, sir."

Knight was stunned. "You didn't see that?"

"No, sir."

The waitress was a washout, and the cashier could not add much. She didn't know if Leslie came in with anyone else, but she watched him leave. She saw him get into a car with his plant.

Knight pushed for more, "Did you notice who was in the front seat of the car?"

"I don't know."

"Was anyone?"

"I don't know."

Knight was back where he started, so he took a break from beating his head against that wall and re-called Mrs. Harlan, the victim's landlady on Griggs Road. When the HPD homicide detectives were on the stand, Knight insinuated Mrs. Harlan had told them she picked up the bayonet and rearranged overturned furniture during the morning after the shooting. The cops would not go along with him, but his questions gave the jury a possibility to ponder. Now, he went to the source. Mrs. Harlan told Knight she had moved a rubber mat. That wasn't enough for him. "Do you recall moving anything else?"

"No, sir."

Strike one. Knight swung again, "Were you familiar with a large bayonet about eighteen inches long with a handle? A type of bayonet you might put on the end of a military rifle?"

"I never had noticed it."

"Do you remember on that occasion seeing one on top of a filing cabinet?"

"No, sir."

"Or behind a shelf?" Knight whiffed again. "Or on a shelf?"

"No, sir."

"You just never did see it?"

"If I did, I didn't pay any attention. I don't remember seeing it."

Instead of creating hidden potentials, Mrs. Harlan's denials demolished Knight's line of questioning. The district attorney did not bother to ask Tones's landlady a single question.

Knight went back to the potted plant he had asked the earlier witnesses about. On the witness stand, the clerk at Grant's said Leslie and Carolyn had left the plant behind, then returned to pick it up later. Knight accidentally was doing the D.A.'s work for him.

"Who was carrying it when they left?"

"I think it was the boy that was with them that day."

"They had another boy with them?" Knight was surprised. "He carried the plant?"

"Yes, sir. I'm pretty sure he did."

Frank Briscoe wanted her to refine that answer. "This was a relatively young man with them that day?"

"Yes, sir."

The identity of Leslie's anonymous friend would remain a mystery over the weekend. Judge Love adjourned the Friday session. Trials were often extended to Saturday, but the judge was still fighting his sensitive stomach. Monday might shed more light on the defendants' unknown companion, but that was not the reason bailiffs were preparing for the biggest, unruliest crowd of the trial to jam the sidewalk on Monday morning. After court adjourned for the weekend, Jack Knight declared the defendants would take the stand on Monday.

18

The crowd that showed up to hear Leslie and Carolyn dwarfed the previous week's spillover turnout. Hundreds of dejected voyeurs were left to pace and squat in the courthouse corridor, which began to look like a fogged-in airport terminal overcrowded with stranded passengers. Putting his clients in the witness chair was a huge gamble for Jack Knight. Leslie was a loose cannon, unpredictable if he felt like camping. Carolyn was part streetwalking tough girl, part teenager with a silver brace across her teeth, who would have to stand up to the D.A.'s merciless bombardment pegging her as a remorseless whore with an itchy trigger finger. Knight had to take the risk. He could not follow a self-defense strategy without letting the jury hear the defendants' side of the story. His case was hollow without them.

Carolyn's face was puffy and her voice was barely audible when she took her oath to tell the truth. Knight had to ask her to speak louder before she gave her name for the trial record. He told her to raise her voice again when Carolyn said she was too young to remember her age the last time she saw her father. She was so nervous she could not recall how long she had gone to beauty school. Nine months, six months, she wasn't sure. She never did graduate. Carolyn talked so quietly when Knight asked her about her first meeting with Fred A. Tones that the microphone had to be adjusted.

"I seen him a lot after that," she recalled.

Armed robbers would not drive a getaway car that did not start, so Knight asked Carolyn to detail the Packard's chronic breakdowns. The Packard even died when she parked along the Griggs

Road feeder. Carolyn said she rang the bell on the Tones Realty door. Mrs. Gutierrez made them wait while she told Tones that he had visitors. The bookkeeper was not gone long. "She said we could go on in there," Carolyn testified.

The trial had finally reached the moment everyone had been waiting for. Lawyers had worked late and scandal addicts beat the sun to the courthouse to be ready for Carolyn's day in court. Reporters were poised to fill clean pages in their notepads with sordid details of an orgy that had turned into a funeral pyre in the mud and weeds near a pile of garbage. Suddenly, Frank Briscoe stood up and asked to approach the bench. His timing was right out of an episode of "Perry Mason"; an Emmy-winning writer could not have scripted a commercial at a more dramatic moment. Judge Love granted the D.A.'s request for a fifteen-minute recess.

Briscoe's interruption was brilliant; he shattered the context of Carolyn's testimony. The abrupt rupture left the fatal party on Griggs Road isolated from the harmless events she had described—the Saturday shopping spree, the Sunday drive to see her mother, leaving the Packard broken down in front of Tones's office. When the session resumed, the most incriminating part of Carolyn's testimony stood in stark relief, separated from the innocuous sequence the defense had been carefully trying to portray.

Carolyn had calmed down after her nervous start and she remained steady, even detached, after the recess. She said Mrs. Gutierrez left the duplex as she and Leslie entered Tones's private office. The trick was sitting at his desk, still dressed in his shirt and slacks. Tones played host, taking drink orders. Leslie asked for coffee; Carolyn wanted a Coke, the last soft drink left in the office refrigerator.

Knight went straight for the trouble, "What else occurred while you were still in the back, that is, in his private office?"

"The knife." Carolyn's answer was too short, like a reminder on a flash card her lawyer had branded into her brain.

"What occurred in relation to the knife?"

"He just picked it up and started to stick me with it and asked me if it hurt." Carolyn said Tones jabbed her just above her right knee. "It wasn't too sharp. It was pretty sharp, but not real sharp." She told Tones that he was hurting her. He asked her to stick him, but Carolyn refused, so he poked Leslie, who took the bayonet and laid it on the desk.

"Did Mr. Tones at any time pick up that knife and make any suggestion to you about cutting him with it?"

"Yes."

"What did he ask you to do?"

"He asked me to cut his penis off." The gallery was all ears. Early birds who had scrambled for seats were not disappointed.

"Was he dressed or undressed at that time?"

"He just had his penis out. . . . He asked me if I would cut it off because it was giving him so much trouble."

Carolyn would not cooperate. "I just wasn't going to do it." Tones was bluffing and he put the knife on his desk. With the aggressive foreplay out of the way, Carolyn said he undressed, removing everything but his undershirt, his socks, and his shoes; then Tones wanted Leslie to French him, but Leslie said no. "He said it was too light in there and he wasn't dressed as a female and he couldn't do it," Carolyn testified. Only Leslie knew why he had put this impediment in front of himself when he and Carolyn kept their date with Tones.

According to Carolyn, who used his middle name, Leslie retreated into the kitchen, but he could not escape. "When Douglas was putting up his coffee cup and saucer in the kitchen, he was putting it in the sink and Mr. Tones was rubbing up against him."

"In what manner?"

"He was behind Douglas." Carolyn said she saw Tones whisper sweet nothings into Leslie's ear. "I was at the doorway when it happened and I didn't hear what he said to him."

Tones spoke louder when he suggested they shift the party into the front office, where the room was darker. He upped his demands after they moved and wanted to have intercourse with Leslie. "He asked if Douglas would let him do it. Douglas said no because he didn't like to." Leslie realized that he had missed his opportunity to get off easy in the private office. "Douglas was trying to talk him out of doing it in the rectum and Frenching him instead." Too late; Tones got mad again. "He started calling Douglas a son of a bitch and things like that, and calling me names too at the time, then he cooled down a little bit."

"By that time had you undressed also?" Knight asked.

"Yes, sir. I had my pedal pushers off and my underwear."

"That left you with what on?"

"My sweater." Carolyn continued, "We were on the white couch or whatever it was there. Me and Mr. Tones were in a sixty-nine position."

"You mean your heads were pointed in opposite directions?"

"Yes, sir."

Knight did not want to lose track of his other client. "While you were in that sixty-nine position where was Douglas?"

"Mr. Tones had his head on Douglas's legs trying to play with him or something." Knight asked her to explain the tangle. "He was going down on me, Mr. Tones was, and he moved out of that position and got another way and he started going down on me again."

"While you were in the sixty-nine position, did Mr. Tones have an erection?"

"Yes, sir."

"How do you know?"

"Well, it looked like it to me." The gallery tittered. Carolyn said she never put Tones's erect penis in her mouth. "I just had it in my hand." They twisted themselves into a pretzel, "He was in a position, I couldn't even get to him." Carolyn said she stayed on her back with her legs spread, while Tones maneuvered.

Knight wanted details. "How was he getting to you? What position was he in? Was he on the couch too or on his knees on the floor? Just tell us."

"He was sort of on the couch and sort of on the floor. He was sitting right up." Carolyn said Tones put his head between her legs. She thought he was going to perform cunnilingus, but the anger Tones had tried to stifle got away from him as he became more aroused. "He started getting real rough, tearing into me." Carolyn said Tones began to pinch her thighs, then he bit her vagina. She screamed and tried to pull away, but he pinned her to the divan and tore at her harder. "Douglas was trying to get him off because he was hurting me, and he didn't want to come off."

Her testimony became more reluctant as the party turned dangerous. "Mr. Tones reached back and hit him with his fist." The closer she came to remembering the killing, the more hesitant Carolyn became. "Mr. Tones got away from me completely and started choking Douglas. Some way or other, Douglas got his hand in my bag and reached for the gun."

"During the time Mr. Tones was choking Douglas did you hear Mr. Tones say anything?"

"Yes." Carolyn's pause filled with tears as she began to cry on the witness stand.

"What did he say?"

Her sobs clashed with her testimony, "I will kill both of you motherfuckers."

The gun went off. Carolyn claimed she did not know where Leslie's shot hit Tones. "They were still fighting with each other." The pistol fell to the floor, but Tones stayed on his feet in this version of the shooting. "Mr. Tones looked away like he was looking for it. I grabbed it before he had a chance to." She still had one knee on the couch. The bayonet reappeared. "I don't know how he placed it. He just got on to it." She said she held the gun with both hands while Tones swung the bayonet. "I told him to stop. I was begging him to stop." Carolyn said she backed away, but Tones kept coming. Wounded and raging, he was only about four feet from her."I pulled the trigger and just kept on pulling." She said Tones did not fall until the last shot was fired.

Knight raced Carolyn through the panic of the aftermath, then prodded her, "Who put the gasoline on the corpse?"

"Douglas did."

"And who lighted the match?"

"I did."

This was the first time they shared the credit for burning the body.

The bailiffs did not bother to clear the courtroom during the long lunch recess. They had no desire to deal with a stampede when court reconvened. One bailiff told a *Press* reporter, "There'd be such a fight when we opened the doors that somebody would be sure to get hurt."

Despite Carolyn's lurid testimony, the hot talk between legal insiders over lunch was not about her performance or predicting the prosecution's best method for destroying her on cross-examination. The courthouse buzzed over word that the United States Supreme Court had denied a petition to rehear the case of Howard Stickney, the necrophiliac killer who was under a death sentence. Jack Knight had been Stickney's original defense lawyer. Against Knight's advice, Stickney made a complete confession and signed a written statement that was admissible in court. After his client ignored him, Knight thought the case was a loser and withdrew. Neil McKay had prosecuted Stickney; now, the assistant D.A. and his boss were planning to expand the range of admissible statements to include oral confessions. Leslie and Carolyn might pay the price if the prosecutors succeeded, and their paths could cross Howard Stickney's on death row.

The secret prosecution plan still lay dormant when Briscoe began to cross-examine Carolyn, "So we won't have any misunderstanding, how do you refer to the defendant Ashley? Do you have a nickname of some kind for him?"

"Cookie."

"You and Cookie began living together there in the apartment at 1205 Truxillo?"

Knight hauled himself to his feet. Anyone with ears could tell Briscoe was going to bludgeon Leslie with ridicule by using this nickname, but the D.A. held the high ground. Having Carolyn speak the nickname had been a slick move. "She has testified that she refers to the defendant by such a name," Briscoe argued. The judge agreed, overruling Knight's objection. Leslie became Cookie during most of the D.A.'s cross-examination of Carolyn.

"You did refer to him as your husband and he did refer to you as his wife?"

"Yes."

"Actually, wasn't your relationship with Cookie something other than man and wife?" Briscoe must have forgotten who was on the witness stand, "Didn't you depend on each other in an economic sense?"

"What do you mean by economic sense?"

"I mean is it true you engaged from time to time in acts of prostitution?"

"Yes."

"Isn't it further true in that regard that this defendant did act as your procurer?"

"Yes."

The D.A. tried to rattle Carolyn, but she was under control, too much under control behind her iron shield. The emotions she displayed during her morning testimony vanished. Her steely facade cast a deep shadow on the jury. Tears might have worked better with them.

"The first time you say Tones exhibited the knife or bayonet to you, isn't it true that he was just playing around, horsing around?"

"He wasn't smiling. I don't know whether he was playing around or not."

Briscoe got the answer he wanted with a different approach. "In any event, there was no argument at that time?"

"No." She admitted that she was not afraid, and made no effort to leave after Tones put aside the bayonet and the party moved to the front office.

"You say you and Tones were in what you refer to as a sixty-nine position on a white couch, is that correct?"

"Yes, sir."

"And your husband was there in the room with you?"

"Yes, sir."

"And you testified that Tones's penis was erect?"

"Yes."

"And you knew that because you had it in your hand, is that correct?"

"Yes, sir."

The D.A. could not ruffle her, so he tried to make her dizzy. "When you took your clothes off were you in the private office or the front office?"

"In the front office."

"Did Tones take his clothes off in the front office too?"

"Yes, sir."

His notes of her testimony paid off. "Didn't you testify earlier at one point that Tones had his clothes off in his office?"

"I think he put them back on before we moved in the other office." She shifted, "He didn't have them all the way off."

"Are you saying he undressed first in his office, then dressed in his office and then undressed again in the front office?"

She repeated herself, "He didn't have his clothes all the way off in the back office."

Briscoe broke his continuity and went for the kill. "You say you picked up the gun when it dropped on the floor?"

"Yes, sir."

"You emptied the gun into him, didn't you?"

"Yes." She kept her balance by turning frosty when she should have thawed.

The D.A. sped to Avenue I. "I believe you testified you were the one who ignited the body, set fire to it?"

"I am." Carolyn was falling into Briscoe's trap. He was scoring as a tough prosecutor, and she was losing by being just as tough.

"Do you recall it lit up like a Christmas tree?"

That remark from her past brought an objection from Knight. Briscoe mocked Carolyn, "Well, it burned, didn't it?"

"It burned."

When the D.A. returned the witness to her own attorney, he had accomplished all of his goals: painting her as a callous prostitute, confusing her memories of the three-way date, and exposing her frozen temper that smoked like dry ice. As a prosecutor asking the judicial system for a life, he was a matador who had turned in a dazzling *faena*, but Jack Knight was the lawyer who stood before Carolyn with a bayonet in his hand. Mrs. Tones had kept her promise and brought the weapon from her home. Knight brandished the bayonet, ready for his moment of truth.

"I will ask you, if you will, to identify this as the bayonet that was in the Tones office on February the sixth, 1960?"

Carolyn did not hesitate, "No."

Her answer punched the blade through the balloon supporting her defense. Knight was shattered, "This isn't the one?"

"No."

There was nothing Knight could do except get rid of her. "That's all." His client had humiliated him. His case had collapsed and he tried to repair the damage by calling his next witness right away. He summoned Leslie Douglas Ashley to the stand without asking for a recess.

Leslie wore his bank teller's suit. He had his hair piled in a wavy pompadour, with a thick curl pulled down the middle of his forehead. He started well with informative, decisive answers. He believed November 20 was the exact date he and Carolyn moved into the Truxillo apartment. Knight tiptoed around details guaranteed to shock the jurors. He used a smokescreen to describe Leslie's Peeping Tom presence the first time Carolyn had sex with Tones.

"Were you aware they were getting acquainted?"

Leslie did not deny he was in the apartment. He never giggled during his testimony, but his dramatic streak began to show as his confidence grew. Rolling his eyes and gesturing with theatrical mannerisms, he treated the witness stand like the stage at the

Desert Room or the Pink Elephant. Although his answers were responsive, he was oblivious to the impact his personality had on the jury. Leslie would not change, even when he could be executed for being himself.

Leslie explained that the Packard died along the feeder street parallel to Griggs. The bookkeeper, Mrs. Gutierrez, told Tones they had arrived. "I think she left as we went back there." Although the time was right for a recess, Briscoe did not interrupt as he had when Carolyn reached this part of her testimony. His ploy worked once, but he had lots of resources. He did not need to repeat himself so soon.

Leslie said they did not stay in the private office very long, but his version did not completely match Carolyn's testimony. He said Tones did not spontaneously ask for a French job. "I was making up to him . . . trying to butter him up to get out of the other." Tones was too hot. "I was pouring coffee when he was rubbing against me." Leslie said Tones held him from behind, pumping a bump and grind against him. "He kind of slick-legged me." The amorous advance continued until the coffee and Coca-Cola were served, then everyone returned to the private office. "Sex was the only thing we talked about," Leslie remembered. "He had an erection. He took it out and was playing with himself."

Knight decided to try his luck with the bayonet again. Carolyn had made him look like a fool when she could not identify the weapon. He spun the wheel with Leslie.

"That's the bayonet I saw out there," Leslie confirmed.

"There is no doubt about it?"

"No doubt about it because I had it in my hands."

Knight could breathe a little easier with the bayonet accepted as an exhibit of evidence, but the rush to certify the weapon had put him ahead of himself. He backtracked to the moment the trio returned to the private office from the kitchen. This time around, Leslie said they broke the ice by discussing paintings Tones had on his wall. "He said some of the paintings were worth about a hundred and some about fifty." After their host quit bragging about his masterpieces, he exposed himself again; he wanted his guests to admire his erection as well as the paintings in his office. Leslie said this was the point when Tones stepped to a filing cabinet, opened a drawer, and pulled out the bayonet. Leslie claimed he, not Carolyn, was the first person poked with the blade.

"I think it was on my right leg, he just punched me." A quick jab. "I felt it," Leslie said. "He was looking at Carolyn when he punched me."

Tones sat beside Carolyn. "He handed her the knife and told her to cut his penis off." Carolyn refused. "I got real nervous and asked for the knife. I got it from Carolyn, she's the one that had the knife." That was a minor difference from Carolyn's testimony; she said Leslie took the knife from Tones. Leslie testified that he put the bayonet on the desk and soothed Tones by placing his hand on the angry man's penis, "It was erect." Tones asked Leslie to drop his Levi's. "I told him we would go into that a little bit later. I got up and got my second cup of coffee." Tones followed him into the kitchen. "He rubbed against me again," Leslie recalled, "from behind." He felt Tones's erection. "I was giggling." He turned around and was surprised to see Carolyn in the doorway.

They all returned to the private office with the tension rising. Tones tried to force Carolyn to French him, but she only stroked his penis with her hand. Tones was not pacified. "He wanted me to French him since she wouldn't," Leslie said. The vibes in the office were so bad Leslie could not get into the mood. "I said there was too much light. I went to the bathroom, still drinking coffee." Nothing had changed when Leslie came back. "He was still sitting there playing with himself." They spent around a half hour in the private office before everyone moved to the front room.

Nerves and coffee kept Leslie on edge. He went to the bathroom again. When he came back this time, Leslie started fondling Tones while Carolyn peeled off her pedal pushers and panties, then pulled her sweater up to uncover her breasts. Tones was silent, "just sitting there enjoying it," Leslie said.

Tones played with Carolyn while Leslie played with Tones. "He wanted me to start Frenching him." Leslie was still reluctant. "I started to and then changed my mind." Leslie could not explain why he would not go down on Tones.

Leslie said he watched while Tones and Carolyn wrapped themselves in a sixty-nine position. He was sitting on the white divan near Tones's head. Carolyn said she never put Tones's penis in her mouth, but Knight wanted a second opinion. "Yes, she did," Leslie said. "That's what he got mad about. He didn't like the way she was doing it."

According to Leslie, they twisted into a different position. Carolyn put her back to the wall and spread her legs. Tones kneeled on the floor. "Then he started biting." That brought Leslie's attention back to the couch. "I was looking at TV, and I couldn't watch TV and watch them too." Tones was not dangerous yet. "It wasn't hurting her too bad. She started squirming and she told him she wanted to do it the old-fashioned way and get down to business and get it over with." That's when Tones turned sadistic. "He told her he was going to open her up and she would be big enough to take a horse." Leslie said Tones began tearing at Carolyn's vagina, "forcing his hands up there."

Carolyn tried to escape. "I pulled on him," Leslie testified. "I said, 'Tones, stop that! Are you crazy?' " Leslie was almost six inches taller, but Tones was ten pounds heavier. "It was like trying to move this building." Leslie could not stop him. "He just kept getting worse and worse." Leslie was not much of a fighter. "He started hitting me, and then choked me and banged my head on the wall." Tones pinned him on the divan. "He wanted me to shut up. He was tired of hearing my voice." Leslie was strangling. "I couldn't breathe. I couldn't talk." He played to the jury, "I thought I would die any minute." Tones knocked him onto the floor. "I grabbed her gun in her pocketbook by the side of the couch." Tones did not back off. "He saw it before I actually got a chance to shoot it. He took it away from me before I could shoot it."

Knight did not like that answer. He wanted the jury to understand that Leslie and Tones were grappling over the gun. "He would've killed me if I hadn't gotten the pistol. He would've killed me with his hands. . . . " Knight could not stop Leslie from adding a disastrous sentence, "And I would have killed him anyway." The D.A. wrote down the sentence for future reference.

Leslie said Tones was choking him when the first shot fired. "We were tumbling. He was over me." Leslie claimed he didn't realize Tones was wounded. "He didn't fall. I didn't know it hit him." Tones kept fighting. "After it went off, he hit me and the gun fell out of my hands." Carolyn snapped into action. "I didn't see her get it, but she got it before he got it." Tones snatched a weapon of his own. "He wasn't over a foot from the desk. He reached on the desk and he grabbed this knife and started to swing it." Knight stepped back. "Like this . . . ," Leslie said as he picked up the bayonet that rested near the witness stand, "just like this . . . "

Leslie clutched the bayonet in both hands and whipped the blade back and forth with all his strength. He wanted the jury to see Tones's fury in their minds' eyes, but the jurors only saw Leslie's capacity for violence when he stirred up the wind with the bayonet.

"She was begging him to stop," Leslie continued. "She was crying." Carolyn had both hands on the gun, "like she was fighting for her life." Leslie could not count the shots, but he heard them. With Tones lying dead on the floor, he recovered and began cleaning the office. "By that time, I was able to get up," Leslie said. "I was all choked up and took the bayonet and wiped it off and took it back where it came from."

"You made an effort to wipe the fingerprints off?"

"Yes, sir."

"And put it back where it had been?"

"Yes, sir."

There was a gaping flaw in these questions that dammed the momentum of Leslie's testimony. The questions about the bayonet stood out like an obvious attempt to clear up Knight's swan dive into quicksand with Mrs. Harlan. If Leslie returned the weapon to the private office, why had Knight tried so hard to prove she had moved it the next morning? And if Jack Knight did not know his client moved the bayonet, he should have. The answers seemed tailored to plug a hole in the defendants' story.

"If I had thought I could've got away from where he was . . . " Leslie paused. "She was nude," he pleaded. "She couldn't go, she was undressed."

When he began his cross-examination, Frank Briscoe asked about the clothes Tones removed, "You say he exposed his person out there to you?"

"Yes."

"That didn't shock you, did it?"

"Certainly not."

"That's what you and Lima went out there to do?"

"We haven't tried to hide what we went out there for."

"Tones suggested that you drop your pants. This also didn't offend or irritate you, did it?"

"No."

Although all twelve jurors swore during the selection process that they could apply the self-defense statutes impartially, even to prostitutes, male or female, these questions by the D.A. were poison. A person who admitted that he was not shocked when another man exposed his erect penis was not about to be judged by normal standards once these blue-collar family men began to consider their verdict. He might have been smarter to claim he shot Tones *because* the real estate man flipped out his penis and demanded anal intercourse, but Leslie never betrayed himself, no matter how much animosity he caused. He was a drag queen and a transvestite hustler, beyond the pale of respectable morality, but he expected to be judged like anyone else, even if he was a pariah to the men who held his life in their hands.

"You say he wanted you to French him. What did you mean?"

Leslie wouldn't bite. "Just what the word means, French."

"And you tried to get out of it and said it wasn't dark enough?"

"I started to, but something held me back."

"You have engaged in such sex acts many times previously?"

"Yes." Before the trial, Leslie had told Dr. Neil Burch that Tones was repulsive to him. Despite his years hooking on the street, Leslie had his limits.

"You testified that you played with Tones while your wife undressed?"

"That's right."

Briscoe made the marriage-that-never-was a weapon for the prosecution. "You say Tones and your wife were on the couch in the sixty-nine position?"

"That's right."

Leslie repeated that Tones did not like Carolyn's technique. "He wasn't enjoying it." Leslie quit watching the portable TV and began laughing at them.

"You thought this was funny, what they were doing?"

"I laugh at everything usually. I have a nervous laugh."

The prosecutors kept close tabs on every answer Leslie gave to his own lawyer. "Did I understand your testimony correctly?" Briscoe asked, "Tones was trying to take the pistol away from you?"

"That's right."

"And you said, 'I would have shot him anyway?' "

Now it was Leslie's turn to carve his own tombstone. "That's right."

"And you did?"

"With his help."

"What's your testimony on that point? Did you shoot him?"

"Accidentally."

"You did not intend to kill him?"

"Nope," Leslie became flip at precisely the wrong moment. "I was trying to take the gun away from him when it went off."

"Despite the fact he was choking you?"

"No, I intended to kill him when he took the gun."

Briscoe had what he wanted. "You intended to kill him when he took the gun?"

"I certainly did." Although Leslie meant that he intended to shoot Tones as an act of self-defense, his answer taken out of context was perilously close to the language of the statute covering murder with malice, "an unlawful act done with intent, means, and ability." With a little twist, the prosecution could make Leslie's answer seem like he admitted committing a capital crime.

"You made up your mind and intended to kill him before the bayonet you identified came into the picture?"

Leslie realized he had made a mistake, "He was trying to take my life with his hands."

The D.A. spun him in circles. "You intended to kill him and then you didn't intend to kill him and then you did intend to kill him?"

The confusing question had no answer, but Leslie agreed anyway. "That was the only way I could do it. I wasn't strong enough to get him off me."

"In other words, the first shot was fired before Tones ever picked up the bayonet?"

"It certainly was." Any shred of progress Leslie had made with his testimony was ruined.

"The truth of the matter was he didn't have his bayonet?"

"He certainly did have the bayonet." Only after Leslie shot him. Carolyn picked up the gun while Tones swung the long blade. "She froze on the trigger."

"Did you know what she was doing?"

"It showed all over her face."

Before Leslie stepped down, his lawyer tried to prove Leslie had to shoot Tones because a hand-to-hand slugfest was a mismatch. "He may have been old, but he was a big fellow," Leslie said. Although Tones was just five feet four inches tall, he was aggressive and that made him large to Leslie. "I'm not very masculine. I couldn't hold up to him."

Jack Knight could not linger over the horrendous mistakes his clients had made. He needed to shift the spotlight as soon as possible, to prove Fred A. Tones was no angel either. It was time to put the victim on trial.

The defense attorney called Mrs. Jerry Lee Parker, who had spent two months working as Tones's secretary in 1959. Mrs. Parker was under twenty-one when she took the job, but Tones liked his secretaries young. Carolyn Lima said he asked her to be his secretary when she was only seventeen.

Knight got straight to the point. He asked the witness, "While you were working with Mr. Tones, did he ever expose his person to you?"

Briscoe was up in a flash, ready to block the defense attempt to air the victim's history of sexual harrassment. Judge Love retired the jury to hear Knight's reasoning before ruling on Mrs. Parker's testimony. Knight said the trial focused on Tones's dealings with the defendants in his office, so the defense was entitled to delve into Tones's sexual behavior with another young person behind closed doors where he worked. "We will try to show this deceased had a proclivity for things of that kind," Knight argued. "We're going to show by this witness that she was forced to quit her employment because of things he did."

Judge Love warned Knight that he would rule against the testimony unless the defense could offer precedent cases to convince him otherwise. Once again, Knight was unprepared. Putting Tones's background before the jury was a major pillar in his strategy. He should have anticipated the D.A.'s objection and he should have been ready to support his position, but his only response was to withdraw the witness and request permission to research the case law and submit his argument the following morning.

With his attempt to reveal the victim's sexual behavior on the shelf, Knight switched to the other flank of his assault on Tones's character. The victim also had a violent temper, the defense contended, but Knight was handicapped by precedents that applied to self-defense pleas in Texas courts. The law gave defendants a lot of room; the "stand and kill" statute said they could advance with lethal force against an adversary who started a fight. On the other hand, courts placed limits on defense strategies and Knight was up against a major restriction: Episodes of violent aggression in a victim's past could only be entered if the defendant was aware of those episodes. A victim's history was relevant only when it influenced a defendant's state of mind; otherwise, testimony had to stick to the incident that caused the trial.

Defense attorneys went through all sorts of contortions to get around this obstacle. With a transvestite and a teenage hooker at his side, Jack Knight did not even try. Carolyn had already told the D.A. that she felt no danger from Tones until he exploded; consequently, her state of mind was not threatened by any knowledge of his past. Since she was not scared of him before he attacked her, bringing up the bad side of Tones's biography was going to be tough.

Knight was in a hole and he needed to make an effort to prove the victim was an unpredictable hothead, but he settled for the narrow questions the precedents allowed. He could ask witnesses if the victim's reputation was good or bad, and he could ask if the victim's character was dangerous or violent. He did not push for more.

Knight called a real estate salesman who worked with Tones for about six months. George Dailey remembered the dead man. "Yes, sir. I knew him as . . . " Briscoe cut off the answer with an objection. Knight asked Dailey if Tones's reputation was good or bad.

"He was a sick man."

Briscoe objected again. The answer was not responsive. The judge instructed Dailey to answer the question that Knight repeated, "Was his reputation good or bad as to whether or not he was a person of dangerous and violent character?"

"It was bad." Dailey was not allowed to mention a beating Tones gave him.

Tones's former employer, George Billingsley, testified next. He answered the same question with an identical answer. "It was bad." Knight tried to bring testimony about Tones's sexual behavior through the backdoor, "Did you know his reputation as to whether or not he was a man of chastity or not?" Briscoe objected, and Judge Love squelched the whole line of questioning. Knight searched for maneuvering room by calling a bartender who had worked at the Pink Elephant and the Desert Room.

The bartender recognized a picture of Tones, "He was alone every time I waited on him."

Another defense witness had seen the victim's dark side. Knight asked Mrs. Frances Todaro if she had ever been involved in a case prosecuting Tones, but the D.A. jumped up before she revealed the alleged offense. The lawyers battled at the bench until Judge Love finally had enough, banged his gavel, and told everyone to come back the next morning.

19

Jack Knight's losing streak continued bright and early on Tuesday when Judge Love ruled the defense could not question any witnesses about Tones's sexual behavior. The jury would never learn if Tones had exposed himself to Mrs. Jerry Lee Parker. Mrs. Todaro could not testify either, so Knight told her story for the record to preserve his objection to the ruling if he needed to appeal the verdict.

"Fred Tones telephoned her residence and used abusive and sexual suggestions," the defense attorney said. The obscene call to Mrs. Todaro was anonymous. "She reported the incident to her husband, who suggested if the party called again he was to be invited to the home at such time as the husband was there."

Tones fell for the trap, the defense attorney said. "When admitted to the living room, he took her by the arm and tried to force her into a bedroom of her home and asked her to go to bed with him." Knight said the man of the house would corroborate this account, but he did not state what had happened when Mr. Todaro got his hands on Tones. (The Todaros restrained Tones and called the police. The arrest produced fingerprints, plus the dual identity discovered in HPD files when the left hand severed from a charred corpse was sent to the HPD lab during the autopsy on Fred A. Tones, a.k.a. Salvadore Pasquale.)

When the jurors were brought back into the courtroom, Knight did not have much to offer them. He called HPD chemist Tom Metz, who said the coroner never sent any scrapings from beneath Tones's fingernails to the police lab. Knight wanted to imply the coroner might have overlooked proof Tones had scratched Carolyn's thighs when he attacked her, but the prosecution got in the last word.

"Did you ever see the body of Fred A. Tones?" Briscoe asked the chemist.

"Yes, sir. I did."

"Do you recall his condition?"

"Yes, I do."

The D.A. did not ask Metz for any gory details. He let the jurors visualize the charred corpse for themselves. Jack Knight did nothing to remove this image from their minds. He had no more questions and he was out of witnesses. He rested his case with the jurors thinking about the scorched remains of the human torch.

Dorothy Tones was the D.A.'s first rebuttal witness. Briscoe was a sniper shooting at a single, tiny target. He was aiming at a phone call the witness had made to her husband after coming home from work on the day he died. Briscoe had tried to get the conversation into the record during Mrs. Tones's first appearance, but the testimony was hearsay and it was one of the few clashes he lost to Knight.

Briscoe was ready the second time around. His staff had located an exception to the hearsay rule in a Texas case called *Porter v. State.* Knight was caught on his blind side again. He asked for time to read the decision that went back to 1908. In *Porter v. State*, a married man was convicted of killing a teenage girl who was pregnant by him. Just before the victim left home on the night she disappeared, the girl's mother caught her packing her clothes. The girl admitted she was running away with the married man; nine days later, she was found drowned in a nearby river with her ankles bound together by bailing wire. The mother's hearsay testimony about her final conversation with her daughter was allowed in the trial and upheld on appeal.

Briscoe argued that the telephone conversation between Mrs. Tones and her husband was covered by *Porter* because the dialogue would reveal intentions the victim expressed to a family member immediately before his disappearance. Judge Love agreed to admit Mrs. Tones's testimony about the conversation.

"Do you recall, ma'am," Briscoe asked, "whether or not there was any discussion regarding the time your husband would come home that afternoon."

"He said to figure on having dinner at six o'clock."

"Where were you having dinner that night?"

"At home."

"What time did this telephone conversation take place?"

"It was just a few minutes after five when I talked to him." The implication was obvious—a man preparing for a three-way orgy would not tell his wife to have dinner on the table in less than an hour.

On cross-examination, Knight tried to show that a sex party and a home-cooked meal were not incompatible. Mrs. Tones acknowledged that her husband's office was just two blocks from their house. A Jekyll and Hyde personality might conclude his business with a pair of prostitutes and waltz home in time for dinner without any guilt clouding his face, but Knight's inference was left dangling because the jury had not heard that Tones exposed himself to his ex-secretary or tried to force Mrs. Todaro to have sex with him after making obscene phone calls to her.

Knight could have continued with his questions, reminding the jury that Mrs. Tones gave her husband plenty of privacy. She did not know the landlady who shared the duplex where he did business around the corner from their house. She had never met a young secretary he employed. A sex party two blocks from home an hour before dinner might be implausible to most men, including the men on the jury. A man like Tones might think differently, but Knight had failed to show the jury that Tones was a different kind of man.

After the widow stepped down, Briscoe used his legal research to pour more pain on the defense. The moment to spring his trap, months in the making, had finally arrived. The D.A. re-called FBI Agent Leo Reuther III, then held up State's Exhibit Number 42. "Did the defendant Lima state anything to you with reference to these automobile keys?"

Knight objected before Reuther answered. The defense attorney argued that oral statements made while suspects were under arrest were not admissible in Texas courts. Any conversation about the keys, plus all the various versions of the shooting and the aftermath that his clients relayed to the police and reporters were not admissible in court. He thought he was on firm ground and so did Judge Love, who sustained his objection.

Briscoe, however, knew exactly where the ice was thin. "Do

you know, Mr. Reuther, the automobile to which these keys belong from any source other than the defendant?"

"No, I do not."

Briscoe believed this answer opened the door for Reuther's entire account of Carolyn's oral confession on the night she was captured in New York. The judge retired the jury, which had been spending most of the morning outside the courtroom. The defense might improvise, but Briscoe and his staff did their homework. The D.A. argued that two exceptions allowed law officers to testify about oral confessions—statements that led to the location of a murder weapon and statements that resulted in the discovery of "fruits of the crime," such as stolen property. If a statement contained any of this information, the entire conversation became admissible.

"It's a subterfuge," Knight moaned. The FBI agent did not need Carolyn to lead him to the Lincoln; the stolen car had already been impounded. Reuther would not have been involved in the case if the car had not been found in his jurisdiction. Knight complained that Briscoe was turning the keys into a crowbar, looking for a loophole to destroy the safeguards against uncorroborated oral confessions.

Knight was missing the point, Briscoe responded. The Lincoln was not "the fruit of the crime" that made Carolyn's statement admissible. The D.A. was not required to show that Agent Reuther needed the keys to find the Lincoln. The keys were stolen too; "fruit of the crime" as hot as the dead man's car. Carolyn's statement was admissible because she identified them for the FBI agent.

Against the D.A.'s legal research, Knight had nothing but his memory. He was reduced to reciting from the Texas Code of Criminal Procedure, "I wish to quote, 'A confession in writing under due warning . . .'"

Judge Love cut him short. He seemed to be fed up with Knight's lack of preparation and his feeble arguments. The judge called a recess and held the rest of the clash behind closed doors in his chambers. Almost an hour passed before everyone emerged and Judge Love ruled testimony about the oral confession was admissible. When the jury filed back into the courtroom, Jack Knight and his clients braced themselves for a firestorm. The D.A. lit the fuse leading to his hidden powder keg. Briscoe asked

Agent Reuther about State's Exhibit Number 42.

"She identified the keys as saying they were the keys to Fred Tones's automobile." Reuther said.

The answer allowed him to repeat the story Carolyn told him, "She stated approximately half an hour after their arrival, Mr. Tones was dressed only in a T-shirt and a blue pair of socks. At that time an incident occurred which constituted a threat to her from Mr. Tones."

"What did she say about that?" Briscoe asked.

"She stated the threat may have been the result of either black-mail . . ."

The word rang in the courtroom like a curse. Blackmail opened a Pandora's box that let brand-new demons slip into the jurors' minds. Blackmail made even more sense as a motive than a robbery gone sour. With their unreliable Packard that needed a screwdriver to get started, Leslie and Carolyn did not come across as convincing armed robbers ready for a quick getaway, but their profession made them naturals for trying to blackmail a family man with a luxury car who paid twenty-five dollars for a date.

Briscoe asked again, "What did the defendant say to you?"

According to Reuther, Carolyn played multiple choice. "She stated the threat was either the result of blackmail or physical assault or insult."

"Did she tell you at that time Fred Tones had his hand inside her private parts and was hurting her?"

"No, she did not."

"Did the defendant Lima at that time tell you of any fight between Tones and the defendant Ashley?"

"No, she didn't."

"Did she mention a knife of any kind?"

"Yes, sir. She did."

Briscoe quickly snuffed this ray of hope. "Did she say at the time Tones was shot that he had a knife in his hand?"

"No, she did not."

"Did she say where the knife was?"

"She said it was on top of the cabinet." Reuther continued, "She stated Fred A. Tones was sitting on a white sofa and he rose from the sofa and started toward her. At that time, either she or Ashley fired a shot from a .22 caliber six-shot revolver." The testimony was a strange mix of vagueness and detail. Reuther said

Carolyn told him the divan was white and her gun was a six-shot .22, but she did not tell him who fired the first bullet. "This shot struck Tones in the side of the head and knocked him back. . . ."

Reuther said Tones fell in the version Carolyn told him. "He arose again from the sofa and started for Miss Lima again and at this time either she or Ashley fired the remaining five shots which also struck him." Again, Reuther implied Carolyn was vague with him except for locating where the bullets hit Tones; his rendition of her statement consistently implicated both defendants equally. "She said when the final shot was fired, Mr. Tones fell to the floor and blood was coming out of his nose and mouth, and his eyes were still open. Either she or Ashley went over to feel his pulse to determine if he was still alive, and it was determined by the person who felt his pulse that he was dead."

Briscoe stopped Reuther to reestablish the reason for admitting the testimony. "Was this all part of the conversation wherein she identified the keys in her handbag as belonging to the Lincoln automobile?"

"Yes, it was."

Knight was wobbling when he took over the witness, "What did you say caused the trouble they had out there?"

"She would not give any one specific answer." Reuther justified his vagueness, "We continued to ask her for the reason, and she stated it was probably one of three. She stated physical assault, blackmail, or insult. We asked her to specify which one it was and she would not specify it."

"Did she say any type of sexual activity had taken place or was taking place?"

"No, she did not," he answered. "We questioned her as to whether some had taken place and she declined to answer."

Knight went back to the cause of the shooting. "Are you sure that she told you it could have been an argument or blackmail or insults or threats?"

"No, she didn't refer to it as an argument." Reuther threw the defense a life preserver, "She insisted on the reason Tones may have represented a threat to her . . . "

Knight broke in, "You mean she thought Tones was going to blackmail her for some reason? Is that what you got out of the conversation?"

A deep silence followed. Reuther said nothing; the judge did

not order him to respond. In the quiet courtroom, a new possibility was born: Tones might have tried to blackmail a teenager
working as a prostitute just a few miles from her mother's home.
Reuther was a prosecution witness and he remained silent until
the D.A. prompted him to answer. "I had a feeling she did not
want to specify what she felt constituted a threat to her," the FBI
agent said. "She was merely listing general items that constituted
a threat to her."

Knight found hope in the wreckage. "Was she saying these
were things that were done to her or that she was doing to somebody else?"

"She did not specify either way."

"But you're sure the word blackmail was mentioned in this conversation?"

"Yes, I am," Reuther replied. Knight could not squeeze more
out of him.

The D.A. had another surprise for his rival. Briscoe's next witness had the power to put the final nails in the defendants' coffins.
When she saw him, Carolyn sat petrified; Leslie began whispering
frantically to his lawyer. The witness gave his name as Richard
Ramirez. Briscoe asked, "Are you sometimes known as Robert?"

The witness nodded, "Sometimes."

He also went by Raymond, the name Leslie and Carolyn gave
to the HPD after they were captured. Early in the investigation,
homicide detectives heard the suspects had a friend, a "Mexican
looking man" in the police report parlance, who was seen around
the apartment on Truxillo during the weekend before the shooting. Leslie and Carolyn did not try to conceal their link to him.
Carolyn thought his name was Riviera, maybe Garcia. That
sounded right to Leslie, although he told the police that Ramirez
was a possibility too. They had trouble with Raymond's last name,
but they knew he shared a room at a downtown flophouse halfway
between the county jail and skid row.

Their friend and his roommate were carpenters and painters by
trade. By inclination, their pal with the elusive identity was a
drifter, arriving in Houston from California a couple of months
before he met Leslie and Carolyn at a cheap second-run movie
theater next door to a penny arcade where trouble always brewed.
Their paths crossed often in dime stores or soda fountains, and
one afternoon they went to the zoo together. They had so much

fun riling up the animals in their cages that they began to clown around a lot.

The cops went to talk to "Raymond" at his cheap hotel and learned the man who fit his description had been registered as Richard Flores Ramirez. The night clerk said Ramirez was gone; he had settled his bill and checked out around three weeks before the cops came looking for him. He left around ten o'clock at night, the clerk recalled. A Sunday, February 5, the flophouse books revealed. He did not give a forwarding address. Ramirez was not the kind of guy who left an easy trail to follow.

"Officers checked a source of information," the progress report said. With help from their snitch, they traced Ramirez to an apartment building where the manager grumbled that he was forty dollars behind on his rent. The manager claimed she had not seen Ramirez for days, but the detectives found clothes and personal papers inside his apartment.

The police staked out the building and surprised Ramirez when he tried to slip in around 1:30 on a dark morning. He admitted he knew Leslie and Carolyn. The next morning, he led the detectives to a stretch of Almeda-Genoa Road where they found .22 shells and slugs in the mud. Under oath on the witness stand, Ramirez tersely described the roadside target practice.

"Who was shooting the gun?" Briscoe asked.

"All of us."

"All three of you?"

"Yes."

Carolyn began to sob, and Ramirez gave her more reasons to cry. He said the defendants were talking about moving to New York when he was with them during the weekend prior to the shooting. Leslie wanted him to come along too, but Ramirez refused. Leslie kept badgering him, according to Ramirez, who never explained why Leslie insisted that he join the trip north. He only said the hassle peaked early Sunday evening while they sat inside the Packard in front of his flophouse.

"He had the pistol and got it out," Ramirez recalled. Rain spattered on the Packard's roof. "I got real mad, I took it away from him and took the bullets out of it."

Ramirez claimed he also removed a box of bullets from the glove compartment before he returned the unloaded gun to Leslie; the fifty-count box of Remington shorts he turned over to a homicide detective a month later was nearly half empty. Ramirez told the cop who picked up the box from him that the missing bullets were fired at the drainage ditch target practice.

The D.A. began working on the motive behind killing the trick with the fancy car. Ramirez believed Leslie and Carolyn only had about ninety dollars between them, not enough for a trip to New York.

"What did the defendant Ashley tell you about getting the money to go to New York?"

"They said they would get it some way."

Robbery or blackmail, it did not matter which scheme the jury bought as long as they believed the defendants went to Griggs Road to coerce money from Tones.

"Why was it you didn't want to go with them to New York?"

"I just didn't want to get involved."

That had a sinister ring to Briscoe, "You what?"

"I just didn't want to go." Ramirez's reluctance implied his friends were headed for deep water.

If Knight had made more headway against other prosecution witnesses, by showing testimony from some HPD experts and detectives had rough edges, for instance, he might have been able to clobber the veracity of a drifter with so many different names. However, Knight had neglected to lay that foundation, and it was too late to start. Even worse, he made a horrendous mistake by plunging ahead, violating a cardinal rule of trial attorneys, and asking questions without knowing the answers in advance.

"They told you, did they not, that Carolyn was going to Austin on Tuesday to take a cosmetology or beauty-shop examination?"

"Yes."

"Did they tell you they were both going up there?"

"Yes."

"You didn't gather the impression they were going to New York then?"

"Yes, I did."

"You did?" Knight was baffled again. He had accidentally turned himself into a prosecutor, "From what?"

"He said he wasn't going to take Carolyn to Austin to take the beauty test because they didn't get enough money from her mother. They were going to New York instead."

Knight was so stunned that he repeated his disastrous question. He used Leslie's middle name, "You say Douglas told you he was going to New York instead of taking her to Austin, is that correct?"

"Yes."

"When were they supposed to leave?"

"I don't know." Ramirez guessed, "As soon as they could get away."

Knight's cross-examination turned up one of the most damaging answers of the entire trial by pinpointing the moment, according to Ramirez, when the defendants decided to skip Carolyn's beautician's exam and leave for New York. Tears poured down Carolyn's cheeks when Ramirez left the stand. Briscoe rested his case with her sniffles as his soundtrack.

After an emergency skull session over lunch, Knight made Leslie the first rebuttal witness for the defense. Leslie was calm, he did not giggle, and he did not camp, but his manner could be flip when he meant to be emphatic.

"I will ask you if Richard Ramirez was known to you as Robert?" The day before, when Carolyn was on the witness stand, she casually tossed out the name Robert to identify the friend who saw the white Lincoln pull up in front of Simpson's late Saturday afternoon.

"Nope," Leslie answered, as if he held the solution that could clear up a minor misunderstanding.

Knight thought he had deciphered Ramirez's multiple identities, "You always called him Richard?"

"Raymond," Leslie responded. Robert was someone else entirely, "blonde and snaggle-toothed," Leslie recalled, because he was missing some front teeth. Leslie said he and Carolyn spent the Saturday before the shooting with Robert, not Ramirez.

"I think we went to Woolworth's or something," Leslie testified. "He picked up some turtles. . . . He had about eight turtles." The turtles may have been shoplifted or Robert might have bought them, Leslie was not sure. As a prank, Robert hid the turtles in strategic locations around a downtown department store. Unfortunately for the defense, he never came forward to explain his sense of humor. Snaggle-toothed Robert, the practical joker, had dropped out of sight, so Knight called Richard Ramirez instead.

The defense had to tread lightly. Knight still had the puncture marks where Ramirez had bitten him before lunch. He steered clear of risky questions, Knight was still wrestling with aliases.

"Are you sometimes known as Raymond Ramirez?"

"Some."

"Did Ashley call you Raymond at the time?"

"He called me Raymond and Robert." Ramirez was not asked why Leslie could not keep his name straight. Knight was content to imply Richard Robert Raymond Ramirez was shifty, with a different name for evey occasion. The defense excused him.

Knight brought back Carolyn for rebuttal testimony. His questions targeted Leo Reuther's version of her oral confession. Knight had given up trying to make the jury believe Tones tried to blackmail her. In this session on the witness stand, Carolyn denied she ever used the word blackmail during her interview with the FBI on the night she was arrested in New York.

"Had you already told any other officer before you told him those were the keys to the Lincoln?"

"No."

That was the wrong answer. If Carolyn had told a different agent or detective about the keys, the argument against allowing Reuther's rendition of her oral confession would have been much stronger. The truth hurt, and the only comfort Knight could take was the knowledge that he was almost finished.

20

Murder trials in Texas, even front-page murder trials, ran on a different schedule in 1961. Speed was a virtue, and both sides closed after only four and a half days of testimony. The jury heard sixty-two witnesses; forty-three for the prosecution, nineteen for the defense.

Judge Love rewarded everyone for their swiftness by adjourning early, just after 2:00 P.M. on Tuesday. He could make up the time he cut this afternoon by shaving an hour off the closing arguments tomorrow. Normally, each side was allotted two hours for its final speeches to the jury. Judge Love decided an hour and a half would be enough.

The lawyers met in the judge's chambers before leaving the courthouse. It was a routine meeting that quickly slipped from Judge Love's mind. Just two months later, he could not recall it. Frank Briscoe said he remembered the conference, but not the substance of the conversation. His assistant, Neil McKay, recalled a discussion, although he could not be specific. Only Jack Knight remembered warning the judge about the possibility of an emotional outburst from Mrs. Tones during his closing argument. "With me, it was an obsession," he said. "I was afraid of it."

With testimony ended, the rule excluding witnesses from the courtroom was suspended. Anyone who could find a seat would be allowed in the gallery on Wednesday. Knight's courtesy was one of his trademarks, but he planned to get tough in his closing argument. He was going to say unpleasant things about the victim, whose widow would not like what she heard. She might break down or blow up. Knight said the prosecutors expressed

163

their doubt that Mrs. Tones planned to attend tomorrow's session. She did not want to expose herself to any more suffering. Knight also recalled Judge Love assured the attorneys he would issue a strong warning against disturbances to the spectators before the arguments began.

A less ethical lawyer than Knight might not have warned his opponents and the judge of his concern. The trial had gone so poorly that Knight had to be pessimistic about the verdict. An emotional outburst by the widow might influence the jury and make his job totally hopeless, or it could give him immediate grounds for a mistrial, and a mistrial might be the best result he could hope for at this point in the case.

The daily ritual of musical chairs began early Wednesday morning. Spectators were not as frantic for seats as they had been when Leslie and Carolyn testified, but space in the gallery was still at a premium because the Rule had been revoked. Unhappy bystanders were left in the corridor.

Sylvia sat with the woman who had been caught taking notes for her. Jim Ayres brought a tape recorder and waved a press card he was issued as a part-time freelance stringer shooting newsreel footage. He did not use the card much anymore, but it came in handy today, earning him a front row seat in a section reserved for reporters and photographers. He set up a microphone and prepared to record the closing arguments.

Mae Lima found an inconspicuous seat near the rear of the courtroom. Leslie Sherman Ashley had never been a witness so he had been in the gallery every day during the trial; for the closing arguments, he brought the female companion he had called his "friend" when the trial started. Now, she was his fiancée. As the prosecutors predicted, Mrs. Tones was not in the gallery when Judge Love gaveled the session to order.

"This trial has been attended by considerable interest and publicity," the judge began. "The spectators on the whole have exhibited exemplary behavior. . . ." Except for a few squabbles over seats, the circus had been in the corridor, not the courtroom. Judge Love promised to maintain that decorum; anyone who misbehaved would be removed immediately.

The prosecution was entitled to deliver the first and last closing arguments. Speaking between his rivals, Jack Knight would have his last chance to save his clients, but the defense attorney's concentration was jarred by a new worry after Judge Love finished his warning to the spectators. Mrs. Tones quietly entered the courtroom through a side door with her older son. A bailiff squeezed them into seats on the second row of the gallery.

Neil McKay, the assistant D.A. who built a career on capital murder cases, rose and stared at the jury. He was a big, ideal image of a Texan, a survivor of World War II combat in a tank division. He sat alertly beside his boss during the testimony, making sure the prosecution never missed an angle. Finally, he stepped out of Frank Briscoe's shadow to practice his specialty—sending killers to meet their maker.

"All of the cowards in the world are not on battlefields," he began, "too often, they get into jury boxes." McKay's wartime experience had taught him how to motivate men to pull a trigger. "Time and again, they say, 'Well, I know I should have done it, but I just couldn't do it. When I was faced with the proposition of doing what my conscience told me ought to be done, I didn't have the guts to do it.'" McKay repeated his word for yellow bellies, "I call those people cowards."

He did not want the jurors to have any false ideas about premeditation. "Somehow or other, in the minds of lay people, maybe it's too much television, radio . . . they get in their heads that here in Texas a man has to premeditate over a long period of time, to plan, plot, and form designs to kill somone. That just ain't the law. If I make up my mind to kill that man and a second later kill him without just cause and excuse, I'm guilty of murder with malice. Malice can form in the mind and heart of a person in the bat of an eye. It can arise as quickly as I snap my fingers, so there is no such thing in Texas as a long period of premeditation. He's just as dead. My heart is just as black with malice at the time I pulled that trigger as if I had thought about it for a month."

Leslie and Carolyn did not shoot Tones in self-defense. "See for yourselves. . . . " McKay gave the jurors photographs of the office on Griggs Road. "There's no evidence of any fierce struggle that these two defendants talked so long and loud about." The office was neat; Mrs. Harlan's mop was still propped by the door. "Where was the knife, the bayonet? Where it was usually kept. Dusty, no fingerprints on it, dusty. I submit to you that knife was never, ever moved off that filing cabinet. I submit to you that's something these defendants cooked up in their minds."

Mrs. Tones remained calm as McKay spoke of her husband's dates with Carolyn at the Truxillo apartment. "Every blessed time he had intercourse with her, it was up there. Why the exception this time? I'll tell you exactly why. Because they went out there for the purpose of rolling that cat who had the Lincoln and the big money, who paid twenty-five dollars for the trick." McKay put his words in their mouths, "Let's go out there and see if we can't roll him. And, he didn't roll. . . . This lad with the golden auburn hair and this lady of the night . . . they were caught with the snuff in their mouths, if you'll pardon that East Texas expression. . . . they got caught with their hands in the cookie jar."

McKay was in high gear. "I don't think if you ever, if you sat on the jury here from this time till doomsday, you would ever hear a more horrid, more sickening, a more stinking story in your life. And where did it come from? Out of the mouths of these two defendants . . . " He went over the horns and straight for the heart. "Are they people who decent society can ever tolerate? A self-confessed prostitute? A self-confessed homosexual? Two people who've poisoned the youth of this land, of this city, and of this county; who made their way by immoral and filthy and perverse conduct." By now, McKay's voice was booming. "Can you tolerate, as a member of decent society, people like that? Can decent convicts who deserve a chance to reform, do they deserve to have to live with people like that."

He seemed to realize he was over the edge, so he got back on solid ground. "I feel as I did when the state accepted you, that you were the men that had the courage, the intelligence, the horse sense to evaluate all of this testimony, to apply the law properly." That meant a pair of death sentences. "I don't believe you are cowards and I don't think I will be disappointed."*

McKay sat down after daring the members of the all-male panel to prove their courage. Knight stood up and reminded them of their duty to be impartial. "I asked you jurors individually, I said suppose a convict comes here . . . and under circumstances of self-defense, has to kill a highly reputable person? You said that certainly it would be self-defense. . . . I told you these persons' character was known to be that of prostitution, that there was doubtless going to be evidence of homosexuality. You said you could extend the same safeguards of the law."

The defense attorney had compared his clients to convicts, so he slashed the victim too. "This man apparently had something wrong with him," Knight frowned. "Tones and these twisted mortals were out together for immoral sexual relations . . . " The widow began to shift in her seat. "While Mr. Tones had an eighteen-year-old son at home, he was out looking for something seventeen years old."

Knight pointed at Carolyn, "He had the price and she had the body." The defense attorney shook his head. He tried to sympathize. "Poor Mrs. Tones. What a burden that woman must have borne with this aggressive philanderer." The widow flinched. "Two days before this man was killed . . . he was out on the night." Mrs. Tones fought to control herself. "He took time to go over to the apartment, leaving Ashley at the Pig Stand, then came back and dropped the girl out."

Knight said no witnesses challenged this version of the tryst forty-eight hours before Dorothy Tones lost her husband. "Don't you know they would have had every member of the Tones family say, Why, certainly not. Daddy came home at six o'clock that evening. He had a cocktail and he put on his house shoes and he watched television. . . . "

"He certainly did," Mrs. Tones blurted from the gallery. They had gone out together Saturday night. "He was with me at the Ben Milam Hotel. . . . " She quickly controlled her tongue, then buried her face in her hands and cried.

Judge Love ordered a bailiff to escort Mrs. Tones from the courtroom, and her son followed her out. While the spectators buzzed, the defense motioned for a mistrial. Knight claimed the jury was tarnished, he could never win them back after the widow's heartbroken plea. The judge refused. He ordered the jury to disregard Mrs. Tones' emotions, and told Jack Knight to proceed.

The defense attorney struggled to recover his broken momentum after the outburst he had feared. "This man had been out on the town, and he'd been out on it for no good." Tones was the culprit. "This man had to have his way, and he wanted his way with this degenerate couple, if you wish to call them that. But they're still human beings." Knight hammered the reason to believe his clients, "These things cannot be concocted by people as ignorant as these two people. . . . They can't stand here under the withering cross-examination of a man like Frank Briscoe and tell that kind of story." Knight roared at the jury, "They just can't do it. They don't have the education for it. They don't have the know-how for it."

Knight got to the core of his case, "There was a class difference between them. They were hustlers, if you want to use the common word in the street. This man was a businessman, who was no better morally than they were, but they feared the implications of what had happened." Sylvia sobbed into her handkerchief as Knight circled his crescendo. "You say, well, there's nobody here to tell Fred Tones's story about what happened in that apartment. You know, that's to some extent Fred Tones' own fault. . . . He asked them to his office. He had a date with them that did not invite wisdom on his part. . . . Remember when you go out and start figuring all the reasons in this case, the reason these two persons with their substantial story holding up under cross-examination, the reason there are two of them and none of him, is that the date was arranged by him."

Knight climaxed by condemning his own clients. "A forty-four-year-old man, with children at least as old as one of these, got out here and got mixed up with two persons that you and I wouldn't walk down the street with for fear that someone would say, 'What's he doing walking down the street with those queers?' "

The district attorney did not need to add much to the final wrecking ball Jack Knight applied to his own case. Although Neil McKay left his boss over half of the prosecution's ninety-minute allotment, Frank Briscoe promised the jury that he would keep his speech brief. Sylvia tried to lock a contemptuous smile on her lips during the D.A.'s closing argument, but tears doused her false grin.

"I'm not here to defend Tones," Briscoe admitted. Some of the mud Leslie and Carolyn slung on their victim might have been true, but *they* had no right to smear anyone. "It is inconceivable to me that this prostitute and this homosexual can, in seriousness, point any finger at anybody and accuse him of being immoral. Tones was victimized by these people in more ways than one. They robbed him of his manhood. They killed him. They burned his mortal remains. There is only one punishment that would fit what these people have done."

The jurors had to shoulder their civic burden. "When you come out of that jury room, don't come out with your chin on your chest. . . . Do this thing that must be done, and take some comfort in the realization that you will have done your share in making this community of ours, this neighborhood of yours, a better place in which to live."

The D.A. justified his wrath with the Bible, "St. Paul writes, 'Be not deceived, God is not mocked. For whatsoever a man soweth that also shall he reap.' On February the sixth, these defendants sowed the seeds of death. . . . Look down within your very fiber, the very being of you, and find within yourselves the strength, the courage, to return that verdict."

Briscoe only used twenty of the fifty minutes at his disposal. The *Houston Press* reported that the hands of the clock on the courtroom wall were pointing straight up at precisely twelve noon when he finished and the jury filed out.

The jurors picked W. F. Pry to be their foreman. He worked for himself as a cost estimator on electrical contracting jobs, so he was a self-starter who could follow the path of complex circuitry and present the details of a bigger picture to other people.

Neither Pry nor anyone else on the jury would discuss their deliberations or reveal how many ballots were taken. At the very least, they gave lip service to the defense claim that the shooting was sparked by a fight. They asked for the photographs the HPD said were taken at the Tones Realty office during the morning after the killing. The furniture was upright; the clutter on desktops was neatly stacked.

Another request the jurors made revealed the direction their verdicts were taking. Pry handed the bailiff a note for Judge Love, "Must both defendants receive the same penalty if proven guilty?" The defense attorney's attempt to bind his clients together seemed to be splintering. The judge instructed the panel that separate penalties could be assessed. At 7:50 P.M., less than eight hours after they began, a buzzer signaled their work was done.

Almost another hour elapsed before the entire cast assembled to hear the verdicts. The families of the defendants had not strayed very far, so they returned promptly. Frank Briscoe and

Neil McKay arrived and took their seats at the prosecution table.
Judge Love stood by in his chambers. Jack Knight was the
holdup. He finally hustled into the courtroom with an unlit cigar
in his hand a little before 8:45. Knight huddled with the families
briefly. The quick verdicts and the jury's note about separate penalties alarmed him.

At least one death sentence seemed likely. "Be prepared. Don't
be upset," Knight whispered. "It might be rough, it might be
very rough."

For the first time since jury selection began, the courtroom was
not completely packed. The sudden notice at a late hour left a few
seats vacant, a final irony at the climax of a trial that had spectators fighting for space. After Judge Love warned the gallery to
remain silent when the verdicts were read, Leslie and Carolyn
shuffled into the courtroom like "sleepwalkers," the *Press*
reported. Jack Knight sat between his clients as the jury entered.
"Keep your composure," he told them softly. "I'm afraid it's just a
matter of how much."

A clerk took the verdict. Knight held each of his clients by a
hand. "Stand up," he said as he helped them to their feet. The
clerk began, his voice was crisp from experience. "We, the jury,
find the defendant Leslie Douglas Ashley guilty of murder with
malice aforethought and assess his punishment at death."

Leslie did not speak or move. The gallery obeyed the judge.
No one moaned, no one gasped, but Sylvia glared through tears
rolling down her cheeks at the twelve men who had voted to execute her son.

The defendants cut a quick glance at each other before the
other shoe dropped. "We, the jury, find the defendant Carolyn
Lima guilty of murder with malice aforethought and assess her
punishment at death."

The electric chair for a teenage girl hit like a thunderbolt. The
jurors did not split their verdicts after all. Carolyn closed her
eyes, her lips trembled out of control. Still, no one made a sound.
The words made sense, but shock built a thin wall against the
reality of their meaning.

Jack Knight used the numb moments to seek relief in a formality. He asked Judge Love to poll every juror. "Is this your verdict, sir?" the judge asked twelve times. Twelve times the answer
was yes, then a bailiff tapped each condemned prisoner on the

shoulder. They turned and followed him from the courtroom. Leslie stared at his mother, but he did not seem to see her. He was deaf to the questions reporters fired at him. Carolyn pressed her trembling lips more tightly together and shook her head stiffly as Knight walked them to the elevator that returned them to jail.

Mae Lima had been calm throughout the trial, but the verdict was too much for her. Knight put his arm around her and guided her to an elevator before she crumbled. A reporter jumped inside as the doors closed. She refused to answer any questions and turned her face to the wall, trying to hide her sobs during the ride down seven floors to the courthouse lobby.

Upstairs, Sylvia Ayres wailed on a bench in the corridor. "Not death, not death . . . ," she repeated. Knight consoled her, "This is just the first step. . . . This isn't the end." The defense attorney's promise to appeal could not stop Sylvia's cries. Her brother, Ted Kipperman, stood pale and powerless beside her. His hands felt frozen, he had never expected a death sentence. Neither had Leslie's father, the harsh verdict surprised him too. Jim Ayres was the only member of the defendants' families who did not give in to shock or sadness. He was angry, and he blamed the district attorney for suppressing evidence about the secret side of Fred A. Tones, "If you've killed a rattlesnake, you should be allowed to prove he carried venom in his fangs," Jim said.

Knight agreed that Tones's hidden background was crucial, but he corrected Jim Ayres. The D.A. did not keep the jury from hearing the unsavory traits in Tones's personality. The rulings were made by Judge Love, and Knight blamed the judge for another decision that cost him the case. Carolyn's oral statement to FBI Agent Leo Reuther should not have been admitted. "Very flimsy," Knight said. He was confident these rulings from the bench gave him ample grounds to overturn the convictions on appeal.

Frank Briscoe was equally confident. "It was a clean case," he said. He predicted higher courts would affirm the verdicts, but the D.A. found common ground with his opponent on one aspect of the trial. He agreed that Reuther's testimony was devastating, but Briscoe and Jack Knight parted company over the second reason the prosecution won. It was not the jury's failure to hear evidence about the victim's volatile temper or his sexual abuses.

"The rebuttal testimony of two surprise witnesses at the end of
the trial was our most telling point," Briscoe stated. A cleancut
FBI agent and Richard Robert Raymond Ramirez, a shady drifter
with a string of aliases, packed a double punch—one high, one
low.

The D.A. did not gloat over his victory. "I never get used to
being congratulated about these things," Briscoe said, in the corridor outside the courtroom, "but it's something that must be
done." Giving a death sentence to a teenager was not easy. "I
think the jury did the right thing," he concluded. "They showed
courage perhaps not one jury out of a hundred would have
shown."

"We decided we wouldn't say anything about the deliberations," the foreman declared. "The verdict speaks for itself." The
twelve men hardly spoke to each other as they lined up to collect
their pay, five dollars per diem. Forty dollars, just twenty dollars
per death sentence, was the salary for their eight days of service,
but money was worth more in 1961.

Neil McKay, the assistant D.A., had the most experience with
capital cases, and he had been pessimistic about winning death
penalties when the trial began. He did not think the tide turned
because the jury never heard details about the victim's sexual misbehavior and bad reputation. And, in his mind, the case did not
pivot on Reuther or Ramirez either. The prosecution's best witness was one of the defendants—Carolyn Lima. "Her answers and
her attitude," McKay said, recalling her testimony thirty years
later. Prostitution, killing a trick, burning his body. Carolyn let it
all roll off her back. "Too casual, like it was nothing," he remembered. "She bought herself the death penalty."

Wednesday night, immediately after the verdicts, Leslie and
Carolyn were transferred to isolation cells, the standard procedure
for prisoners under death sentences.

The guards said Leslie was shaken, but none of them saw him
cry. When Carolyn woke up around eight o'clock the next morning, she wanted to read the headlines she had inspired. The day-
shift matron told her that inmates in isolation cells were not
allowed to have newspapers.

A psychiatrist with an interest in the case did not miss the
front-page coverage of the death sentences. On Thursday, May

25, Dr. Howard Crow sent a letter to Frank Briscoe:

Dear Mr. Briscoe:

Dr. Jack Tracktir and I evaluated Leslie Douglas Ashley, white male, 23 years of age, and Carolyn Lima, 18 years of age, in the Harris County Jail, Houston, Texas, March 22, 1961. We felt they were legally incompetent as we understand the laws of Texas referrable to this kind of problem. Again on April 8, 1961, I evaluated Leslie Douglas Ashley and Carolyn Lima alone, and again felt they were legally incompetent.

As you may recall, I offered to talk with you and wanted to talk with you about this prior to their recent trial, and ultimately I discussed this by telephone on the day of the beginning of their recent trial.

Find attached bill for my services and a bill for Dr. Tracktir's services.

Respectfully yours,

Howard G. Crow, M.D.

Dr. Crow made sure that he created a record of his diagnosis, but the district attorney slipped the letter into a file where it languished as though it had never been written.

THREE

A Prophet and the First Lady

21

Missionaries spread their message in the Harris County jail, and the ground for converts could be fertile in isolation cells where condemned prisoners were locked. A woman evangelist gave Leslie a Bible and religious tracts he began to read, and he started listening to a Baptist minister building a flock behind bars, but the vivid visions conjured by Pentecostal preachers mesmerized him.

"I really took to the way them holy rollers carried on," Leslie remembered.

The Pentecostals watched for signs predicting Christ's return. Their sermons mixed a promise of rapture and redemption with apocalyptic fire and brimstone. They believed in miraculous faith healing and they sometimes spoke in tongues as earthly evidence of the power of the Holy Spirit. Leslie looked for an epiphany to rescue him from the electric chair. He needed the hand of the Lord to boost his strength in his death cell. When he was baptized in the jail chapel by a missionary from the Assembly of God, the largest Pentecostal fellowship, a choir of female inmates sang, but Carolyn was not among the voices celebrating his salvation.

Jack Knight tried to save both his clients with the laws of the land, not blind faith. Within weeks of the verdicts, he filed a motion for a retrial with Judge Love that argued the convictions should be void because of three judicial mistakes: 1) letting the FBI agent repeat Carolyn's oral confession; 2) allowing Mrs. Tones's hearsay testimony about the final phone call from her husband telling her to fix dinner; and 3) failure to grant a mistrial after the widow's outburst during the closing arguments.

Since the alleged trial errors challenged his own rulings, the judge was not likely to reverse himself, but Knight had something new that was not based on a decision from the bench. In his motion, the defense attorney also said Richard Ramirez lied under oath and Knight accused the prosecutors of knowing that their star surprise witness had altered the truth. The charge persuaded Judge Love to call a hearing barely two months after Leslie and Carolyn received their death sentences. If Knight could prove his allegation, they might win retrials.

The day before the hearing, Leslie said he went through a religious transformation. He saw himself born again "as a little boy from a white cloud." He had five Bibles in his isolation cell. "I'm a changed person," he announced. "I don't want to die in the electric chair, but, if I do, I believe I'll go to heaven."

The cast reassembled July 28 in District Court Number 3 for the hearing on the defense motion for a retrial. Leslie and Carolyn were not scheduled to testify, so plenty of seats were left in the gallery. No extra bailiffs were needed. Knight put Richard Ramirez on the witness stand.

The last time he sat in the same chair, Ramirez had said Leslie threatened him with the .22 pistol. While Ramirez testified, Leslie was whispering a different story to Jack Knight. After the trial, the defense attorney decided to see who was lying. Knight claimed Ramirez not only came into his office and confessed to giving false testimony, the drifter also revealed he had told the truth in a secret affadavit that he signed for the homicide detectives who questioned him. Now, Jack Knight was ready to set the record straight.

"At the original trial, do you recall that you testified Douglas Ashley pulled a pistol on you?"

"Yes, sir." Ramirez nodded.

"And that you took the pistol away from him and unloaded it and gave it back to him later?"

"Yes, sir."

"Did that actually happen, Mr. Ramirez?"

Ramirez didn't blink, "Yes, sir."

Knight went after him. "Didn't you tell me at my office that you held up Douglas Ashley on the night of Sunday, February the fifth and took forty-five dollars away from him?"

Before Ramirez answered, the D.A.'s chief assistant stood up. Sam Robertson was an expert on legal research to block appeals, and his courtroom tactics were sharp as well. He reminded Judge Love that Jack Knight had called Ramirez. The defense attorney was trying to impeach his own witness. "That procedure is not proper," Robertson emphasized. A lawyer was not allowed to dispute his own witness.

Knight rephrased his question, "In the period of time that you knew Ashley, did you at any time hold him up and take some of his money?"

"No."

"You did not do that?"

"No."

Knight had subpoenaed the pretrial affadavit Ramirez signed for the HPD. The statement was lying on the counsel table in front of Frank Briscoe. Knight called the district attorney as a witness to ask him about discrepancies between Ramirez's murder trial testimony and the tale the drifter told the HPD. The defense attorney was hoping the D.A.'s answers would persuade Judge Love to release the document; as usual, the prosecutors were ahead of him.

Sam Robertson rose again and asked his boss if he ever mentioned or displayed the affadavit at the original trial. Both answers were no. Robertson argued the negative replies meant the affadavit that might have vindicated Knight did not have to be surrendered under higher court rulings that applied at the time. The defense attorney had not researched any legal precedents to contradict him.

Receiving the wrong replies was a familiar tune for Jack Knight, but he heard more sour notes when he dismissed Briscoe and recalled Richard Ramirez. Knight could not challenge him, so Ramirez was safe as long as he stuck to his denials. Robertson jumped up with objections whenever Knight tried to argue with the witness. Ramirez swore he had never robbed Leslie and said he told the truth when he testified that Leslie threatened him with the pistol.

The drifter admitted he was hauled into the D.A.'s office just four days after Knight filed his retrial motion, but Ramirez said his session with Neil McKay was short. McKay did not pressure him, Ramirez claimed, the prosecutor merely wanted to make sure he was telling the truth. The pressure was implicit—if Ramirez admitted he lied at the murder trial, he could be charged with perjury. He needed to keep his testimony consistent.

The defense attorney was fighting opponents who had cracked his code. Whichever direction he turned, the prosecutors were waiting to block him. Judge Love denied Knight's motion for a retrial. Although the decision merely meant the case would move up the judicial ladder to the Texas Court of Criminal Appeals, Carolyn cried when she heard the ruling. She also learned Leslie had changed his story and said she fired all six shots.

"I'm scared of him," Carolyn said. "He's a little feminine, but he's as mean as he can be." Their romance was over. "I couldn't marry him now," Carolyn sniffled. "I could have at one time but not now, never."

Leslie found other outlets for his amorous energy. Despite his death sentence, he worked his way out of his isolation cell, earning a promotion to "tender," the jailhouse term for an inmate janitor who swept up the cell block and delivered food or water to the other prisoners. Leslie's status gave him the run of his ward, and the jailers thought he was doing a good job until they found him going down on another inmate. After that, they put him back in isolation with his Bibles.

22

Lloyd Lunsford was looking for a camera, not a new client, when he walked into Ted Kipperman's store. Lunsford had built a jack-of-all-trades legal practice based in South Houston, a ragged, mostly lower-middle-class enclave on the side of town where trees do not grow unless people plant them. His professional peers usually called him Lucky, a nickname he had picked up as a navigator on B–24 bombers during World War II. When Lucky Lunsford was guiding the plane, the crew always came home. The monicker stuck because Lunsford's unorthodox courtroom strategies often defied common sense, but his batting average stayed high.

Lunsford liked to reminisce about representing a drunk driver charged with killing a pedestrian. The defendant had signed a confession admitting he was intoxicated when his car hit the victim so Lunsford faced a tough trial, but he came up with an ingenious argument. He agreed that his client had been drunk, so drunk, in fact, that the guilt-stricken defendant signed his confession without realizing an anonymous hit-and-run driver had made the first, fatal impact that launched the unfortunate pedestrian into the air. His client, Lunsford contended, merely struck the dead body on the fly. The picturesque theory and Lunsford's powers of persuasion raised enough reasonable doubt to carry the day with a jury despite the written confession. The victory had been doubly difficult, Lunsford bragged, because sentiment was strong for the victim and her surviving spouse, an ex-chief of the Houston police department. (In a less colorful version, a neutral observer said Lunsford won because he damaged the credibility of the device used to perform the sobriety test on his client.)

While Lucky Lunsford was browsing through the inventory at Kipperman's Camera Shop, Sylvia gave him an unsolicited sob-story about her son's plight. She no longer felt any loyalty toward Jack Knight and she begged Lunsford to get involved. The odds were long, but the case fascinated Lunsford, and climbing aboard a front-page death sentence struggle would not hurt his practice. Most lawyers considered the case a surefire flop, so his reputation would not suffer if he could not save the defendants.

Jack Knight still felt he could handle the case alone, but Luns-ford found a way to bypass him. Since neither defendant's family had enough money to fund the black hole of a marathon appeal, Knight had convinced Leslie and Carolyn to sign pauper's oaths so the courts would pay their bills, but this maneuver also gave the courts more influence over the case. By arguing that one attorney could not represent two defendants without being caught in a con-flict of interest, Lunsford was named Leslie's court-appointed counsel. The coup created a glaring irony—Knight had always been Carolyn's lawyer by default. Her mother had never wanted him and refused to pay him a penny. Now, Carolyn became his only client.

Both sides went to Austin to make their oral pleadings before the Court of Criminal Appeals in the spring of 1962. Sylvia spoke to the judges also. "If you will show mercy, it's all I ask," she begged. "There's been a change in my son's life since he became a Christian." It was a tough pill for a Jewish mother to swallow, but she would drink poison to save her only child.

Despite the new lawyer on his team, Knight continued to push the same three judicial errors that were in his failed motion for a retrial, but the defense was through with Richard Robert Ray-mond Ramirez. Knight's attempt to discredit the shifty witness had backfired, and he was not eager to replicate the humiliation on a higher rung of jurisprudence. He dropped Ramirez from his appeal strategy and substituted a new complaint—Judge Love had erred when he excluded testimony about the victim's background, especially the incident when Tones showed up at the Todaro home after the barrage of obscene telephone calls.

Nothing worked. When the decision came down in June, the Texas appeals court found no reversible errors in the trial. Carolyn's oral confession and Mrs. Tones's hearsay testimony were properly admitted; the victim's background was properly excluded. The trial judge cured any damage done by the widow's outburst with prompt instructions ordering the jury to ignore her grief as soon as she was led from the courtroom. The convictions were upheld, so were the death sentences.

Leslie refused to accept defeat. "God wouldn't give me salvation, then sit me down in the electric chair." His conversion sustained him. "It would be like leading innocent lambs to the slaughter block," he said. "The law is as crooked as can be. Our jury was selected from a common mob like the one that condemned Jesus Christ. Juries should be made up of our superiors, bankers and wealthy businessmen."

The fresh disappointment brought Leslie and Carolyn together again, and she had her own words for the men who had voted to execute her, "Our jury thought prostitutes were the scum under the earth." Figures of speech were not her forte. "They convicted us for what they thought we were, not for what we did."

Leslie agreed, "We should have been freed of murder and convicted of car theft."

They were no longer angry at each other. "We still want to get out, get married, raise a large family, and bring in lost souls," Leslie said. When Carolyn went along with him, he stuck out his hand, "Put her there, kid."

As they shook hands, his optimism waned, but his bravado rose even higher. "When it comes time to burn somebody, I want to burn for both of us. I want to sit in it by myself. I don't want any shots or pills and none of that 'It's okay, pal' from anybody either." A messiah complex was beginning to show, "I'll take it just like Jesus Christ—forgive 'em all."

Carolyn was always the realist of the pair. "You have too much faith," she told him. "You're talking too much."

Lloyd Lunsford was ready to step forward and inject fresh blood into the appeal, but he could not take control as long as Jack Knight remained on the case, and he did not want to repeat Knight's initial mistake by working alone. Lunsford said he approached a classmate from his law school days at the University of Houston about coming on board as Carolyn's counsel.

Clyde Woody had graduated the same year as Lucky Lunsford,

but Woody was younger, young enough to have missed World
War II and to have blazed straight through school. He was short
and pugnacious, with the build and temperament that might cause
a coach to call him a fireplug. His tongue was sharp and salty;
profanity could be his palette. His down-home drawl did not conceal a fierce ambition to win, and he liked to shake up cross-
examinations and social conversations alike with outrageous
openings or non sequiturs that put listeners off balance while he
carefully sized up their reactions to his intentional gaffes and slurs.

Woody said Lucky Lunsford did not talk him into entering the
case. Three female reporters who covered the trial for local newspapers had been disturbed by the verdict. Death sentences
seemed extreme to them, given the facts of the case and the mental condition of the defendants, especially Leslie. The reporters
ganged up on Woody. "Those damn women were riding a broom
on me," he moaned. "I had to do something to get them off my
back."

Woody had built his reputation on drug cases that made headlines in the mid-1950s. Vipers and hopheads were his specialty.
Early in his practice, he was on the legal team that took a heroin
case all the way to the Supreme Court, winning a reversal
because the arrest warrant was issued without sufficient probable
cause.

That victory near the beginning of his career gave Clyde
Woody a taste of triumph at the highest level of his profession.
Neil McKay, the assistant D.A. who specialized in capital cases,
believed the Supreme Court success ruined Woody. McKay
trusted verdicts voted by juries, and he thought the heady experience of winning in Washington made Woody too dependant on
twisting trials to create possibilities for appeals. "He's not a lawyer's lawyer," McKay scoffed. "Clyde doesn't care about the jury."

Neil McKay faced a formidable adversary when Clyde Woody
joined the defense team. Woody's combative drive at this stage of
his career was not his only asset, he was also fueled by a visceral
dislike of McKay's boss. Clyde Woody despised Frank Briscoe,
and the feeling was mutual.

"Me and Frank have never been the best of friends," Woody
smiled, remembering their battles.

23

"At the time of the crime, my client was only seventeen years old," Clyde Woody told the *Houston Press*. "At the time of the trial, she was only eighteen. She was only a child. She didn't know what she was doing." Woody hit his predecessor with a flamethrower. Jack Knight "was never hired by my client or my client's mother," Woody continued. "As far as I'm concerned, she's never been represented." The remark came close to charging Knight with malpractice. The original defense attorney withdrew from the case, but nursed his anger against the colleague who bumped him.

Despite his cocky confidence, Woody's start was no better than Jack Knight's finish. The new defense team suffered a defeat when the Texas Court of Criminal Appeals denied a leftover motion of Knight's for a rehearing, which Woody and Lunsford had amended with arguments of their own. The court ruled again no damage was done by Mrs. Tones's hearsay testimony of her final telephone conversation with her husband. The appeals court came up with a scenario all the defense attorneys had missed. Telling his wife to have dinner ready at six o'clock "could have been beneficial," the decision read. "It could be construed as an effort on the deceased's part to keep his wife from coming to his office while the sexual date was being consummated."

Woody could not stifle his sarcasm. "Counsel for the appellants is in the unfortunate position of being unable to speculate on the quantum of time necessary to consummate such a sexual date," he wrote in a motion asking the court to reconsider. "The record appears to be silent as to the usual, customary, and expected

duration of such a relationship." Unless the appeals court judges
could speak from experience, they should not put a clock on
three-way dates with prostitutes. "It is not within the realm of
matters of which this Honorable Court may take judicial knowledge."

Woody did not wait for another rejection. "This is only a minor
skirmish, not the war," he said. He and Lucky Lunsford were
already working on a new lead that launched them in a more
promising direction—Dr. Howard Crow's eighteen-month-old
medical opinion was no longer a secret. Clyde Woody conven-
iently forgot who leaked the word to him about the shelved psychiatric report, but he knew Dr. Crow and the clinical
psychologist, Jack Tracktir, who also believed Leslie and Carolyn
had been incompetent to stand trial. "I had used those two birds
before," Woody said.

Crow and Tracktir were fairly new to forensics. Woody believed
they had only handled one other capital case before they examined Leslie Douglas Ashley and Carolyn Lima. By coincidence, he
happened to be the defense attorney on that case. Woody had
stayed on good terms with both of them, retaining them for his
own cases, and they both confirmed they had notified the district
attorney's office that Leslie and Carolyn were legally insane before
the murder trial began. Woody did not fault them for failing to
publicize their conclusions. Crow and Tracktir were "new to the
system," he noted. He was happy to have a fresh angle to pursue.

When Sylvia visited Leslie, she said that she had to speak with
him through the metal door of DC–6, short for Death Cell 6, an
isolation cell for condemned prisoners on the sixth floor.

Leslie fought his demons with religion, and the struggle had
escalated. He told his mother about another visitation. "He said
he was kneeling at a rock," she recalled. "He said he was kneeling
down praying, and he said a cloud opened up and the sun came
out of this cloud and took him by the hand and led him away."
Leslie was always a child when he saw his sacred fog. "He was a
little boy," Sylvia continued. "He said after the cloud closed up,
the lights in the jail went off. That was one of his visions."

Sylvia remembered, "He said Jesus takes over his mind." Leslie
made his savior in his own image. "Jesus, he told me, was a man
and Christ was a woman." The power of his dual-gender Lord

made Leslie immortal. "They can't kill him in the electric chair, that's what he told me," Sylvia said.

Leslie devoured his Bibles and religious tracts. He was drawn to Elijah, the ancient Hebrew prophet who fled to a desert cave where he saw flames and wind and earthquakes before the Lord appeared and told him to gather an army to slay the followers of a false god. "I will call on the name of the Lord, and the God that answereth by fire, let him be God," Elijah raged at his enemies. He won his religious war and never died, instead he was carried to heaven in a blazing chariot.

As a legacy, Elijah became a special benefactor to Jews in distress with a chair reserved for him at circumcision ceremonies and a glass of wine at Passover seders. Despite his conversion to Christianity, Leslie could see the connection. Elijah also promised to reconcile fathers with their children, according to scripture in the Prophecy of Malachi, "before the great and dreadful day of the Lord." To both Jews and Pentecostals, this quote made Elijah's reappearance a harbinger of the messiah's arrival. With a seat in Old Sparky waiting in his future, a messiah was exactly what Leslie needed.

He also developed a special affinity for Elijah's protégé, Elisha, who performed many miracles during sixty years as a holy man. Elisha cured a leper and restored life to a dead child; he struck thieves blind, then restored their sight. Leslie decided he was the reincarnation of Elisha, only his Elisha was a woman. His mentor was Sylvia, to whom he gave the peculiar title Misrus Elijah when he was in the grip of his religious fervor.

When he felt more earthbound, Leslie kept himself occupied with a pair of cockroaches he had trapped inside a cigarette box in his death cell. He tried to train his insect companions to do tricks. "He said he was lonesome," Sylvia explained. "He didn't have anyone to talk to." She shook her head as she repeated, "He didn't have anyone to talk to."

After the old psychiatric reports surfaced, Clyde Woody wanted recent opinions, so he asked Dr. Eugene Tips to examine Leslie. When Dr. Tips hired Jack Tracktir for a battery of clinical exams, he did not realize the psychologist had evaluated Leslie once before. Tracktir did not think his prior involvement was worth mentioning. No conflict was created. In fact, Tracktir believed the previous evaluation was an asset. He could compare Leslie's current mental condition to the findings eighteen months earlier.

Tracktir began his session with Leslie in a sheriff's office at the county jail. Leslie was angry and refused to cooperate. Tracktir scribbled the gist of the tirade in a notebook. "I'm not going to talk to any nut doctor," Leslie had fumed. "I see nobody but my mother. I'm not crazy. I'm not going to look at any ink splotches, they make me nervous and I'll sound crazy. I'm not going to be found crazy and go to any insane asylum, and I'm not going to talk to you anymore. I've talked too much already. You don't need any ink splotches to tell I'm not crazy."

After his harangue, Leslie met every question with silence until he was told that going along with the tests might help his cause. Leslie did not want Tracktir's help, "I don't need any nut doctors or lawyers," he answered. He put his faith in the personal religion he had developed in Death Cell 6. "I've been reborn," Leslie stressed. "I was reborn as a little boy and flew off in a cloud."

Tracktir could see Leslie had "deteriorated quite a bit" from his condition nearly a year and a half earlier. "He is delusional and there is some evidence of hallucinations." The diagnosis was unequivocal. "He is insane," the psychologist concluded.

When Dr. Tips arrived, Leslie refused to let the interview be recorded, so the psychiatrist had his tape machine removed from the room. "He knew where he was and the approximate date," Dr. Tips recalled. Beyond those objective facts, Leslie lived in his own private reality. "He felt there was a great deal of evil in the world, and one of the great dangers was that rats were taking over the world, eating away at the vital structures."

Rats were a problem, but people were not. "I didn't feel he was cognizant of the fact that he had received a death sentence. He said I was in grave error if I felt anything was going to happen to him because he was above and beyond punishment by any human hand."

Leslie had absolute confidence in divine intervention. "He completely ignored the possibility of his death sentence and very mysteriously stated that he knew it would not be carried out," Dr. Tips said. "He gave me the impression that something miraculous would keep him from going to the chair." His Lord would not let him down. "He would be saved by something supernatural from above." Dr. Tips believed Leslie was seriously ill. "His psychosis is, in my opinion, incurable." The psychiatrist rendered his specific diagnosis, schizophrenia–paranoid type, and submitted a bill for two hundred fifty dollars.

The defense team paid the same fee to send a another psychiatrist to see Leslie. "Mr. Ashley was an extremely tense young man. He was obviously under a great deal of pressure," Dr. Exter Bell reported. "Mr. Ashley, I found, to be suffering from delusions of persecution and abnormal religiosity. He had hallucinations of various kinds. . . . The giggling and laughing were quite striking." Dr. Bell noticed another survival mechanism, Leslie's "almost complete detachment from his real situation. He didn't seem to be personally involved, but rather looked upon this as something happening to somebody else."

The psychiatrist continued, "I think part of his detachment from his situation is because of the belief that some supernatural force will save him. In other words, he cannot be hurt. The prospect of his electrocution does not mean anything to him because he feels at the last moment some miracle will take place which will take him away from electrocution."

Leslie discussed his religious visions with Dr. Bell, but the psychiatrist was more impressed with Leslie's faith in himself. "One of the most inappropriate things in the whole interview was his insistence that he was sane," Dr. Bell remembered. "He insisted he was sane. Of course, the signs were to the contrary, but he seemed much more perturbed by the idea that he might be found insane than by the idea that he might be electrocuted."

Armed with the two new psychiatric reports, the defense team saw a way to block the executions. Texas law was explicit— inmates who became insane after their convictions were transferred to an asylum until they recovered. Executions for insane convicts were postponed until they were deemed mentally fit to understand their punishment before they sat in Old Sparky. With the new psychiatric opinions, the defense lawyers believed they had a decent chance to stall Leslie's death sentence.

Alone, the psychiatric reports could not get the job done. A jury's verdict after a court hearing was required to declare Leslie legally insane, but the pair of psychiatric opinions gave the defense lawyers the leverage they needed to push forward. Judge Love scheduled a sanity hearing to begin two weeks before

Christmas 1962. The stakes were high for Carolyn as well. If Leslie went to a mental hospital, the defense lawyers felt certain that she would not be executed as long as he was alive. Woody and Lunsford were reversing the old strategy—Jack Knight had tried to use sympathy for Carolyn to spare Leslie. The new lawyers made him the wedge to save her.

24

Medicine and law hardly dovetail, but a sanity hearing is the crooked seam where they join. Strictly speaking, the psychiatrists called to testify did not even use the word insanity in their daily practices. "I think it was used several hundred years ago," Dr. Exter Bell said. "We don't use it today except when we're talking with lawyers."

Doctors have more precise categories for the disorders they diagnose. Dr. Eugene Tips, who also saw Leslie just before the hearing, put the distinction simply. "If you want my medical opinion of this man, he's psychotic. If I'm talking about it in a courtroom, I might say he's insane." The difference did not bother Dr. Tips. "We talk a little different language, but it's interchangeable. We all know what we're talking about."

But doctors and lawyers were not deciding the verdict. That task rested with members of the jury, who would have to funnel conflicting opinions and dense jargon from a crash course in psychiatry through the criteria for legal insanity under the M'Naghton Rule, the common standard that asked whether "a defect of reason from disease of the mind" kept defendants from understanding the consequences of their actions or the difference between right and wrong.

The burden of proof was on the defense at sanity hearings, and Texas law made Leslie's current mental balance the only question open for judgment. On the surface, this sanity hearing was simply a method to defer the death sentences by moving Leslie from jail to an asylum. To plead not guilty due to insanity, defendants had to raise the issue at their trials. After the original jury's verdict was in, prior insanity could not be used to reverse a conviction, but Woody and Lunsford believed they had a witness who might give them the power to make the clock spin backward.

Carolyn had a lot riding on the hearing, but she brooded in jail without realizing an insanity verdict for Leslie would help her too. "They're ditching me," she charged. "I guess I was born to lose."

Leslie entered the courtroom on December 10, the opening day of his sanity hearing, wearing blue jeans and a silver religious medallion hanging outside his white T-shirt. He carried a Bible with his full name stamped in gold on the cover, and he trembled when he was not giggling. "I don't want to go the nuthouse," he told reporters. "I just want to go home." Before he sat beside his lawyers he informed them he was Elisha today. "I don't know who Leslie Ashley is," he blared.

The jury candidates were questioned about their religious backgrounds because Leslie's obsession with mystical prophecy was at the heart of the hearing. Unlike at the murder trial, jury selection here flowed smoothly. Eleven men and one woman were quickly picked and sworn in by noon. Frank Briscoe rose to recite the status of the case, "Leslie Douglas Ashley was convicted in this court, Criminal District Court Number 3 of Harris County, Texas, on May 23, 1961. . . ."

"I believe the verdict was returned on the twenty-fourth," Judge Love corrected him.

"That's according to the record I have," Clyde Woody added.

"All right, Your Honor. It was the twenty-fourth," the D.A. grumbled. The mistake was a petty clerical oversight, but Frank Briscoe had never been this careless before.

Sylvia Ayres was the first witness, and Lloyd Lunsford handled the direct examination. (Although they represented different clients, the two defense attorneys worked the sanity hearing together.) Lunsford started with questions about her unhappy marriage to Leslie Sherman Ashley. "He gave me a venereal disease," Sylvia said. Her ex-husband had not made the trip from Arkansas so he was not around to refute her.

"Were you suffering from this disease at the time this boy was born?"

Briscoe rose to object, but Sylvia was too quick for him. "Yes, sir," she answered.

Briscoe finished his objection; the question was immaterial, he argued. Lunsford let Clyde Woody handle the technical wrangling. The defense double-teamed the district attorney, a change from the murder trial when one lawyer represented both defendants.

After questioning resumed, Sylvia cried as she described Leslie's suicide attempts as a teenager and his bachelor apartments where pets that were not housebroken roamed amid kitsch disarray. Lunsford wanted to hear more about her son's interior decor. "He had a large number of statues and idols?"

"That's right."

"Do you have those statues or idols in the courthouse?"

She did, and Lunsford ordered crate after crate carried into the courtroom. Leslie winced, visibly irritated as the treasures from his past were cermoniously unwrapped, filling three tabletops. A bailiff tripped on a courtroom spittoon, splashing water on Leslie's shoes. "Don't baptize me right here and now!" he yelled.

Wax and plastic flowers, fat Buddhas, lithe Asian dieties. Leslie's treasures included benevolent lions and chimeras with their long tongues hanging out as gestures of good fortune. Svelte ceramic women wore sheer, flowing robes. Lunsford asked Sylvia to step down from the witness stand and go through the items on the tabletops. They all belonged to Leslie, she said. Briscoe was sick of the showboating. He wanted the kitsch entered as evidence or removed from the courtroom.

"We're going to enter them," Lunsford shot back. "We'll offer them for the purpose of showing the extremes to which this defendant went beyond the normal realm of reason." Sylvia testified that Leslie went hungry to save money for his treasures.

An old pattern repeated. Sylvia sobbed when she was questioned by a friendly attorney. As soon as Frank Briscoe took over, she choked back her tears and they clashed. "At the trial, you did not testify to anything regarding insanity?" the D.A. asked her.

Sylvia turned to stone, "No, sir."

Briscoe dipped into Leslie's youth, "You took this defendant to a Dr. Taylor?"

"Yes, sir."

"He suggested you take him to a pyschiatrist?"

"Yes, sir."

"The reason for that was because of some homosexual tendency, wasn't it?"

"Yes, sir."

Briscoe wanted to know about Leslie's criminal history. "You say he's had trouble with the authorities regarding his dressing as a woman?"

"Yes, sir."

"You said here in Houston, but he was actually convicted of some similar offense in New York, was he not?"

"Yes, sir."

Her son was hustling on the Upper West Side in 1958, when he claimed that he scuffled with a trick who welched on his debt, but the police charged Leslie with robbery by assault. He was booked wearing high heels, dangling earrings, and a blue knit dress. Leslie said he plea-bargained a reduced charge sentencing him to a few days on Rikers Island, where his hair was clipped short. "I lost my confidence," Leslie complained. After his release, he packed his bags and headed for home. "I just couldn't work without my hair."

Even under a death sentence, the Harris County jailers let Leslie keep his wavy black locks. He sat in the courtroom staring into space or reading his Bible, ignoring the kitsch from his past that was supposed to be evidence of his insanity, while Frank Briscoe questioned his mother.

"Have you appeared on the radio or transmitted messages by radio?"

Sylvia played cagey, "What type of messages?"

"Any type on behalf of your son, appealing for funds and other help."

"By mail."

"Haven't there been some radio programs in that connection?"

"I believe once."

Sylvia made most of her pleas to Christian groups impressed by Leslie's conversion. The Jewish mother stepped to the pulpit beneath a cross in their churches and begged for donations. Sometimes her emotions conquered her memory and she lost her lines. The first time her mind went blank, she flashed on a solution. "I just closed my eyes, bowed my head and asked for a moment of silent prayer." She laughed as she remembered rummaging her brain for the speech she had forgotten.

Woody took over the questioning when Dr. Howard Crow was

on the stand. The psychiatrist was the defense team's witness who might change the future with his account of the past. Dr. Crow said he saw Leslie twice for the prosecution prior to the 1961 murder trial. He described Leslie's facetious attitude, his inappropriate emotions, his giggling, his emotional ambivalence, and the broken logic that scattered answers like shotgun pellets—all symptoms of schizophrenia. To Dr. Crow, Leslie's persecution complex was an obvious expression of paranoia. "I feel he was insane, and made a record of it on 3–22–61 and 4–8–61."

"Did you report your findings to Mr. Briscoe?" Woody asked.

"Yes, sir. I talked to him about it and I told him in a letter." Dr. Crow used Leslie's middle name, "I stated that I felt Douglas Ashley was incompetent. He was sick, and, in talking with Mr. Briscoe, I told him I felt this man, Douglas Ashley, needed treatment in a hospital. He was sick and a schizophrenic, and I did that on 3–22–61 and 4–8–61."

Woody wanted to clench Dr. Crow's memory, "There is no question in your mind that prior to the trial Mr. Briscoe knew of your opinion?"

Briscoe objected. Dr. Crow might be a psychiatrist, but he wasn't a mindreader. He could not testify about conclusions the D.A. reached in his own brain.

Woody tried again, "You did discuss fully with him your findings?"

Briscoe was on his feet again, contending Woody was leading his witness, and Judge Love agreed. Woody rephrased his question, "I believe you said that you had a discussion with Mr. Briscoe on at least two occasions."

The new phrasing tied the D.A.'s hands. No objection blocked Dr. Crow's response. "Mr. Briscoe got my findings and professional opinion that Mr. Ashley was a schizophrenic and incompetent to understand what the trial would be about. I felt he was chronically ill and had been for a long time. We discussed this, and I wrote him an opinion about Douglas Ashley being incompetent."

The lasting power of Dr. Crow's replies remained hidden. Although his medical opinion could be contradicted by other psychiatrists with equal credentials, a critical fact his words put into the transcript could not be refuted—Frank Briscoe had known of Dr Crow's findings before the murder trial. The impact of this testimony lay ahead. For now, the questions returned to the present.

Since Leslie's current mental condition was the issue at the hearing, Dr. Crow had seen him more recently, just yesterday and the day before, at the request of the defense team. He had talked with Leslie's mother as well. Dr. Crow saw traces of Leslie in Sylvia. "She kidded with me and I was quite serious," he said. "I'm here as a physician, trying to get serious information. She kids with me about his illness and thinks it's funny, then weeps and comes back and laughs again."

Sylvia's traits were magnified in her son. "He's like his mother. He talks like her and laughs like her and thinks like her." Dr. Crow continued, "He's male as far as his genitals are concerned, but he dresses like a woman and walks the streets of a town. . . . He induces men to make passes at him as though he were a female. He cannot help himself. He cannot consciously control himself, no more than you can̄ stop breathing."

The psychiatrist said the treasures Leslie went hungry to collect soothed his troubled personality. He identified with the breasts on the fat Buddhas and the fragility of the feminine figures, but the statues and jungle of artificial flowers offered a deeper satisfaction. "This is his family. These are things that cannot hurt him, but people can. He can look at these things and feel these things in his room alone."

Leslie never had that peace with his mother. "He doesn't tear loose, and she can't either." Dr. Crow offered his view of their bond, "A son will love his mother too much if the mother lets him." A virgin birth had even become part of the personal mythology Leslie wove into his new biography. Dr. Crow paraphrased him, " 'I am like Jesus Christ because we have the same origin, the same genetics, and the same kind of mother.' . . . Then, he tells me a very interesting thing. He says, 'I'm married, you know, and she comes to see me, you know. I can leave the jail any time I like, spiritually or physically, and we spend time together.' "

Dr. Crow called this delusion a mystic marriage, and Carolyn Lima was not the bride. Leslie had begun a pen-pal romance with a Kentucky teenager, a high school senior who had read about him in *The Voice of Healing*, an evangelical magazine aimed at believers in faith healing and miraculous intervention. Leslie said he and his favorite pen pal would spread the word together when he got out of jail. They would speak in many languages, including Pentecostal tongues.

"It matters little what you do to me," Leslie challenged Dr. Crow. "I will live always." God had anointed him as the reincarnation of Elisha, but Leslie had more names in his new identity. "He laughs about it and says 'My first name is Lillette.' Then another word comes to him and he said, 'Gold U.S.A.' I asked him 'What's your last name?' And, he said, 'Elisha,' so his name is Lillette Gold U.S.A. Elisha," Dr. Crow testified. "He says he's a prophet, a seer of visions, and if you don't agree with him you will die."

Clyde Woody wanted to backtrack. He asked Dr. Crow to explore Leslie's virgin-birth theory. "He says, 'Misrus Elijah is my mother and God is my father,'" the psychiatrist answered. Dr. Crow thought Sylvia's hostile attitude toward her first husband was the key. "In talking with the mother, she said, 'You know, I was just like a virgin when he was born. I had not been exposed but one time.'"

Dr. Crow allowed himself to speculate, "Do you suppose that in her feelings for her son, she denied that she ever touched his father because she hated him so? Maybe this is where he picked up the virgin birth. She did not like his father and did not live with him. . . . She would say facetiously, 'I married my first husband because he was good-looking.' And, she looks at her present husband and says, 'Obviously, I didn't marry him for that.'"

Running down her mates could have influenced her son. "She was cruel," Dr. Crow said. "How uncomfortable would that make her son? I think she made him very uncomfortable, and he resorted to schizophrenia protectively."

Leslie boiled at the defense table. His mother did not make him insane. He believed he was not insane at all, but that was not Dr. Crow's professional opinion and Clyde Woody wanted a prognosis. "What is your best estimate of his chances of ever recovering his sanity again?"

Assistant D.A. Neil McKay rose to object, but Leslie's voice rang louder. "Indeed, I'm not . . . " he screamed. The rest of his brief tirade was garbled as he waved his Bible, claiming the proof of his fitness was in its sacred pages. As soon as he made his point, Leslie quickly calmed down and sat quietly again.

"He's the messiah," Dr. Crow explained. "He's not on trial, you are."

The outburst did not disturb the prosecutors. They did not bother asking Judge Love to remove or discipline Leslie, much less stop the hearing and start over with a new jury. His rage helped them. He claimed he was sane, an opinion the prosecutors shared, and his outburst proved he understood what was going on around him.

Tuesday, December 11, began with Jack Tracktir, the ex–Air Force psychologist who had seen Leslie with Dr. Crow in March, 1961, and nineteen months later with Dr. Eugene Tips. The psychologist testified Leslie was psychotic and paranoiac during the first visit, even worse during the recent session. "Much more ill," Tracktir concluded.

When Judge Love called a brief recess, Leslie uttered his first word of the morning. As he was led from the courtroom, he stared at a bailiff and said "Boo!"

After the break, Dr. H. Newell Taylor took the stand and described treating Leslie as a teenager. Frank Briscoe had a few questions for the general practitioner. "He admitted to you that he was a homosexual?" the D.A. asked on cross-examination.

"That's right," Dr. Taylor answered.

"It was for this reason that you referred him to a psychiatrist?"

"That was part of the reason," Dr. Taylor replied. "His responses were abnormal in other fields as well as sexual."

The D.A. locked onto Leslie's sexual preference, "Outbursts such as you've described and immaturity, isn't this common among homosexuals?"

"I presume it is, but I don't think the emotional outbursts indicated homosexuality."

"Aren't homosexuals given to emotional outbursts?" Briscoe tossed a wide net.

"I don't believe I can answer that," Dr. Taylor said.

The D.A. wanted to create the notion that a hysterical streak capable of generating religious delusions and murder was linked to being gay. The prosecutor used a homophobic stereotype in an attempt to create animosity toward Leslie with the jury. The defense would have to counter that tactic, but the battle was delayed for a bittersweet burlesque, a comic interval built on a human disability.

Leslie began giggling as soon as his grandmother stepped into the courtroom. Elizabeth Kipperman's spine was bent and cerebral palsy hobbled her. With two escorts flanking her, she returned Leslie's laughter when she saw him. She could not remember her age, sixty-two or sixty three, she was not sure, and a speech impediment made her difficult to understand.

"Have you suffered with your present condition all your life?" Lloyd Lunsford asked.

"Yes, all my life, yes sir." She smiled. Leslie's chuckling grew louder.

His grandmother laughed as she said her late husband "had syphilis, something like that." She claimed Joe Kipperman suffered from the venereal disease when Sylvia was born, and Sylvia had testified that her ex-husband gave her a venereal disease before Leslie was born. It was either a family tradition or a fantasy they shared. Leslie and his grandmother both howled.

The shrill hilarity hypnotized Clyde Woody. "She'd start laughing, then he'd come in too, back and forth all the time," the defense attorney remembered. "They sounded just alike." When Leslie and his grandmother hit identical notes, a resonant chord vibrated in the courtroom. "It was eerie," Woody said. Lucky Lunsford seized the spooky moment to rest their side of the case.

Frank Briscoe began his case with Dr. Benjamin Sher. As consulting psychiatrist for Harris County, Dr. Sher had seen Leslie on "at least a half a dozen occasions" during his regular rounds through the jail prior to the murder trial in May 1961. "I was always having trouble somewhere," Leslie told him. Dr. Sher reported the defendant was not psychotic.

After Judge Love granted the motion for a sanity hearing, Dr. Sher gave Leslie a pair of extensive exams. The first session was not quite two weeks before the hearing. "The interview was a little bit unsatisfactory," Dr. Sher recalled. "The defendant didn't wish to discuss anything, but after about five minutes he stated he was sane." With that declaration, Leslie began to talk. "He didn't want to be examined for fear that he might have to go to a state hospital, and the other person involved in this episode might get a commuted sentence and after he got out of the hospital he would still have to go to the electric chair."

Leslie was not willing to burn for Carolyn anymore. "He wanted to be in the same position as the girl. If one sentence was commuted, he wanted both commuted. He understood what was going on, he had no defective reasoning."

Dr. Sher believed any evidence of insanity Leslie displayed was fake, "In the beginning, he put on a pose." A second visit over a week later confirmed that conclusion. "The defendant has always been an actor more or less. He's acted out some of his feelings, dressing up in clothes of the opposite sex, but he was aware of what was happening. I found him of sound mind."

Before he challenged that judgment, Clyde Woody started his cross-examination by mocking Dr. Sher's accent. The psychiatrist was a New Yorker who had begun his pre-med studies at Brooklyn College.

"You were an Italian doctor or in the Italian army," Woody asked one of his trademark questions from the moon.

"I said I was a battalion surgeon," Dr. Sher replied.

After his stab at ridicule, Woody switched directions. "Doctor, isn't it a fact that homosexuality in many instances is a basic factor of schizophrenia?"

"No," Dr. Sher was certain. "I think it's an inadaquecy within oneself pertaining to the opposite sex."

Woody was fighting the D.A.'s charge that gays were prone to tantrums which made them unstable, even homicidal. If Briscoe pounded that theme, Woody pushed it to the extreme, trying to forge a connection between being gay and schizophrenia, a form of legal insanity. Neither side bothered to make the distinction between Leslie's transvestite fixation and gay lifestyles that did not involve drag hustling. At the sanity hearing, all homosexual behavior was lumped together, and it was all either reprehensible or crazy.

"You would agree with me that homosexuality isn't normal?" Woody asked.

"It's not normal by our standards," Dr. Sher replied. In December 1962, the American Psychiatric Association still classified homosexuality as a mental disorder. "Since there are both sexes on the earth, I conclude the good Lord didn't want us to engage in homosexual practices."

Woody tried the same question when he cross-examined the next witness, Dr. Neil Burch. "Will you agree that homosexuality is not a normal thing?" Woody asked.

"Yes, sir," the psychiatrist answered.

"And will you further agree with me that it's not unusual to find homosexuality in a paranoid schizophrenic?"

"Oh, no. I don't agree with that," Dr. Burch responded. "The individual who is a homosexual is not a schizophrenic."

In his original 1961 report, Dr. Burch called Leslie "a caricature of a homosexual and so overdoes the girlish effeminate pose that he seems to be advertising himself. He acts out all of the characteristics that society attributes to the homosexual, but which in fact are rarely seen in such a pure culture." The psychiatrist learned why Leslie hung out in lesbian bars, like the bar where he met Carolyn. Leslie said he spent a lot of time with gay women, starting when he was a teenager. The women liked to "show him off in their crowd because he was prettier than most of the other sissie boys," Dr. Burch wrote.

Leslie had always lived on the social fringe. Spurned by the mainstream, he seemed to revel in the animosity he inspired. "I think he provoked it," Dr. Burch said. "I think he's proud of being deviant, and in some strange way I think it's a mark of success. He can really push people around with this."

Woody saw an opening, "You really mean he can control people and manipulate them?"

"Yes."

"And that's absolutely one of the symptoms of a paranoid schizophrenic. He's known to have this very ability, isn't he?"

"Along with ninety-nine and nine-tenths percent of the human race."

The D.A. had jailers make copies of letters that Leslie wrote to his network of pen pals. The grammar, spelling, and punctuation left a lot to be desired, but Leslie's script was neat with round, flowing curves, like perfect examples traced from a handbook on penmanship. Briscoe wanted the jury to hear that the letters were not incoherent ravings from a lunatic so he began to read in the courtroom.

Leslie was chipper when he received a picture from a steady pen pal in Michigan: "You sure do have a good-looking set of hair. I do believe it appears to be more curly than mine." Another correspondent got a rundown of Leslie's radio habits. He mixed Christmas carols with gospel music in his isolation cell, but he also tuned in a country station. "I do like hillbilly music. Guess that is because I come from Ark. And am a hillbilly from A-way back." He was spreading the word about his sanity hearing. "You may catch a few scenes on TV so try and see the telecast news. And for sure it'll be carried on the radio . . . cause they carried all of my trial. Guess you know they also carried Howard Stickney's. I wonder how his mom is." Stickney was the necrophiliac whose trial made front page news two years before Leslie's case. After fourteen reprieves and spending more time on death row than any other prisoner before him in Texas history, he had been executed in May, 1962.

In another letter, Leslie believed faith would save him from Stickney's fate. "I am a new person in Christ and have put off my mind and have indeed put on the mind of Christ! . . . I was well on my way to hell but Christ saved my soul and he will not let me down and will deliver me like he did Daniel from the lion's den." He did not want psychiatrists to be his salvation. "I just can't hardly bear the thoughts of being judged insane. It is just plain injustice. This is getting me out of the way to clear Carolyn for a life sentence. . . . Pray that I shall not be judged insane cause I don't feel this is the will of the Lord."

Leslie's confidence soared when he wrote to Gail Rash, the Kentucky high school senior who was the bride in his mystic marriage. "They are going to fight me down to the finish line to set me in the electric chair. I am afraid they are in a losing battle cause they are going to lose and I am going to live!"

The D.A. rested his case when he finished reading the letters. As a rebuttal witness on Wednesday morning, the defense lawyers called Dr. Eugene Tips, who had examined Leslie before the hearing and determined he was a paranoid schizophrenic, insane under the law.

Woody held out a sample of the damaging evidence, "Would this impair his ability to write a letter as you see here?"

"I think it's a common fallacy, when a person is pronounced psychotic, that he's confused in all areas," Dr. Tips responded. "They're not."

Leslie ignored the testimony. He sat quietly reading a religious tract titled The Last News—Christ Is Coming. In his cross-examination, Briscoe returned to a familiar topic. "Doctor, when you first saw this man wasn't it pretty obvious from the beginning, from the effeminate characterstics and matters of that kind, that he was a sexual deviate, a homosexual?"

"Yes, sir."

Woody rose, "Doctor, is homosexuality consistent with paranoid schizophrenia?"

"Yes, it's a frequently associated phenomenon."

Briscoe got up again. "Are all homosexuals schizophrenics?"

"No."

"Are all schizophrenics homosexuals?"

"No."

"What percentage of homosexuals are schizophrenics?" Briscoe demanded. "You say it's consistent, would you say half?"

Dr. Tips did not have an answer. "I wouldn't give a statistical account of it."

The hearing had degenerated into an unenlightened inquiry into sexual preference and mental health. The defense attorneys wanted to convince the jury that a generalized gay psychosis should save their client from the electric chair, while the D.A. tried to execute Leslie by generating homophobia.

Both sides rested before noon on Wednesday, December 12. Above the caption BATTLE OF THE PSYCHIATRISTS, the afternoon edition of the *Houston Press* ran photos of all five M.D.s who had testified at the hearing. "Sane" or "Insane" appeared beneath each doctor's picture. The score was three to two in favor of schizophrenia, but the tally that mattered was being deliberated in the jury room. The members of the panel only had one choice to make: sane or insane at the present time, but the verdict took nine hours, over an hour longer than the jury at the murder trial had spent before coming back with two death sentences.

Thursday morning, Leslie was the only person on his side of the aisle who seemed satisfied when the clerk of the court announced the jury had found him sane. "I'm glad." He chuckled and hugged his Bible. "That's what I wanted. I'm not crazy."

Sylvia kept her composure until Leslie was led away, then she stepped to a corner of the courtroom and cried quietly while a circle of sympathetic friends tried to console her. She broke down completely as she packed away her son's kitsch treasures. "They just can't kill this boy, they just can't," she wept.

Sylvia offered Lloyd Lunsford a memento—a fat, smiling Buddha, green to look like jade, with its arms raised high. Sylvia said she planned to auction off the other statues, about sixty in all, to raise money to continue the legal fight.

Carolyn lost a chance to delay her execution with Leslie's sanity hearing verdict. The jury's decision surprised her. "If he's sane, he's changed quite a deal since the last time I seen him," she said in the women's jail. "I feel Leslie does need help."

Carolyn was still hoping for a long life, "to have someone that would really love me and take care of me, that I could give all my love to and just stay at home and take care of them." She missed her family. "I'm not cold," she assured the reporters who came to visit her.

25

The winter that began 1963 was bad by Houston standards. The temperature rarely rose above freezing during the weekend before Leslie and Carolyn were due in court to learn their execution date. A few flakes of snow, the first in almost three years, fell during the hours between midnight and dawn on Monday, January 14.

The crowd at the courthouse saw a van parked along the curb when they arrived that morning. A sign on the roof said A MOTHER'S PLEA—IN THE NAME OF GOD, PLEASE HELP ME SAVE MY SON. Silhouettes of a cross and the electric chair flanked her message. "If you will find it in your heart to help, please call or write." Sylvia included a telephone number, along with a post office box, and added a partial quote from the New Testament. "For God so loved the World . . . " She assumed the people who saw her sign knew more of the verse from the gospel according to Saint John, "that he gave his only begotten son."

Leslie wore a thin sport shirt decorated with a bright yellow and green pattern when he was led into the warm courtroom. He could have been headed for a spring picnic instead of waiting to hear the date he might die during a bone-chilling winter. He giggled and laid the Bible, with his name embossed in gold letters on the cover, on the table in front of his chair.

Although Carolyn was not fat, twenty months of sedentary life in jail had put more flesh on her voluptuous figure. She emphasized her expanding curves in a tightly wrapped sheath dress with a neck that rose to her throat. She left a cardigan sweater unbuttoned across her breasts, and her black hair was crimped in a wave. She whispered a greeting to Clyde Woody, then swapped quiet remarks with Leslie.

Judge Love asked the defendants if they had anything to say. Their lawyers answered for them. Lloyd Lunsford wanted the judge to grant Leslie a new trial because the D.A. had suppressed psychiatric evidence prior to the murder trial. Clyde Woody made the same motion for Carolyn.

Judge Love refused. "Hearing nothing in bar of the sentence, I direct that you be taken to the county jail and thence to the Department of Corrections. . . . " Carolyn held her head high. She closed her eyes, but could not stop her tears. "That an electric current shall be caused to pass through your body sufficient to cause your death." Leslie stared straight ahead with an empty look in his moist eyes. "And that it be continuously applied until you are dead."

"Frank Briscoe, turn around and look at me!" a woman's voice screamed from the gallery. "You're a blood-thirsty killer! God is going to punish you for killing these children!" The outburst came from Sylvia Ayres. "The people of Texas won't let you do it! God won't let you do it! You're going to be punished for this!"

The D.A. did not move, but a member of his staff finally snapped into action and grabbed Sylvia by the elbow. "Show some respect," she yelled as she was hustled out the door. Mae Lima remained under control in her front-row seat. Her face was forlorn, but her eyes were dry as the echo from Sylvia's tirade faded.

Judge Love announced the execution date, February 28; just over six weeks away. "I don't know how I feel," Leslie answered when reporters asked him about the limit on his lifetime. Carolyn was more talkative. "Sometimes you can almost forget about death hanging over your head, but all this today brought it home." She had adjusted to life behind bars. "I've made it this far. I can make it the rest of the way."

The execution date was just five days after Carolyn's twentieth birthday, but she and Leslie had longer to live than they realized. By custom, the governor automatically granted one thirty-day reprieve to all condemned prisoners. Carolyn would not be a teenager, but she could still be the first woman to die in the electric chair in Texas.

Two days after their sentencing, Leslie Douglas Ashley and Carolyn Lima were transferred to the Texas prison system. They were both driven seventy miles due north to Huntsville, where Leslie's destination was the Walls Unit, the central penitentiary for men near the middle of town, a red brick fortress next to an arena for the annual prison rodeo that allowed inmates to blow off steam riding broncos and bulldogging steers.

Carolyn was just a few miles away in the women's prison called Goree, a structure of generic institutional architecture that could have been an early-twentieth-century library or high school, except for the bars on the windows and the barbed wire topping the fence surrounding the grounds. To celebrate her status as the next candidate to break Old Sparky's gender barrier, the other inmates gave Carolyn a nickname—the First Lady. Some of the "Goree girls" sewed her a special death gown from regulation prison cotton, dyed blue, and cut with a deep decolletage to emphasize her ample cleavage.

The warden went along with the design, "It's a horrible garment really, but a woman wants to look her best even when she's going to be executed."

Her death gown offered Carolyn grim distraction, but she also looked for comfort in the Book of Psalms and she learned to paint by numbers. Biblical scenes appealed to her. Carolyn was a docile inmate, "a model prisoner," the warden said. She sedated herself with food. The closer she came to death, the faster she put on weight.

When Leslie entered the state prison system, he was given an admission interview by a psychiatrist. "There's no doubt in my mind that he was feigning insanity," Dr. C.A. Dwyer said.

Leslie was hostile, and laughed during most of the exam. "It really doesn't matter to me if I'm electrocuted or not," he blurted, brushing off every question. "I don't know nothing about no murder or being a queer or wearing female clothes."

"Are you what's known as a 'he-whore'?" Dr. Dwyer asked.

"No."

"Did you ever hustle?"

"I deny it all."

"Did you pimp for Carolyn Lima?"

"I most certainly did not. Vice versa."

"What do you mean by vice versa? Did she pimp for you?"

Leslie threw back his head and howled. He said his father warned him that Carolyn would turn against him. Leslie Sherman Ashley had cautioned his son to beware of Carolyn.

"How do you feel about turning out young girls?" Dr. Dwyer challenged him.

"She said I did that? She was a prostitute long before I knew her."

"How do you know?"

"I just know." Another parent was the source of that information. "My mother told me."

Dr. Dwyer brought Sylvia into his questions. "Who is your mother? Is she normal?"

Leslie lost himself in a giggling fit. "Wheeee!," he shrieked. "She's normal just like me."

"They tell me that she's carrying on down there in Houston?"

"She's a minister."

"What faith?"

"Pentecostal," Leslie answered. He said Sylvia had jettisoned the religion of her birth. "The Jewish turn to other things," he remarked. "They can turn to anything."

Sylvia made the most of the automatic thirty-day stay of execution that delayed her son's death. She visited churches, drove around Houston with her conspicuous MOTHER'S PLEA billboard and mobilized a petition drive that collected more than ten thousand signatures supporting clemency for Leslie and Carolyn.

Less than a month before the execution date, she helped organize a prayer meeting headlined by an evangelist named William Branham, who was one of the most prominent faith healers in America during the years after World War II. Brother Branham delivered simple, understated sermons describing the vision of an angel only he could see that was standing on the stage beside him. The angel brought him a divine gift allowing him to diagnose an illness through vibrations he felt in his left hand.

In 1950, at the peak of his popularity, Branham had come to Houston for a series of revival debates with a Baptist minister who doubted his message. Ted Kipperman and Jim Ayres were hired to photograph the event. During one session, every roll of film Ted snapped came out black, except for a single exposure that showed Brother Branham standing at the podium with a halo-like aura glowing above his head. "Supernatural light," his followers labeled the phenomenon.

Ted thought the streak came from a leak in the faulty camera, but his skepticism did not stop him from renewing an old connection when his nephew received a death sentence. Ted was the member of the family who wrote to *The Voice of Healing*, an evangelical magazine that had started as a promotional vehicle for Branham's ministry. Ted's letter raised money, widened his nephew's network of pen pals, and began the momentum that brought the famous preacher back to Houston to pray for Leslie's survival.

By March 1963, William Branham was past the crest of his popularity. He had moved away from faith healing to focus on his self-proclaimed ability to see the secret sins that others hid inside the dark corners of their souls. A preacher who helped cripples toss away their crutches was in demand; a mystic who exposed buried vices was not.

At Sylvia's prayer rally, only eight hundred people spread themselves around four thousand seats at the City Auditorium, a downscale hall that was a frequent site for wrestling matches. The audience saw film footage of Leslie in his death cell and heard Brother Branham urge them to have faith in miracles. The slogan of his ministry was "Only Believe, All Things Are Possible."

After the prayer rally, Sylvia and Lloyd Lunsford led a "mercy committee" that appeared before the State Board of Pardons and Paroles in Austin. Sylvia presented her petitions asking the board to commute both death sentences to life in prison. The long list of signatures included the first juror selected at the murder trial. He said that he would not have voted for either execution if he had known about the suppressed psychiatric report, but his ballot could not be retracted despite the new evidence.

The decision came down—no clemency. A double execution was scheduled for 12:01 A.M., Saturday, March 30. Leslie would die first. As soon as his body was unstrapped and lifted away, Carolyn would be buckled into Old Sparky's warm seat.

The defense lawyers churned out a blizzard of writs and motions. Stress and exhaustion caused Lunsford's gallstones to flare up. He collapsed, then checked into a hospital. In Austin, Sylvia convinced a state legislator to give her the floor in the capitol. She made a passionate plea to the politicians, reading a tele-

gram the prison system sent to every condemned prisoner's next
of kin. The message notified Sylvia that she was responsible for
the cost of a hearse to remove her son's body from the penitentiary after his execution. Otherwise, Leslie would be buried
among the graves of unclaimed corpses in the prison cemetery.

"I hope you never have to read this telegram about any of your
children," she sobbed to the lawmakers.

Leslie spoke inside the Walls. "I certainly have a good mother
to stand by me through all this." He refused to give up. "A pleading mother sure can win."

Lloyd Lunsford conquered his pain and pressed on. He and
Clyde Woody put together a writ of certiorari, the standard term
for the petition asking the U.S. Supreme Court to consider a case.
The lawyers packed their request with every argument they could
brainstorm, from the D.A.'s suppression of evidence to the contention that Jack Knight's legal strategy denied Carolyn a fair trial.
Although Woody was the member of the pair with prior experience before the highest court, Lunsford got out of his hospital bed
for a flight to Washington.

"Clyde sent me up there," he recalled. Woody wanted a clear
field for some solo maneuvering with federal judges he knew in
Houston. "I had to get Lucky out of my hair," Woody said. The
tension grated on both of them.

Leslie Douglas Ashley was Lunsford's first death-row client in
the ten years he had been practicing law, and the emotional effect
of the fight had already driven the defense attorney past his limits
of physical endurance. Lunsford's wife was so worried about him
that she asked a neighbor to look after their three children and
boarded a plane for the first time in her life. She was afraid her
husband would push himself too far if he went to Washington
alone.

Lunsford arrived at the Supreme Court on March 25, late Monday afternoon; so late, the building was about to close. He
ignored the ache from his gallstones and hopped a barrier to get
inside. The guards were not impressed with his physical feat of
mind over matter. "They damn near shot me," he remembered.

With the writs on file in Washington, Woody labored over a
written brief running more than one hundred pages to build arguments buttressing his plan of attack. He attached affadavits from

Dr. Crow and psychologist Jack Tracktir, both swearing the district attorney was informed of their insanity findings prior to the murder trial. Woody wanted to be ready when the Supreme Court ruled on the writs Lundsford had delivered, but he needed an affirmative result from at least one justice before he could switch from research to action.

Tuesday and Wednesday passed with no response from the solemn chambers behind marble columns. Lloyd Lunsford was nervous. "It's like rushing to a fire station to tell them a house is burning down and waiting while they consider the truth of the statement before sending somebody down a pole."

26

By Thursday, March 28, preparations were beginning for the two executions scheduled to start at the first minute after midnight on Saturday. Leslie tried to keep his composure inside the Walls. He was proud of himself for not banging the bars or yelling at the guards. "Not everyone on death row is a nice person," Leslie recalled. "Some of them are really mean."

Carolyn was waiting on the outskirts of Huntsville in the women's prison. Goree did not have a "capital wing," a formal penal term for death row, so a separate cell had been rigged for the First Lady. "A special cubicle," the papers called it.

"I've been a good girl," Carolyn said. "They've treated me nice in here. I've gained ten or fifteen pounds, the food is so good." Packing extra inches onto the weight she gained while she was in jail in Houston had destroyed her figure. At her formal sentencing just six weeks earlier, she was beginning to bulge, but the extra flesh did not distort her appearance. Now, she was a butterball at one hundred sixty-five pounds, forty pounds more than her weight before the shooting.

"All I really think about is getting out." She tried to laugh. "It helps to laugh. I've found it's good to laugh." She could not sustain her false cheer and she started to cry. "I feel so helpless now. I just can't believe it. These people are taking my life, and I can't fight back."

Thursday, her mother, as well as her grandmother and her older sister, shared her tears in the special cubicle when the first word came from Washington. Justice Hugo Black had denied the writ of certiorari and refused to grant a stay of execution. The dark mood in Goree grew even darker. "It sure was tough hearing that," Carolyn said. "I still have faith. It's all I've got, and I'm trying to hang onto it."

She shifted her mind away from herself. "I feel so sorry for Douglas though, I just know he'll crack up." She locked her thoughts on him. "I pity that boy," she whispered. "Kook" was her frequent word to describe him. "Sure, we're guilty. I know I done wrong, but I don't think I deserve death and I don't think I'll die. I'll have hope right up till the minute they strap me in that chair."

Carolyn could not predict her reaction if she was wrong. "I hope they'll give me something for my nerves though. I'm going to try to hold my head up, but there's no telling what I'll do really." State law prohibited condemned prisoners from being sedated before executions. Doomed inmates had to face Old Sparky straight, but no regulation prevented medication this far ahead of schedule, so prison officials rewarded Carolyn with a few pills on Thursday night.

"Having her here has been a problem," the warden said, "but she herself has never been a problem."

Before Justice Black refused the reprieve, Leslie allowed reporters into his death row cell. The green door leading to the electric chair was just twelve feet beyond the bars. He crossed his ankles beneath his lap as he giggled and described his burial plans, "I don't want a service in a funeral home. I want it in a church where I'll be among my friends."

His first choice was a Pentecostal church in Houston where the pastor and congregation had stood by him. "I want everybody to wear white or red because black indicates death. I won't be dead, my spirit will live." Leslie said he preferred an open-casket ceremony, although his hair would be shaved to guarantee skin contact with Old Sparky's electrodes. Leslie asked his Uncle Ted to buy a toupee for him so he would not have a bald head in his coffin.

Leslie had never met his teenage pen pal from Kentucky, but he kept her picture in his cell. "She's really pulled me over the hump," he said beaming. "We're in love." Carolyn was in the past. "She's crazy, you know." He scowled. "I would've married her though, except for my mother. I was going to marry her anyway toward the end, because I was away from my mother, but they caught us." Unlike Carolyn, he still maintained their innocence. "Neither of us are guilty," Leslie said.

He would not discuss his religious visions. "I don't know anything about that," he replied frowning to questions about them. Leslie refused to remember his claims to be Elijah or a female version of the prophet's protégé, Elisha. "I have amnesia once in awhile," he shrugged. "I'm perfectly sane if that's what you mean." Leslie was not thinking about being saved by a miracle anymore. "I can go like I'm supposed to go," he said, although he wanted the prison chaplain to stand beside him. "If he isn't, I may not be able to make it." After the straps were pulled tight around his wrists, he wanted everyone to leave. "I'm not going to let anyone watch. It's going to be a horrible thing. I hear it turns you black and blue."

Like Carolyn, Leslie was with his family on Thursday when he learned Justice Black had denied a stay of execution. He and his mother and uncle absorbed the shock together, then suffered a second blow when they heard that Justice William Brennan also had refused to consider the case. His relatives were silent when they left the Walls, and Leslie asked for privacy.

"He's feeling pretty sorry for himself," a prison employee said.

After his writ was denied by two justices, Lucky Lunsford said a Supreme Court insider advised him to quit. He had not been able to see either justice, they had just scanned his paperwork and turned him down, so the insider who knew how the high court worked told Lunsford to go home. Rejection by two liberal justices was a sure sign he was headed for failure.

"I could never sleep a good night's sleep again if I let that lever be pulled knowing I didn't do everything humanly possible," Lunsford said. He thought he might do better with Justice Arthur Goldberg. Although Lunsford could not get into Justice Goldberg's chambers, the jurist agreed to look over the the thick brief, which included a request for the right to file a writ of habeas corpus in lower federal courts. Like his two colleagues, Justice Goldberg relayed his denial, but he added two words, "without prejudice."

Those two words meant the case was still alive. Denying the writ without prejudice allowed the defense team to continue the fight, moving from the highest court in the land to the lowest rung of the federal judicial ladder, where Clyde Woody was ready to begin his final push to jerk Old Sparky's plug from the socket.

The battle started with an uncooperative judge. Ben Connally, the jurist considering Woody's plea, sat on the federal bench for the Southern District of Texas. The crusty son of a former U.S. senator, Ben Connally "wasn't the easiest person to get along with," in Clyde Woody's opinion.

Judge Connally (no kin to former Governor John Connally) was used to being obeyed, and his philosophy was not likely to expand the scope of constitutional freedoms. Another attorney who began adding his skills to the defense team had more to say about him. James Hippard Sr. was in private practice and he was executive director of the Houston chapter of the American Civil Liberties Union; that was the hat he wore when he began helping Woody and Lunsford. Hippard called Judge Ben Connally "bright, brilliant," but he was also "a son of a bitch and you can quote me on that."

Hippard was deeply involved in the legal wrangling to desegregate the Houston public schools, and Judge Connally was the jurist who supervised the local plan. Hippard said Connally went to great lengths to present an image of prudence and fairness in public. In private, he dragged his feet, slowing integration as long as he could. "Which nigger is your client?" was the Honorable Ben Connally's standard opening question for Hippard when they were behind closed doors with no African-Americans around.

Clyde Woody got an unwelcome midnight surprise from Judge Connally on Friday morning, March 29, the last day before the midnight execution. They lived only a couple of blocks apart in an affluent part of town, and when Woody saw a familiar car in the judge's driveway he assumed Connally was home. His years of trial experience should have taught him not to trust assumptions. The judge was out of town, and Woody spent precious time before learning Connally was in Austin for the day. Over the telephone, Woody finally tracked him down. The judge scheduled a hearing for five o'clock, which meant the defense would only have a few hours left to implement an alternate plan if the request for a stay was rejected.

Woody raced to the airport and hopped on a private plane to Austin. Frank Briscoe, however, was in no rush. The D.A. drove.

An easy three hours on the road, the trip from the coastal flat-lands into the slow pace and history of the hill country deep in the heart of the Texas was always therapeutic for an old-guard native.

"I'm scared now," Carolyn said as she waited for the results from the Austin hearing on Friday. "I know how precious life is." The sedative she had taken before bed had bounced off her strained metabolism. "I didn't sleep a wink last night. I was too nervous." On second thought, she admitted, "Maybe I got two hours of sleep."

She wanted to be baptized again, so the Goree chaplain, a Methodist minister, performed the ritual in her cell. "I think I'll die saved because I've been forgiven," Carolyn said. "I feel it in my heart." After the quick service purged her soul, she showed off her latest paint-by-numbers masterpiece: a vivid tableau of Moses hearing the voice of the Lord from the burning bush.

Carolyn asked the chaplain to witness her execution, and she wanted the Goree warden to come along as well, "to be with me when I take that long walk." Mrs. Velda Dobbs had been a warden for ten years, but she had never seen an execution. "I dreaded it," she recalled, but the First Lady's composure astonished her. "She hasn't had a cross word with anyone since she's been here. She wasn't even annoyed when we cropped her hair last night," Mrs. Dobbs said. "I just wish I had more like her."

Clyde Woody had his own memories of his client. "She was the coldest woman I've ever met," he said. "She was filled with ice water." She never acted afraid of the electric chair when he went to visit her. She bragged that she "could take it better than any man," Woody remembered. He turned on the purple language when he repeated her spiel. "She told me, 'If those motherfuckers are going to do it to me, I'm going to walk in there by myself without anybody to hold me up and look those motherfuckers in the eye and say, 'Okay, strap me in.' " Another time he told the story, Woody said Carolyn promised to buckle herself into the chair.

"She even invited me to see her burn." He was appalled. "Can you imagine that? Inviting your own lawyer to see your execution." No defense attorney wanted to climax futility with that gruesome sight.

Leslie met his teenage pen pal from Mortons Gap, Kentucky, for the first time on Friday morning, a little more than twelve hours before his life was to end. Gail Rash had no makeup on her face, and she was wearing a pink plaid dress with a tight waist that emphasized her thin figure.

Sylvia whisked her past the photographers and reporters stuck outside the Walls because Leslie refused to admit them. His mother recalled the visit as "calm and pleasant." Sylvia chatted with the guards while the youngsters got acquainted. The prison chaplain, a Baptist, watched them talk. Gail swapped her gold high school ring with a bright red stone for a Star of David on a necklace chain that Leslie gave her.

The teenager finally spoke to reporters after her quick trip to death row. "It was so exciting," Gail said. Leslie's charms worked on her. "He was everything I hoped for," she gushed. "If he gets out, we're going to be married." She did not bring a chaperone, but Gail had not made the trip alone. "I came with God," she proclaimed, fingering the Star of David around her neck.

Leslie was now calling himself a "Christian Jew," putting his faith anywhere he could find relief. At the end of the death-row cell block, beyond the only green door in the entire prison, guards were getting the electric chair ready for him. Over three hundred and fifty men had died in the chair since the lethal contraption had arrived at the Walls in 1924. The high-backed seat was a relic from an earlier era, oak stained dark, with more belts and straps than a straitjacket. The electrode coils were primitive, as if they had been salvaged from a mad scientist's basement laboratory in a Victorian horror novel.

One electrode was clamped around the prisoner's head; another was wrapped around the left ankle. The condemned inmate was used as the conductor to close the circuit for a sixteen-hundred-volt jolt. A single blast should be fatal, but the law required three doses just to be thorough. On Friday, March 29, the guards began testing Old Sparky. The lights flickered and Leslie heard each surge of current. "I'm not afraid to die, but I'm a little bit nervous," he told the only reporter he allowed into his cell. "If I live, I'll spend the rest of my life witnessing my faith in God," he promised. The lights flashed on and off as the executioners perfected their drill.

Leslie talked about ordering a kosher last meal, but he changed his mind and took the standard fare. He had not eaten in two days and his appetite was gone. He let a tray of ocean trout, hash brown potatoes, corn, peas, celery sticks, green salad, and peach pie grow cold.

The ice in a tall glass of tea melted and a hot cup of coffee slowly cooled. Leslie asked for a glass of fruit juice, which he sipped. When he learned Carolyn had willed her Bible to Frank Briscoe, he decided to leave the D.A. two rambling religious tracts he had written while he was in the Harris County jail.

Mae Lima was allowed to stay with her daughter until five o'clock on Friday afternoon, the same time the hearing for a stay of execution started in Austin. Mae did not know what to do with herself after the visit, so she drove seventy miles south from Huntsville to Houston. She planned to turn around and go back to Huntsville about ten, then complete her second round-trip of the day following the hearse she had hired to carry her daughter's body home in the darkness after midnight.

In her cell, Carolyn sat down for her final meal. Condemned prisoners were allowed to order a special feast, whatever they wanted. Carolyn ate a banquet of fried chicken, mashed potatoes dripping with gravy, English peas, scoops of cottage cheese mixed with chunks of pineapple, hot rolls lathered with butter, a chocolate malt and a slice of banana cream pie. She also bit off her thumbnail while she waited for word from Austin.

27

Prior to the hearing, Judge Connally ordered all reporters from the room, but since he was a member of a dynasty he wanted to preserve, he let his son remain to watch the wheels of justice grind behind closed doors. According to Clyde Woody's memory of the event, before the arguments began, the stern jurist said he would probably deny the stay of execution, as well as a writ of habeas corpus asking him to overturn the death sentence convictions or allow an appeal to advance.

The lawyers battled for an hour and a half. The D.A.'s failure to disclose Dr. Crow's psychiatric report was the wild card that still hung over the convictions. No damage was done, Briscoe contended, since two other psychiatrists, including one hired by the defendants' original lawyer, believed Leslie Douglas Ashley and Carolyn Lima were sane. None of the three psychiatric reports he had received before the trial was hard evidence that had to be revealed. The D.A. said they were only potential "opinion testimony" from experts he could use or ignore as he saw fit.

The D.A.'s arguments persuaded Judge Connally, who did not see any constitutional issues in Clyde Woody's position. The judge ruled the case belonged in the state courts that had already upheld the verdicts. The stay of execution was denied.

Word of the rejection reached Goree at about seven o'clock, just five hours before the planned executions, at almost the same time Carolyn was scheduled to make her ride to the Walls. She climbed into a station wagon sandwiched between two prison cars packed with armed guards, and flanked by Highway Patrol vehi-

219

cles that completed the circle of security. The calvacade did not
stop for streetlights. The First Lady was mobbed by the media
when she arrived at the men's prison.

"I felt pretty blue on the way over here," she sighed. "Tears
came to my eyes, but I kept pushing them back because I knew if
I let go I'd break up."

No woman had been executed in Texas for a hundred years, not
since Chepita Rodriguez was convicted of murdering a horse
trader and strung from a mesquite tree near the banks of the
Nueces River on Friday, November 13, 1863. Her grave disappeared, but *vaqueros* who worked ranches in the south Texas cattle country remembered Chepita Rodriguez in their *corridos*,
ballads celebrating outlaws and unrepentant victims of injustice.
Their lyrics said Chepita's ghost roamed the mesquite groves wailing on nights a woman was scheduled to be executed in Texas.
Her mourning had saved them all, and the ghost of Chepita
Rodriguez was wailing once more while Carolyn Lima waited in a
wire cage inside the Walls listening for the phone call that could
spare her life.

As soon as Judge Connally signed the ruling that denied the
stay of execution, Clyde Woody launched his backup plan. Now
that he had been denied at the district court level, Woody could
move up to the next level in the federal system. Before he left for
Austin on Friday, Woody had contacted Judge John R. Brown of
the U.S. Fifth Circuit Court of Appeals, which, at the time-cov-
ered the south, ruling on verdicts from Georgia to Texas. (Population growth has sliced the Fifth Circuit in half since 1963.) Woody
tested his arguments on Judge Brown, who agreed to look over a
copy of the huge brief.

Judge Brown had a Friday night dinner date with visitors from
Canada at the posh Petroleum Club in Houston, so he told
Woody to have Judge Connally call and page him if the Austin
hearing did not work out. Judge Connally did not like making
phone calls for losing lawyers, but he had no choice. A judge on
the next rung up the ladder wanted to hear the result of the hearing.

As soon as he relayed the message about the denial, Judge
Connally jabbed the receiver at Woody. "He wants to talk to
you." When he recalled their clash, Woody put pure cowboy con-

tempt in his imitation of the seething judge's wrath. The anger amused Woody. He did not mind stomping on Ben Connally's toes. Clyde Woody still relished topping him almost thirty years down the line. "That asshole denied me my writ."

Friday night, Leslie's family and his teenage pen pal waited for 12:01 in a bus station near the Walls. Checking into a hotel room would have been a waste of money, nobody would sleep. Sylvia saved a few more dollars by refusing to hire a hearse for her son's body. She could not believe Mae Lima surrendered to pessimism and rented the morbid funeral home vehicle for Carolyn. When Sylvia learned a reporter had accepted Carolyn's invitation to watch her die, Sylvia marched up to him and said he was not going to see anyone executed, not tonight, not any other night.

A light fog shrouded Houston. The mist of warm humidity that hung over the flat city prevented Clyde Woody's plane from landing on his return from Austin. The countdown continued while he circled, but Woody was covered. The stakes were too high to be defeated by weather in a place where the climate was always unstable.

The defense team relied on the new member who had signed on for the final drive to save their clients. The thick stack of paper Woody and Lunsford assembled had been joined by a short amicus curiae brief written by James Hippard Sr., executive director of the Houston chapter of the American Civil Liberties Union, who said he decided to get involved because the D.A.'s behavior was "so outlandish." Executing defendants after suppressing psychiatric evidence involved a broad judicial issue that justified jumping into the case as a "friend of the court," an interested third party.

Hippard's brief gave him the status to make arguments, so Woody phoned before leaving Austin to say he would not reach Houston in time to see Judge Brown. Hippard was already home for the day, but he was not surprised at the outcome of the Austin hearing. He had expected Judge Connally to deny the stay, so he was ready to rush to the Petroleum Club to deal with a more reasonable jurist.

Judge John R. Brown was a midwesterner, born in Nebraska. He came to Texas during the depths of the Great Depression and he found a job as a trial attorney specializing in maritime law with a Houston firm. As Brown rose in his profession, he also became involved in politics.

"A half-assed Republican," he labeled himself. Brown had backed Dwight Eisenhower, and, after Ike won the presidency, his supporters received their rewards. GOP headhunters asked Brown if he was interested in a seat on the federal bench. At first he said no, then he went on a weekend meeting with his presbytery council; he was always more attached to his Presbyterian faith than to politics. At work on Monday, the future judge had a change of heart while reviewing a lawsuit filed by a sailor claiming he had caught gonorrhea from a defectively laundered towel on a freighter owned by one of Brown's corporate clients.

"I thought, my God, am I going to be doing cases like this for the rest of my life?' " Brown recalled.

He snatched the phone and put himself back in contention for the seat on the Fifth Circuit Court of Appeals. On the bench, he was regarded as open minded and even handed, easing the fears of liberals worried about his past as a lawyer for large steamship companies. "A fine man," James Hippard called him, high praise for a former chairman of the Republican party in Harris County from a lawyer who moonlighted for the ACLU.

Defense attorneys often brought their motions for stays of execution to Judge Brown, and he heard many of their arguments at exclusive clubs around town where he unwound after work. "We had quite a little circuit going," he recalled with a twinkle. Almost a year earlier, Howard Stickney's execution was delayed nearly thirty minutes while Judge Brown listened to a late night plea from the condemned man's lawyer at the Houston Club, an upper-crust enclave downtown. The judge did not come through for Howard Stickney that night.

James Hippard hoped for a better outcome for Leslie and Carolyn as he took an elevator on the long ride up to the Petroleum Club, perched forty floors above the ground, atop the Humble (now Exxon) Building. It was the tallest skyscraper west of the Mississippi River in 1963. Suspended in the mist, Judge Brown could not entertain the visiting Canadians with the view, but he could treat them to a lesson in American jurisprudence. He was pleased Clyde Woody was delayed by fog. "I liked Clyde," the circuit judge said, "but I could never shut him up." Frank Briscoe did not rate as well. "I never met anyone with so much gall in my entire life." Judge Brown was over eighty years old when he offered that evaluation.

James Hippard said the judge "commandeered" a private dining room for the hearing. Judge Brown had reviewed the heavy defense brief, but he was only interested in one point—the suppression of evidence by the district attorney. Hippard remembered that he was up against the D.A.'s top assistant, Sam Robertson, an appeals expert. (Robertson, who left prosecution and became a state appeals judge, had "no independent recollection" of the dramatic evening three decades later.)

A tap on the door of the dining room interrupted the pleas; a deferential waiter wanted to know if anyone cared for a drink. Hippard was thirsty, but Judge Brown would not allow alcohol in his improvised courtroom. The arguments did not last long, just fifteen or twenty passionate minutes. The judge had prepared two typed opinions; one granted the stay, the other was a denial.

The arguments ended. Hippard waited. The fog rolled slowly past the swank club cloistered above the flat concrete far below. The clock stood at 7:50 P.M. when Judge Brown gave his decision, "The state had obtained from two professional, competent experts the opinion that each of the defendants, petitioners here, were mentally incompetent." The affidavits from Dr. Crow and Jack Tracktir had convinced him. "This information, though known to the district attorney, was not disclosed to the state trial court, to the defendants, or to their counsel. It came to light some time later. This, in my opinion, raises some substantial questions."

Judge Brown ruled those questions should be decided by a three-judge panel from the Fifth Circuit Court of Appeals after a hearing to be held in late April or early May. He signed the opinion granting the stay of execution, then stepped outside the dining room to use a pay telephone to dial a secret number in the prison director's office at Huntsville. He rummaged his pockets and discovered he did not have ten cents to make the lifesaving call.

"I gladly lent him a dime," James Hippard recalled.

"I just knew it was going to come through," Carolyn said. "Everytime I could hear that phone ring, I just knew it was going to come through." Blind optimism had kept her from cracking. "I just knew it." She paced in her cage for forty-five minutes before she saw the chaplain who had baptized her racing up the hall with the message she wanted to hear.

"Ain't it wonderful," Carolyn whooped. A Catholic priest standing beside her said, "She bowed her head and murmured a prayer of thanksgiving." Then, Carolyn Lima looked up and winked at a reporter. "I ain't going to be the First Lady." She lit a cigarette. "You can't say God isn't with me." Carolyn propped herself against a wall and finished her smoke. "Take me back to my little old home in Goree," she told the warden. "I'll sleep tonight."

Not far away, Leslie was listening to a tiny transistor radio in his cell. "I was just a-prayin'," he said. When he heard a bulletin about the stay, he began to cry. "Thank the Lord," he wept. "Nothing is impossible with the Lord."

He was sobbing when a Catholic priest and a Baptist chaplain came to confirm the good news. "Oh, Lord, I've had all kinds of blessings today." His appetite was back. "I'll eat tomorrow, you can bet." He gazed at the memento from his teenage pen pal. "I'm going to give this ring back to my fiancée now. I was going to take it with me." Reporters who joined the death-row celebration said Leslie never giggled once.

A call to the bus station brought Sylvia Ayres speeding to the Walls. She rode shotgun, her brother was at the wheel of a cream-colored Cadillac that screeched up to a barricade in front of the prison gate.

"Thank God, honey!" she yelled as she stuck her head from the window. "Leslie's got a stay! Go tell them I want to see my son!" The guards had not heard about Judge Brown's decision, so the commanding officer radioed for his orders. Suddenly, a siren began to howl. "It's the Lord a-singin'," Sylvia cried. The guards thought the siren was probably from an ambulance or a fire truck, surely a coincidence, because the prison didn't crow over stays of execution.

"I want to see my boy," Sylvia repeated, "I want to see my boy."

Word came back from the warden—no visitors tonight. "He didn't say I couldn't come back tomorrow, did he?" Sylvia asked. The guards thought that was fine. "I'm all excited!" she yelled. Sylvia was bouncing up and down on the springs in the Cadillac's soft seat as the big car turned around and drove away.

In her small home on cinder blocks, Mae Lima was too tired to kick up her heels. She had not yet left on her return trip to Huntsville. When she heard the news, she went to bed. Like her daughter, worry had kept her awake. "Mother is asleep now for the first time in days," Carolyn's little brother told a reporter who called. "We're thankful and very happy."

Frank Briscoe kept his cool. "It's our position that the prosecution is not required to turn over to the defense everything they know about the case." The D.A. had merely exercised his prerogative; "failing to inform," he called his tactic. "Every time a case is tried, the prosecutor must decide what to present and what not to present," he said. "This simply was not suppression of evidence."

The D.A. knew the setback might be temporary. Leslie and Carolyn were safe for the moment, but they were living on borrowed time unless their convictions were permanently overturned by the federal appeals court. One score by the other side would not defeat Frank Briscoe.

Clyde Woody's blue eyes flashed at the memory. "Frank really wanted to burn 'em,"

28

"The conviction is for murder with malice aforethought. The sentence is death."

The defense team began its brief to the U.S. Fifth Circuit Court of Appeals with those stark facts. The pages that followed tried to show why the verdicts should be reversed. Affadavits from Dr. Howard Crow and psychologist Jack Tracktir confirmed they had diagnosed both Leslie Douglas Ashley and Carolyn Lima as legally insane prior to the murder trial. More important, they had notified the prosecutor of their conclusions. The defense team also included a transcript of Leslie's sanity hearing, where Crow and Tracktir repeated their allegations under oath on the witness stand.

A short amicus curiae brief from the ACLU was part of the package too. James Hippard's argument was a frontal assault on Frank Briscoe for suppressing the psychiatric report; "passive nondisclosure of exculpatory evidence" in legalese. (Exculpatory evidence is evidence that benefits the accused.) Hippard charged the D.A. with robbing the defendants of their right to pursue an insanity defense by sitting on the report.

"This conduct on the district attorney's part was a serious violation of his duty to provide appellants with a fair trial," Hippard wrote. He quoted from the Canon of Professional Ethics of the American Bar Association: "The primary duty of a lawyer engaged in public prosecution is not to convict, but to see that justice is done. The suppression of facts or the secreting of witnesses capable of establishing the innocence of the accused is highly reprehensible." The ACLU attorney had to look beyond Texas for his language. In 1963, the state's Code of Criminal Procedure did not

226

give explicit instructions decribing a D.A.'s duty to be fair, instead of playing tricks to pile up convictions.

"The law was more of a game back then," Clyde Woody said.

Frank Briscoe tried to shore up his side of the appeal by minimizing his knowledge of the suppressed report, saying a telephone call was the only pretrial contact that his office had with Dr. Crow. The D.A. also denied the concealed evidence would have changed the outcome of the murder trial. Dr. Crow's diagnosis was contradicted by other opinions; the conflicting reports canceled each other, the prosecutor argued.

Briscoe attached a copy of the report by Dr. Burch, who had been sent to examine the defendants by their original lawyer. In the report, Burch said he heard a full account of the shooting. Leslie told him Fred A. Tones "looked like an ape coming at me he was so horrible," wounded and wild, wearing nothing but his T-shirt and socks, swinging the bayonet before Carolyn finished him off with the .22 pistol.

Briscoe added the report from the county's consulting psychiatrist, which included results of psychology tests performed by a University of Houston graduate student. The defense team mocked the Ph.D. candidate's lack of credentials, but the tests turned up insights about their clients.

Leslie had refused to cooperate with the examiner. "If you're not going to answer my questions, I'm not going to answer yours," he sulked and said he had a toothache, but he seemed eager to have his answers reinforced before he broke off a Rorschach test. Leslie saw a map of the United States in one ink blot and promptly asked, "Is that what other people see?"

During the comprehension section of an IQ test he did not finish, Leslie answered questions about hypothetical situations by separating what he would do from what he should do. If he saw smoke in a crowded theater? "He should call the fire department," the examiner reported, "but he would be the first one out." Or if he found a letter, stamped and addressed, lost on the sidewalk? "He should put it in the mailbox, but he would open it." The answers were egocentric, the examiner concluded.

Despite the incomplete test results, the psychology report determined Leslie was "a childish person who, although he makes feeble attempts at presenting a facade of strength and self-confidence, is really passive, immature, and inadequate."

Unlike Leslie, Carolyn cooperated. The report described her as "spontaneous and uninhibited, giving no evidence of anxiety." Her only complaint was a petty worry that the testing would make her late for lunch. Her IQ measured eighty-seven, fifteen points above her junior high school score, pushing her near the top of the dull-normal range. She had no problems with motor skills when she copied simple spatial designs, so she did not appear to have any organic brain damage.

The examiner said Carolyn seemed to be enjoying herself. He labeled her as "very hedonistic . . . is preoccupied with appetite gratification." Food was prominent in her interpretations of ink smudges: "looks like a cat . . . his tongue is hanging out . . . like he's seen a bird or something; a fish with his mouth open . . . going to swallow little fish; two bears . . . waiting for someone to throw them some peanuts."

Carolyn's immediate desire to satisfy her appetites made her "unable to use her past experience to edit her thinking." She relied on impulsive instincts, and her instincts could be aggressive. A big fish ate little fish, sea gulls swooped on their prey, and hats had horns in her Rorschach responses. The combination of instant appetite gratification and aggression, along with her reliance on instinct and impulses created frustration, "and the patient, at least partially aware of her inadequacy, occasionally expresses those feelings of inadequacy and frustration in a bitter, resentful approach to the world." Carolyn saw wilted flowers and blood-sucking mosquitoes in other ink blots.

Asked to tell a story about a picture she was shown, Carolyn said, "This is about a girl that couldn't get along with other people. She really tried, but some way or another she made them mad. She always said the wrong things to people and everybody was against her. No friends at all. She always moved town to town, place to place. One of these days, she'll find someone just like herself and have a friend."

As a final description, the examiner concluded, "under pressure she could either panic, become childish, or both."

On May 9, the lawyers went to New Orleans, the seat of the Fifth Circuit, to make their oral arguments before three federal judges. Lucky Lunsford was ready for his day in court. He recalled that he arrived early and Frank Briscoe was not around.

The hour to start the session passed with the prosecutor still absent. Lunsford said the venerable men on the bench were seething at the D.A.'s tardiness and the lack of respect he showed them by his willingness to waste their valuable time.

When Briscoe was finally there and the hearing began, the defense team tried to capitalize on the judges' anger. Clyde Woody claimed the D.A. knew Leslie and Carolyn were legally insane, but tried them anyway. In front of the Fifth Circuit judges, he accused the district attorney of attempted murder.

Judge Elbert Tuttle stopped the animosity from boiling out of control. As chief judge of the Fifth Circuit, overseeing appeals across the south, all the way to the Panama Canal Zone, he held the highest job a jurist can have without being on the Supreme Court. A conscientious servant of justice, Judge Tuttle had read the transcript of the sanity hearing, as well as the defendants' testimony at their murder trial. From his perch at the center of the bench, he said Leslie and Carolyn seemed like "logical, reasonable people, just like anyone else."

However, the issue in question was not the actual sanity of the defendants. The issue was whether the suppression of psychiatric evidence impinged upon their constitutional right to mount any defense that should have been available to them. One of the judges on the panel asked Briscoe pointblank if he was informed of the reports rendered by Dr. Crow and Jack Tracktir before the trial. The D.A. had to answer yes; the opinions had been given to him before jury selection began.

Any optimism that Briscoe's admission gave to the defense team was obliterated when Judge Tuttle spoke again, "The posture of the case at the time it went to trial appears to have been equally balanced as to the opinion of the doctors regarding the sanity of the defendants."

The defense needed two votes to win the appeal, and Judge Tuttle was flanked by a pair of senior jurists from Florida. Judge Warren Jones of Jacksonville had put in his military service during World War I; Judge Dozier DeVane had also been around awhile. Although Judge Brown, who signed the stay of execution, was not on the panel, he knew his peers in the Fifth Circuit. He said Judge DeVane was "nice, but not real sharp," a courtroom veteran who liked a shot of bourbon and believed in conservative causes, not the kind of judge who favored the rights of defendants.

At the hearing, Judge Tuttle offered his own pessimistic predic-
tion by announcing that the Fifth Circuit had never overturned a
conviction in any similar case during its one-hundred-year history.
Prison officials in Huntsville agreed with him. The people who
ran the Walls could remember lots of death sentence reversals by
the Texas Court of Criminal Appeals, and prison lore even
counted one date with the electric chair reversed by the Supreme
Court, but Leslie Douglas Ashley and Carolyn Lima had already
failed before both of those benches. No one could recall removing
a single condemned prisoner from death row because of an order
from the Fifth Circuit.

Six weeks passed with no word from the federal appeals court.
Every day, customers at Mae Lima's beauty parlor asked about
Carolyn's case. Mae had nothing to report so she developed a
standard reply. "No news is good news, I would have to tell
them." On Mondays, her day off, Mae drove to Huntsville to see
Carolyn.

Although she received crank calls at odd hours, Mae refused to
have an unlisted telephone number. She would not change the
way she lived, and the address next to her number in the telephone book brought snoops driving by her home to point and
honk. A police officer who recognized her told Mae he wanted to
pull Old Sparky's switch on her daughter himself.

Then, on June 25, the Fifth Circuit ruled. The decision was
close; the court split two-to-one. Judge Dozier DeVane, the most
conservative member of the panel, did not cite any precedents in
the opinion he wrote, "This is not a case where the district attorney was guilty of any misconduct." Judge DeVane held the
defense responsible for building its own case; Frank Briscoe
should not be blamed because his opponent chose a strategy that
failed. "I am confident that had Mr. Knight sought from the district attorney information as to the reports of Doctors Sher, Crowe
[sic] and Tracktir, he would have been advised fully with reference to them."

Brady v. *Maryland,* a landmark Supreme Court decision, barely a month old in June, 1963, had just clarified the standard for
disclosing evidence that would benefit defendants. *Brady* required
prosecutors to reveal "exculpatory" evidence requested by defense
attorneys, but the ruling did not apply to Leslie and Carolyn
because Jack Knight had never made that request. "I believe the

district attorney would have withheld the evidence," Knight explained. Free disclosure was not the way the law worked in Harris County. "That contradicts everything in my twenty years of experience with the district attorney's office," Knight said.

Chief Judge Tuttle, who delivered negative signals during the May hearing, wrote the majority opinion without using *Brady*, "The facts upon which the appellants base their claim for a new trial are not seriously in dispute." Judge Tuttle quoted Dr. Crow's letter to Frank Briscoe, sent the day after the murder trial verdicts. In the letter, Dr. Crow reminded the D.A. of their conversation prior to jury selection reporting that he and Jack Tracktir believed both defendants were legally incompetent.

Judge Tuttle also cited Dr. Crow's testimony at Leslie Douglas Ashley's sanity hearing. Under oath, the psychiatrist said, "In talking with Mr. Briscoe, I told him I felt this man, Douglas Ashley, needed treatment in a hospital. He was sick and a schizophrenic, and I did that on 3–22–61 and 4–8–61." The trial had not begun until May 15. "Mr. Briscoe got my findings and professional opinion that Mr. Ashley was a schizophrenic and incompetent to understand what the trial would be about."

The chief judge chastised the prosecutor, "The fact of the opinions of Drs. Crowe and Tracktir, favorable to the defendants, is of such vital significance to the accused persons in planning and conducting their defense, the failure of the district attorney to inform their counsel of this fact amounts to such fundamental unfairness in the trial of a criminal case as to amount to a denial of due process."

The swing ballot was cast by Judge Warren Jones, the World War I veteran who founded the first blood bank in Jacksonville, Florida, when he came home from the carnage on European battlefields. He let his vote speak for itself.

"The stay of execution heretofore entered by Judge Brown is continued until a final disposition of the matter," the ruling said. The guilty verdicts and death sentences were all overturned and the case was sent back to lower courts for retrial.

Carolyn Lima heard the news in her special cubicle in Goree. "Boy, that makes me feel real good," she said. "I knew God was with me all the way." She sat in a chair and clutched a prayer book. "A new chance at life," Carolyn smiled, but she did not laugh. "I don't know what to say. I'm so happy and thankful." She was still overweight, with bags beneath her eyes and acne on her cheeks. "I always had my faith and hope."

Her mind latched onto a boilerplate phrase of legal formality near the end of the Fifth Circuit's order. "The case is remanded to the trial court with directions to issue the writ, and discharge the prisoners." "Didn't it say we were discharged?" Carolyn blurted. "Well, let me out!"

"Oh no, it doesn't mean that," the warden laughed. "It's just a figure of speech." The Fifth Circuit had overturned the conviction, not the indictment. Despite winning a writ of habeas corpus, Carolyn was still charged with murder. The warden knew the procedure. "You'll probably be returned to the Harris County jail."

"I want to get back to Houston and hug that lawyer." Carolyn grinned.

A reporter reminded her another trial might repeat the original verdict. She could still be the First Lady to die by electrocution.

Carolyn replayed her familiar refrain, "I'll hold my head high and take it better than any man. At least better than Leslie."

Leslie pored over a letter from his pen pal fiancée inside the Walls around four o'clock that afternoon. "I read down to the part in her letter when she said that she hoped I'd be free soon." His little radio kept him company. "A newscast came on the radio about the court ruling from New Orleans." His attention was split and he missed the crucial facts. "I heard something on the radio, but it was garbled. I thought they ruled against me." He was still feeling blue when the warden slid back the cell-block doors. Leslie ignored the warden's announcement, he just sulked on his bunk and listened to his radio.

The warden brought Leslie into his office. But even after hearing about the reversal again, Leslie still did not understand. Too many disappointments had made him ornery.

"What does it mean?" he snapped.

"I think it means you'll get a new trial," the warden answered.

Slowly, the new reality began to sink into Leslie. He started to giggle, then dropped into a chair and laughed even harder. "Wow!" he yelled. "Oh, Lord!" Tears began to mix with his happiness. A telegram arrived from Hot Springs, Arkansas. "YOUR CASE HAS BEEN REVERSED. DON'T TALK TO ANYONE, ESPECIALLY

REPORTERS. REPEAT. DON'T TALK TO THE NEWS MEDIA. LOVE, DAD."

Leslie waved the message. "It says 'Dad,' but I don't have one of them." His spirits were too high for him to sit still. "I was surprised. I thought I'd been turned down." The good news restored his arrogance. "I've been telling them I'll get a new trial and I'll be out of here by the Fourth of July. Freedom Day!" The holiday was his latest fixation. "It's the workings of the Lord. Everything up to now has been the work of the Lord. It's been a good revelation and I'm going to let the spirit guide me."

Leslie's piety was fleeting. "Haven't you noticed my hair?" he flirted. "I had the curls cut." He showed off a religious medal engraved with his pen pal's name, but the reporters asked him about Carolyn. "We're no longer close," he said, dismissing her. "I don't care to have any further contact with her." He wanted to call his fiancée. "I don't need Carolyn anymore."

Leslie hoped his lawyer was not thinking about using an insanity defense for the retrial. "I don't want anything like that. I may be off sometimes, but I'm not crazy. I don't want to go to any asylum."

Sylvia and Jim Ayres had moved from the house on Wentworth. The extended family that shared the red brick cottage had split apart under the pressure of the two-year fight to keep Leslie out of the electric chair. Sylvia's brother, Ted Kipperman, needed some distance to build a life of his own. Sylvia and Jim moved from the shade of mature trees growing near the bayous at the center of town, out to the flat, featureless prairie that became mud and marsh during the long, relentless stretches of wet weather that covered the calendar.

When the Fifth Circuit decision came through, their home was being pelted by a deluge that had lasted almost two weeks, turning the streets into rivers and the lawns into swamps. A reporter from the *Chronicle* braved the torrent and found Sylvia drained, wearing a wrinkled housecoat, and surrounded by Leslie's Buddhas and artificial flowers. "Aren't they beautiful?" she asked. Despite her plan to auction off the treasures to defray legal expenses, Sylvia had not been able to part with the memories they held for her.

She tried to make sense of the good news on a dark day. "The Lord worked hard for Douglas." Sylvia was not ashamed to beg for help from above. "A lot of people scoff at people in trouble turning to God, but Jesus did when he was on the cross."

Mae Lima had just finished her grocery shopping during a break in the storm when she saw her youngest son running up the street. "The way he was waving his arms, I thought the house was on fire." Mae pulled over and heard the welcome news. Her joy turned the short trip home into a wild ride, two blocks became an obstacle course. "She was so excited we almost had a wreck," her son remembered. "She kept asking me if it was appealed or if Carolyn got a new trial, and I kept telling her I didn't know."

Her son said the Fifth Circuit decision cracked Mae's stoic facade. "When we got home, she was still so excited that she let the dog out of the car, then ran around to the other side of the car and got back in." Mae's head was spinning. "I don't know who I am even now," she said that happy afternoon.

Neighbors flooded into her small home. Two and a half inches of rain fell on Houston in a single hour, but the downpour did not blot the sunshine from their mood. "I felt in my heart Carolyn was going to have another chance," Mae said. "I'm so thrilled. I expected it, but I'm still thrilled."

Frank Briscoe was stunned. "I can't believe that's the holding of the court." The mistake that overturned the convictions was hung on him.

Clyde Woody was glad to see his rival stumble. The fault belonged to Briscoe, no one else, especially not his assistant, Neil McKay. "Neil was just doing what his boss made him do," Woody said. "Never was there any doubt in my mind about the appeals court's decision in this case." Woody spoke with the confidence of hindsight, considering one swing vote, the thinnest possible margin, was the difference between new trials and two dead defendants.

FOUR

Bobo the Clown

29

"She's in a position to develop the true facts now," Clyde Woody said, signaling a new direction for Carolyn's defense. By mutual agreement, Woody and Lunsford decided she would be first on the docket. The motion for a severance to try Carolyn separately was granted automatically, and jury selection began in Houston on Monday, February 17, 1964, after Frank Briscoe failed to convince the Fifth Circuit or the U.S. Supreme Court to reinstate the convictions.

When Carolyn Lima appeared in the courtroom, most of the forty extra pounds she had put on were gone. "I haven't been dieting," Carolyn said. "I'm just too nervous to eat."

By Thursday, one slot remained open on the jury when the panel of candidates was exhausted. Five hundred potential jurors were available in other state district courts in the building, but Clyde Woody refused to consider them. Under the law, he did not need a reason to exercise this privilege and he did not give one. Judge Love was forced to fall back on a contingency that existed in Texas law: He dispatched deputies from the Harris County Sheriff's Department to round up fifty more candidates.

The deputies fanned out through downtown, where the streets still smelled like a stable after the previous day's grand parade to open the annual rodeo. Hundreds of horses had left their mark on the concrete, and the deputies needed to watch where they stepped as they hustled across intersections to scour the sidewalks for potential jurors. One team got away from the odor of horse manure by ducking into the palatial lobby of the Texas National Bank of Commerce, a marble cavern of art deco opulence.

A courteous account executive approached them with his customary question. "May I help you?" he asked. The deputies
answered yes and escorted him to the courthouse, where the
banker eventually joined nine other men and two women to
become the twelfth member of Carolyn's jury.

Although snow is rare in Houston, a light dusting fell the night
before testimony began, just as it had the previous winter in the
dark hours before Carolyn and Leslie heard Judge Love set the
date for their execution. Snow seemed to match the icy facade
Carolyn showed to outsiders.

Many familiar faces were back in the courtroom, and the D.A.
asked for the death penalty again, but a new wrinkle appeared when
Frank Briscoe deferred to his second chair, allowing Neil McKay to
handle most of the early questioning. Retrials can be sticky. Memories fade, witnesses evaporate, defense attorneys have seen where
pitfalls lie. Permitting his subordinate to take over allowed the D.A.
to distance himself from a possible unfavorable verdict.

Despite any prosecution misgivings, the retrial was walking in
worn shoes. Robert Reyna sat in the witness stand and described
reporting the blaze on Avenue I. The veteran fireman, F. E. Blysard, had retired; he recalled discovering the flames were burning
on a human, not a dummy. Clinton McDaniel, the pharmacy student who lived next door to the duplex on Griggs Road, was man-
aging a drugstore now. He could not remember if Carolyn was
carrying a purse, where she allegedly kept her pistol.

"Your attention was on Ashley because he was such an oddball,
wasn't it?" Woody asked.

"That's true," McDaniel replied.

Leslie lived up to his billing when he was led into the courtroom to be identified. "Goodness! I see no gathering of the Lord
in here," he blurted. "Mercy!" he yelled as deputies hustled him
away. "Judge not that ye be not judged!" Neither side brought
him into the courtroom again.

The trial was recessed on Sunday, February 23, Carolyn's
twenty-first birthday. She celebrated by attending a church service in the jail chapel. "To ask for help," she said.

Three years had brought changes to many people involved in
the case. Richard Ramirez was living in Los Angeles. The drifter

with the unreliable testimony was not ordered back to Houston. Mrs. Hortense Cooke did not return either. The lyrical landlady no longer ran the Golden Age Mansion. She had left New Orleans and moved to Florida. She claimed that she was too ill to travel.

In court Monday, Frank Briscoe read Mrs. Cooke's testimony from the first trial, then Sergeant Cornelius Drumm of the New Orleans police department took the stand to describe finding blood-smeared Levi's left on the floor and shells from six .22 caliber shorts fished from a dirty ashtray inside the room in the slave quarters of the Golden Age Mansion.

Carolyn's confidant from the FBI was in town too, but Clyde Woody managed to limit Special Agent Leo Reuther III's testimony and reduced the damage from his rendition of her oral confession.

Mrs. Tones sat through more questioning. She identified her husband's clothes that had been strewn along Polk Street in Houston; she also recognized his cuff links decorated with musical notes and the portable TV stolen from his office.

When the widow stepped down, the prosecution had one major goal left. Carolyn had been her own worst enemy at the first trial, and the D.A. wanted her working for him again. He could try to convict her with her own words, so he asked for permission to read her three-year-old transcript.

With the jury out of the courtroom, Woody argued that his client's first trial testimony was invalid. Carolyn was incompetent in 1961, Woody said. The conviction did not stick because the D.A. hid the evidence of her condition. Carolyn was not only legally insane when she gave her first trial testimony, Woody added, she was improperly represented by a lawyer she did not want.

The fight carried over to Tuesday morning, when Carolyn herself took the stand. With the jury still away, she recalled the visits Racehorse Haynes paid to her jail cell before the original trial. She believed he was going to be her lawyer. Haynes appeared too, confirming Carolyn's memory. Mae Lima caught stares with her flaming red hair at the first trial, now she was a blonde, and nervous as she recalled the history of her hassles with Jack Knight, but she was forced to admit that she eventually had accepted him as the lawyer representing her daughter.

Judge Love ruled in favor of the prosecution and allowed Frank Briscoe to read Carolyn's transcript. The D.A. could not emulate her cold detachment, but he did plenty of harm with his rhetorical flourishes. A teenager turning tricks; the sixty-nine on the couch; playing with a man's penis before she shot him. The D.A. had her words on the record. "I pulled the trigger and just kept on pulling." After Briscoe finished reading her testimony, the prosecution rested.

Carolyn had to save herself. Her lawyer made her the center of his strategy, a daring risk since her first trial testimony had been so disastrous. The D.A.'s damning replay still rang in the courtroom Tuesday afternoon when Carolyn swore to tell the truth as the star witness in her own behalf.

"I took the blame then," Carolyn admitted. "Douglas told me to." She did not call him Cookie anymore. "He told me if I didn't, he'd put all the blame on me and see that I went to the electric chair."

Carolyn switched from Leslie's middle name to his last name as her new version unfurled. "Ashley told me what to do and what to say." He was her Svengali. "He said I was such a young girl that I wouldn't get the death penalty if we split the blame, and he'd get off too."

Carolyn testified that she did not meet Tones while she was shaking a rug on the porch of her apartment; Leslie introduced them. She didn't pay for the gun either; Leslie did. Her name was on the pawnshop Rental Agreement because he made her sign for the pistol. She did not bring the .22 to the three-way date; she did not even bring her purse. Her lawyer made sure the jury remembered the pharmacy student who lived next door was not positive Carolyn had a purse when he saw her in front of the realty office. Carolyn swore she was not aware Leslie had the gun.

"If I'd known, I wouldn't have gone," she asserted.

Clyde Woody asked her to stand up and step to a diagram of the duplex, then he put a pointer in her hand while he steered her through the sequence of events that had led to the shooting. As part of her geography lesson, Carolyn waved away the difficulty with the bayonet. In the original self-defense scenario, the weapon mysteriously moved from the back office to the front office, then returned to the back office where police dismissed it during their investigation. When she failed to recognize the bayonet on the witness stand at the original trial, Carolyn had looked like a liar and made a buffoon out of her lawyer.

In her revised version of the shooting, she disposed of the long knife's importance. Tones was just playing when he poked her, and the weapon stayed in his private office. It was never used during a fight in the front office because there was no fight in the front office.

The shooting was not self-defense, Carolyn explained. She and the trick were stripped and pretzeled on the couch. "Ashley suddenly moved Mr. Tones's head. . . . " She had no hint that anything was wrong. "Douglas looked at me and sort of smiled." Something about her sex with Tones made Leslie jealous. "I turned my head the other way for an instant, and then I heard the gun go off." She did not see the bullet hit Tones's skull. "I heard the shot and heard Mr. Tones grunt. Douglas jumped up and had the pistol." She had not realized Leslie was armed until he pulled the trigger.

"Douglas was giggling and giggling right after the shot. He acted like he was enjoying it," Carolyn continued. "Mr. Tones fell off the couch. I screamed and jumped up. I hollered to Ashley, 'You killed him!' " She tried to see if the trick was dead. "I was bending over Mr. Tones with a mirror to see if he was still breathing when Ashley said, 'Shut up or you'll get the same.' " He ordered her away from the body. "He told me to stand up beside him, then he fired five more shots into Mr. Tones as Mr. Tones was laying on the floor."

Carolyn said Leslie came up with the idea of burning the body, but she had to account for eyewitness evidence that she bought the gasoline. "He made me," she swore. In a trance, she followed him to the East End. "We drove the cars to a spot he said he knew." Leslie dictated every move she made. "He told me to get him some matches and stay in the car and I did." Carolyn was a witness, not an accomplice, "Then I saw it all flash up."

She told the jury that she was so disoriented after the shooting that she did not realize they were running away until she and Leslie were on the highway to New Orleans. He forced her to stay with him. "In New York, he grabbed me around the throat and threatened to kill me if I didn't share the blame," she said. "He was threatening me all the time after the killing." She was caught between Leslie and her fear of the law. "I lied the first time because I was afraid."

Carolyn stayed on the witness stand until the session ended at six o'clock. Frank Briscoe had his chance to cross-examine her on Wednesday morning. "I was not a prostitute," she answered his accusation. Carolyn claimed she was not really a hooker because she never collected any money for sex. The tricks always paid Leslie, she said.

Briscoe scoffed at the idea that she was Leslie's terrified puppet. The D.A. introduced the heartbroken "Dear Cookie" letter Carolyn had written when tension tore them apart in New York. "I miss you very much. . . . I love you with all my heart. . . . " The jury heard her teenage pain. "Does this sound like a letter from a person who's scared of another person?" Briscoe asked.

"I don't know," Carolyn mumbled. "I don't remember saying all those things," she stalled. "I wrote that letter because I thought if I told Douglas I cared for him, he wouldn't tell a lie on me about the killing."

Briscoe wondered why she did not break away from Leslie when they were driving separate cars after the shooting. "I don't know," Carolyn said again. The D.A. pushed harder. "I couldn't," she wailed. "He said he would see I got the chair. I didn't want to die for something I didn't do. I didn't kill that man."

Her icy facade cracked. "I was afraid of Douglas," she pleaded. "Please believe me. . . ." She broke down and the D.A. remained silent as she sobbed.

Carolyn Lima cried in the courtroom on the third anniversary of her arrest in Manhattan. It was exactly three years since the FBI had trapped her on the stairwell in Hell's Kitchen. She had told a different story in New York, and much of it remained inadmissible in court.

The morning after her capture in 1961, Carolyn spoke with Detective John Thornton, the HPD's homicide expert. Carolyn refused to make a written confession and she was vague about a motive for the shooting. "He may have been trying to hurt me with that large knife or he could have been trying to rape me," Thornton paraphrased her in his report, which could not be submitted to the jury because it was not linked to the discovery of a "fruit of the crime."

She refused to say who poured the gas and struck the match that lit the corpse. "I won't tell you" was her standard answer, but "she stressed the point that Leslie had not forced her to do any-thing and anything that she had done was voluntary," Thornton wrote in his account of the interview.

Carolyn was more talkative when the homicide detective saw her later in the week. She told Thornton that "she carried the pis-tol in her beige purse all of the time," including the trip to see Tones in the duplex on Griggs Road. "She and Tones sat on the little couch in his private office. Ashley moved from chair to chair, part of the time on the couch with them. Carolyn stated that Tones wanted to have intercourse with her, also sodomy by Les-lie, but stated that he only had a hundred-dollar bill and wanted to charge this one."

In his report, Thornton did not say whether Leslie and Carolyn agreed to work on credit. The detective wrote, "Carolyn stated that all this time Tones had his penis (DILLY) out and would ask Ashley to eat it, and at one time sat down on the couch, pointed to his dilly and asked them which one wanted to sit on it." Pickles were the inspiration for Carolyn's phallic imagery. "Carolyn stated that some way they moved into the waiting room and that Tones had removed his clothes and would walk up to both she and Ashley and shake his dilly at them."

The date began to go sour. "Carolyn stated that she finally con-sented to let Tones commit oral sodomy on her and while he was committing the act he kept pushing his dilly into her face. Caro-lyn stated that Tones became so rough by biting her and 'felt like he was putting his head in it' that she tried to make him stop and when she was unable to stop him, Ashley tried to stop him."

A scuffle started, and Leslie knocked Tones to the floor. Caro-lyn never explained how the bayonet appeared. "Tones got up fighting and picked up a long sword-like knife and started at Ashley." Leslie grabbed the gun from her purse and shot Tones in the head, then quickly put down the pistol. The trick kept strug-gling, so Carolyn reached for the .22 and emptied it into him.

"Carolyn stated that Tones fell, but his eyes stayed open and they didn't know whether he was alive or dead." After they real-ized he was dead, they started their getaway. They financed their trip with his hundred-dollar bill, but they tossed away Tones's clothes, including the charcoal-gray topcoat and shadow-plaid jacket that were never found. "Carolyn stated the reason for burning the body was to destroy it, and she believed it was Cookie's idea."

The homicide detective added a few miscellaneous claims that Carolyn threw into the interview. "Tones told her of going to the gyms (like the YMCA). He enjoyed watching the young men and boys walking around without any clothes on, and also would state that he just wanted to get his hands on their 'keester' (slang for buttocks)."

Near the end of their talk, she threw in a last-minute memory about the fatal date on Griggs Road. Finances were a sore subject with the real estate man. "Carolyn further stated that at the time in the private office Tones would have his dilly hanging out of his trousers and that it was very stiff, but when she would ask about the money, the stiffness would go out of it."

Without Carolyn's signature on a written confession or a link to a "fruit of the crime," the version she told Thornton in New York could not be entered as evidence. Both sides rested at ten o'clock Thursday morning, and Judge Love allotted two hours for closing arguments. The gallery was packed, but Mrs. Tones stayed away, so the danger of another outburst from her was not a threat. Just as three years before, Neil McKay spoke first. The assistant D.A. called Carolyn's new version of the shooting "one of the biggest layoff jobs in the history of this courtroom."

When Clyde Woody got his chance with the jury, he steered attention away from his client. The defense attorney put the harsh light on his adversary. "Briscoe has to have a death penalty this year," Woody charged. Politics made the prosecutor warp Carolyn's role in the shooting. The D.A. had an election campaign on his calendar and death penalties were popular at the ballot box.

"I'm standing for reelection," Briscoe admitted in his closing argument, but winning votes was not the reason he wanted to punish Carolyn. "I'm honest first with myself. I could never be part of a trial if I didn't believe the defendant was guilty."

Carolyn was a killer, "cool and calculated," he said. On the same witness stand, three years before, she confessed that she carried the pistol in her purse; in her new version, she claimed that she had gone to Griggs Road empty-handed. At both trials, Carolyn said she used a mirror to see if Tones was still breathing after the shooting. "It would be interesting to know where she got the mirror when she testified that she had no purse," the D.A. wondered.

"They were in this together from the beginning. She's lying to you when she lays all the blame on Ashley." The D.A. was willing to absolve Carolyn's perjury. "I don't blame her for doing so," he told the jury, "but I'll be sorely disappointed in you if you believe it."

The ten men and two women began their deliberations around six o'clock Thursday evening, and they did not reach a verdict before their bedtime.

At nine-thirty Friday morning, the jurors sent a letter to Judge Love. The single sentence read, "We are unable to resolve the definition of 'reasonable doubt' and 'malice aforethought.' " The judge brought them into the courtroom and told the members of the panel he could not give them a firm definition of "reasonable doubt." They had to find the standard in their own consciences, he advised, but if they had reasonable doubts about a murder with malice verdict, they should consider a lesser crime.

"This pretty much rules out the death penalty," Woody explained after the jury retired again. "It sounds like good news," Carolyn grinned and crossed her fingers.

Less than two hours later, just before 11:30, the buzzer from the jury room signaled the decision. Everyone was back in the courtroom within fifteen minutes. Carolyn's hands wrestled each other as she waited for the clerk to read the verdict. "Guilty . . . " the word slapped her, then her spirits rose, "of murder without malice." The jury gave her the maximum, but the maximum sentence for murder without malice was only five years in prison.

"This is the happiest day of my life," Carolyn sobbed with joy in the corridor after the verdict. "It's a lot different from the electric chair." She gave Clyde Woody the credit for restoring her future. "I was tried separately and I had a lawyer who had my interest at heart," she said.

Woody praised his client. "She convinced the jury that she was telling the truth." Woody didn't expect to appeal the five-year sentence, instead he planned to ask Judge Love to give Carolyn credit for the three years she had already spent in prison. The judge had the power to reduce her debt to society to just two years, and Carolyn could cut the short stretch in half if she behaved herself. Inmates received two days "good time" credit for every day they stayed out of trouble.

A year behind bars would be a snap. "You can throw that in no time," a reporter told her.

"That's right." Carolyn laughed. "This is really great." Her mother stood beside her. "I hoped and prayed for this," Mae Lima wept. "Now I can rest."

A reporter asked Carolyn about Leslie before she returned to her cell. "He's sick, very sick." She scowled. "He can't even conduct a conversation. He's always been that way. I always knew it, but let's say I overlooked it at the time."

Less than two weeks after the verdict, Carolyn was back in Criminal District Court Number 3. She could not stifle a smile when Judge Love asked, "Do you have anything to say before sentence is passed before you?"

"No, sir," Carolyn chirped, "but I'd like it if . . . "

Clyde Woody silenced her. Protocol required *him* to ask the judge to credit her with the time she had already served. "She has grown up, she has matured," Woody argued, "she's not the same girl who sat here three years ago." Neil McKay wanted Carolyn to do the full five years. "She's a self-confessed perjurer," the assistant D.A. said. By retracting her testimony from the first trial, Carolyn admitted that she lied under oath, McKay charged.

Judge Love weighed the arguments, then sided with Carolyn, granting her credit for the entire time she had spent in jail since her murder indictment—exactly three years, plus one week. "I'm so happy," Carolyn purred. "I just can't find the words to express it."

The prospect of watching Carolyn Lima get off so lightly was too much for the district attorney. After personally prosecuting her twice, Frank Briscoe stayed away, conspicuous by his absence during the formal sentencing procedure.

30

A week after Judge Love reduced Carolyn Lima's sentence, he decreed three years of publicity had made justice impossible for Leslie Douglas Ashley in Houston. On a motion of his own, without being asked for a change of venue by either side, the judge transferred the case sixty miles southwest to Wharton, a sleepy town with a population in four figures, where the installation of new parking meters or the tenth anniversary of a local supermaket made front-page headlines in the weekly newspaper.

Lucky Lunsford exploded. Wharton was separated from Houston by a single county, and that buffer county happened to be Frank Briscoe's native home. The D.A.'s ancestors settled along the Brazos River in Fort Bend County when the Mexican flag still flew over Texas; the family's blood and influence stretched across the landscape into neighboring counties. "Everybody in Wharton County is kin to Briscoe," Lunsford railed. "I'd just as soon try the case with Briscoe's assistants on the jury."

In early April, Lunsford came to court and accused Judge Love of caving in to pressure from the D.A. On March 23, 1964, "persons acting under Briscoe's direction," in Lunsford's opinion, arrived at the judge's home with a search warrant to look for a stolen six-and-a-half carat diamond brooch. The piece of jewelry allegedly was given to the jurist by a lawyer named Sam Hoover, a shady stringpuller who worked on both sides of the law. Hoover had been mayor of Pasadena, the aromatic petrochemical suburb known as the City of Smells, and he was currently under indictment as the mastermind behind the torture and robbery of an affluent family tormented in the privacy of their comfortable home.

247

Frank Briscoe claimed one of the accomplices in the crime told Houston cops the whole story, adding an extra detail—Hoover supposedly offered a missing diamond brooch taken in a different robbery to Judge Love, who gave it to his wife. The pin was not found when the judge's home was searched, but the episode forced him to admit Hoover had helped him buy tires at a discount for his Mercedes-Benz. "I don't see anything wrong with obtaining merchandise at wholesale prices," Love said. The judge also admitted that he took a one- hundred- dollar campaign donation from Hoover, but returned an expensive pair of cuff links Hoover slipped to him across the tabletop in the courthouse cafeteria.

During the controversy, Love received some negative mail, including a letter Leslie sent from the county jail. "You can feel the viles of Satan. Now you know what it means to be falsely accused. You are about to become a bouncing ball as the elections draw near." Leslie's imagery was strong, but his political knowledge was weak. Judge Love was running unopposed on the ballot.

He was not in immediate political jeopardy, but Judge Love was determined to get rid of Leslie's retrial. He denied Lunsford's "absurd" motion to vacate the change of venue, pointing out the motion to move the trial was made a week before his home was searched. Judge Love named the new jurisdiction, the Twenty-third District Court of Wharton County, where Judge Thurman Gupton set the retrial for May 11, just a month away, and ordered the local sheriff to send out five hundred jury notices.

Leslie was moved to the Wharton jail in the middle of April. "I'm anxious to get this show on the road," he said, giggling as he was removed from his cell in Houston. "I will be acquitted because I was only an innocent bystander." He sounded like he wanted to try the strategy that had worked for Carolyn.

His lawyer still believed an insanity plea was Leslie's best chance. His mother had called the Jewish Family Service and asked the center to pay for a new psychiatric exam for her son. Her request was denied. "Thank God we don't have any family problems," Sylvia screamed and slammed down the receiver, according to the record the center kept of her call.

Lloyd Lunsford found another source to pay for the psychiatric examination, so he was able to present a new insanity diagnosis, as well as Leslie's long psychiatric record to Judge Gupton, who agreed to change the Monday, May 11 proceeding from a murder trial to a mental fitness hearing. Because his conviction had been overturned, Leslie was starting fresh, and Texas law permitted his attorney to raise the question of sanity at the time of the shooting, a possibility that had not been allowed at the earlier hearing when the conviction was still valid. With enough votes in Wharton, Leslie could wind up in a mental hospital and he would not have to go back to prison at all.

The day he was due in court for his second sanity hearing, Leslie sat down over a cup of jailhouse coffee and wrote one of his pen pals, a woman living in Nova Scotia. "I've been thru so much, a trial, a sanity hearing, and been to court on scores of motions and seen death nearly and been persecuted. I sure feel I've been punished but Mr. Briscoe strives to electrocute me."

On May 11, Leslie walked into the courtroom wearing dark slacks, a white shirt with the sleeves rolled up to his elbows, and a necktie knotted around his collar. He could have passed for a streetcorner evangelist except for the chewing gum he snapped between his teeth.

He sat beside Carolyn, who had been brought to Wharton to testify. She had put on a little weight since her sentencing, but she was still shapely in a brown print dress. Although she had condemned Leslie at her retrial, he did not hold her harsh words against her. He smoked while they whispered and giggled together for half an hour, just like old times, until Frank Briscoe had his fill of their friendly reunion and asked Judge Gupton to separate them.

The jury selection ritual began again; six men and six women filled the panel before the end of the day. Around seventy-five spectators, less than capacity, were in the gallery when testimony started. Leslie did not have such a big draw on the road. "Whartonians like to gossip about themselves more than outsiders," a librarian at the local junior college explained.

The roll call of witnesses had a familiar ring. The general practitioner who examined Leslie as a teenager was back, so was psychologist Jack Tracktir. A trio of psychiatrists—Howard Crow, Eugene Tips, and Exter Bell—all labeled Leslie "a schizophrenic of the paranoid type." Dr. Bell said a medical education was not required to see Leslie suffered from a psychotic illness. A new

psychiatrist added his observations. Dr. Alfred Bolch believed
Leslie smothered thoughts of returning to death row by acting
"like he's at a county fair, and he also acts like a schoolgirl."

Sylvia took the stand. "He didn't know right from wrong as a
little boy," she sobbed. "I don't think he does now." She wept at
the recollection of Leslie's teenage jobs—paper boy, movie theater usher, delivering eyeglasses. He never lasted long. "They
were just too complicated for him," she sniffled. She was sorry
that she didn't listen to the doctor who advised her to take Leslie
to a psychiatrist. She felt differently now. "I want my son
treated," she wept.

Frank Briscoe was riding high, surging on a wave of confidence
after his latest election victory less than two weeks before the
hearing. But he made a mistake when he asked Sylvia Ayres why
she began to claim Leslie was insane after his death sentence,
although she had never raised the possibility during his trial.

"You wouldn't let me, Mr. Briscoe, remember?" she clawed
him. "You were the only one who had that information."

Lucky Lunsford put Carolyn on the stand. During his direct
examination, she catalogued her life with Leslie. "I know he
didn't know right from wrong," she said.

After Briscoe took over, Carolyn was not as talkative. "Didn't
Ashley pour gasoline on the body?" the D.A. asked her.

"I refuse to answer on the grounds that it might tend to incrim-
inate me." Carolyn had the language of the Fifth Amendment
down pat, but her answer was a surprise. Every other time she
testified, she had freely said Leslie poured the gas that burned
Fred A. Tones.

The D.A. moved on. "Didn't you change the license plates on
Tones's car after Tones was shot to death?" Carolyn took the Fifth
again. Briscoe asked about the getaway to New Orleans. Again,
the Fifth. Carolyn would not answer and the sanity hearing hit an
impasse.

Judge Gupton ordered her to respond, but Carolyn remained
stubbornly silent. She had never been tried for stealing the Lincoln or any of the other charges that could stem from burning a
corpse and fleeing to avoid prosecution. The light sentence at her
retrial might motivate the D.A. to dredge up those old raps, and
Carolyn had learned her lesson about loose lips.

The judge threatened to hold her in contempt of court if she did not cooperate. "I still refuse to answer," Carolyn said, smiling at Leslie who grinned back at her without laughing. Judge Gupton did not share their sense of humor. He fined Carolyn one hundred dollars and sentenced her to three days in the Wharton County jail.

After Lunsford rested his case, Frank Briscoe began by calling Dr. C. A. Dwyer, the psychiatrist who had performed the exam when Leslie entered the state prison system. "It was obvious to me that he had been advised not to talk to me," Dr. Dwyer recalled. He labeled the inmate "a sociopathic personality without psychosis."

Called by Briscoe to testify in Wharton, Dr. Neil Burch said Leslie was "an unusual person, but not psychotic." Dr. Burch reviewed his findings, "He knew right from wrong, but he suffered tremendously from a social persecution complex."

As the hearing progressed, Leslie began giggling for no visible reason. During one snickering fit, he nearly fell off his chair. Briscoe countered Leslie's performance by calling the Wharton sheriff. "I've seen nothing from his actions or conversations to cause me to think anything but he's sane," the lawman said. Leslie had been in his jail for nearly three weeks. The D.A.'s final witness was his own assistant, Neil McKay, who sat in the witness stand and read Leslie's responsive, logical testimony from the first trial.

A change of venue required a local prosecutor to be part of the state's team. Wharton County D.A. Bob Bassett addressed his neighbors during the closing arguments at the sanity hearing, "Don't you know if you and I had a death penalty staring us in the face, we would realize the only way to save our skins would be to play crazy?"

After three days of jury selection and testimony, Judge Gupton turned the case over to the panel around 6:45 on Wednesday evening. The jurors were facing two decisions: Leslie's legal sanity when the shooting occurred and his current mental condition. They elected to have dinner before beginning their business, but they were not shirking their responsibility. After they finished eating, they worked until 2:30 in the morning without reaching a consesus on either verdict.

The panel members had an early breakfast and got back to their deliberations by eight o'clock the next morning. The foreman, a car salesman who knew how to cut deals, said the jury stuck on a dozen or more votes when both questions, prior and current sanity, were coupled on the same ballot. The breakthrough came after the panel split the choices before them.

In Wharton, juries did not buzz the courtroom when they reached a verdict. The courthouse lacked that technology. A note to the judge signaled a decision, and Judge Gupton received the message just three minutes before 11:00 A.M. on Thursday. People get places quickly in a small town, and everyone who needed to hear the verdict arrived in less than ten minutes. Leslie was dressed for the occasion in a charcoal-gray suit with a blue tie. He chewed gum and smiled at his mother, who sat in her customary front-row seat as the clerk read the verdict.

"We the jury find the defendant is now insane, now at the time of the trial." But while one hand gave, the other took away. "We the jury find the defendant was sane at the time of the commission of the alleged offense." The split decision left the murder charge in suspended animation. Leslie was going to a mental institution until he was declared fit to stand trial for homicide again.

"We had no trouble finding him sane at the time of the shooting," the foreman said. Two out of three psychiatrists who had examined him in 1961 reported Leslie knew right from wrong when Fred A. Tones was killed. "Our biggest problem was his sanity or insanity at the present time." The spontaneous giggling jags tilted them.

Sylvia burst into happy tears. She crossed the railing and hugged her son. "This is what I wanted all the time," she sobbed as she stroked Leslie's hair. "I wanted my son to get treatment, and now he's going to get it."

Leslie stayed in his seat. He began to giggle again, then he quickly steadied himself by lighting a cigarette. Reporters asked him for his reaction. After a long pause, he finally mumbled, "I agree with the jury."

31

Frank Briscoe assumed Leslie would be assigned to Rusk State Hospital, an outdated prison that had been converted into a maximum security asylum for the criminally insane deep in the east Texas pine forests. The D.A. did not realize Rusk was overcrowded with an ample population of violent psychotics and unhinged felons, so Judge Gupton found a spot for Leslie at a state mental institution in San Antonio.

"This is a hospital, not a jail," the San Antonio clinical director said. "We don't have a truly maximum security unit." No fence surrounded the grounds. The guards were medical orderlies who used medication and a reasonable amount of muscle to control patients who ranged from sedated lunatics to stressed-out depressives looking for a rest. The orderlies were not trained to discipline criminals through intimidation. They preferred to cultivate friendships by playing cards with the patients and including them on beer drinking excursions to a neighborhood cantina.

Leslie was assigned to the hospital's equivalent of confinement, a third-floor dormitory with approximately fifty beds called ward 8, where the doors and windows were supposed to be locked. Ward 8 patients were not allowed to wear their street clothes; instead, they were required to remain in pajamas and robes around the clock. Unlike other patients in the hospital, they were not permitted to stroll the grounds without supervision. Sealed windows, slumber-party attire, and light-handed surveillance were the extent of the security measures at the unfenced asylum in San Antonio.

The dog days of 1964 were tough on Frank Briscoe. Judge Miron Love got even with the D.A. for having smeared him in the spring. That summer, a grand jury empaneled by Judge Love charged Briscoe with perjury, indicting him for lying when he testified before them. Frank Briscoe told the summer grand jury that he had had no advance knowledge of the warrant issued to search the judge's house for a stolen diamond brooch in March. But two police officers testified that the D.A. was behind the warrant all along. The indictment also accused Briscoe of knowing the HPD had located the missing jewelry before the judge's home was searched. (The brooch had been fenced to a San Antonio jeweler who sold it to an unsuspecting rancher. No evidence ever linked the brooch to Judge Love.)

Grand juries normally work with the prosecutor's staff to draw up their indictments, but the D.A. himself was under investigation, so outside counsel was hired for Briscoe's case. The grand jury, with Judge Love's blessing, picked James Hippard Sr., the attorney who had won the stay of execution for Leslie Ashley and Carolyn Lima at the Petroleum Club hearing. Briscoe chose a blue-chip corporate law firm staffed with his patrician peers to defend him.

The case was too volatile for a local judge to handle, but many substitutes sat on Houston benches during the summer. An out-of-towner could make a decision, then return home without being mired in the political crossfire. Briscoe's high-priced lawyers put the matter before a judge visiting from Williamson County, a thinly populated jurisdiction in central Texas named for a colorful figure from Texas history called "Three-Legged Willie" Williamson, a backwoods lawyer and preacher who dealt with a dead right foot by jamming a pegleg on his knee and letting the useless real limb drag along behind him. Three-Legged Willie delivered the invocation before the Battle of San Jacinto, where Texas won independence from Mexico, and legend claimed he asked the Lord, "If you can't help us, please don't help those Mexicans."

The substitute judge from Williamson County quashed the indictment against Briscoe. In his complicated ruling, the judge decided perjury could not be committed unless a grand jury was investigating a crime. He said the police officers who asked for the search warrant from the spring grand jury at the D.A.'s request had not accused Judge Love of knowing the brooch was stolen.

They were merely looking for hot property innocently received by a third party. Briscoe did not obstruct justice when he misled the summer grand jury, the substitute judge said, because the solution to a crime was not being pursued in the spring.

Fancy footwork saved the D.A., but James Hippard believed the indictment he wrote was rock solid.

While Frank Briscoe slipped out from under his perjury indictment, Leslie Douglas Ashley worked his way out of ward 8 in the San Antonio mental hospital. He started a romance with an orderly, "a tall good-looking Mexican, that Castillian type of Mexican," Leslie recalled. His *enamorado* was ambitious, with dreams of becoming a doctor, so the orderly worked hard to please the medical men who ran the hospital. They treated him well in return, and he could pass on favors like putting in the good word that helped move Leslie from ward 8 into the general population.

Leslie thought he was in love with the orderly, but love did not keep him faithful. He said he was having a clandestine affair with a female patient too, then added a third lover to his list, also a woman, when a rancher's wife checked herself into the asylum. "You'd never believe a queen like me could crawl all over them women, but it's true," Leslie bragged.

At twenty-five, Mary Lou Wiederkehr was ending her second marriage. While her husband ran cattle on the scrub-brush range near the bottom of the Lone Star State, Mary Lou had worked at a motel. Like Carolyn Lima, she wanted to be a beautician. She plucked her eyebrows into high, narrow arches and she had the skill to shape and spray her hair into any style that pleased her. Sometimes she wore a perfect spitcurl coiled down the center of her forehead like a comma, almost long enough to reach her tweezed eyebrows.

Mary Lou came to the San Antonio hospital on a voluntary commitment; no one forced her into the asylum. She met Leslie at a Friday night dance, and they did not hide their relationship from his family. Leslie's mother and stepfather drove to San Antonio about once a month. During one of their visits, Leslie introduced them to his new girlfriend. "She was very pretty," Sylvia recalled. "She had a lot of class and she was obviously very fond of Douglas."

In the fall, Mary Lou started feeling better. As October began, she was released, "furloughed" in the hospital's term. She moved in with a friend, a beauty-school classmate, in hospital parlance her "guardian," although they were almost the same age. Cora Lee Hobbs, like Leslie, was twenty-six; she was married to a Marine captain stationed in Japan. Cora Lee said her classmate was "adjusting nicely" to psychiatric treatment.

Mary Lou was in a good mood shortly after her release when she phoned her stepmother, who lived in a small town in the Ozark highlands, a sunny plateau below the hilltops in southern Missouri. They chatted about Mary Lou's cosmetology lessons. "She seemed very happy. Her greatest wish was to finish that school," her stepmother said. She mailed Mary Lou a check for ten dollars.

Leslie called home during that time also, but he was brooding, scared he was headed back to ward 8. "He lived in horror of that ward," his stepfather explained. "He said they were putting him back there because he watched a poker game between orderlies and inmates." Jim Ayres was proud Leslie would not snitch. "When the hospital authorities asked him who was playing, he didn't feel like he should tell them."

The clinical director scoffed at the poker game story. "Ward 8 is not a punishment ward, but it is kept locked." He said Leslie had to be confined "because an attendant believed he might try to escape."

Leslie was under supervision in ward 8 when Mary Lou and Cora Lee drove to the hospital to visit him on Tuesday, October 6. They arrived around 9:00 P.M. Although the windows on the third floor were supposed to be locked, Cora Lee said Leslie stepped onto a balcony and waved to them, shouting he would be down soon. The women waited about fifteen minutes, but Leslie never came out to greet them. They left without seeing him again.

Mary Lou and Cora Lee stopped at a store for some quick shopping, and they were startled when they returned home and found Leslie waiting for them. Instead of his pajamas and robe, he wore ordinary street clothes—a green corduroy jacket, blue jeans, and a plaid shirt. He brought along a Bible with his name on the cover. "I asked him about the Bible," Cora Lee recalled. "He said something real cute. He said he was going to 'play the missionary.'" Cora Lee could see why her friend liked Leslie. She described him as "personable."

Leslie told the two women that a friendly orderly had let him out, and his liberator was going off duty at eleven, so he had to beat the clock and return to ward 8 quickly to stay out of trouble. "I told Mary Lou to take him out to the hospital and come right back," Cora Lee said. She turned over the keys to her three-year old light blue Dodge Lancer station wagon, a sensible car, economical on the open road.

Leslie was supposed to be in the hospital earlier than he admitted. He missed a 10:30 bedcheck, and a search party found his robe and pajamas tossed away on the unfenced grounds outside the building. Around midnight, the San Antonio police got a call from the hospital. Because of the murder charge hanging over Leslie, the description of the missing patient listed the trait "homicidal tendencies," but the warning was a formality. "He's been a quiet patient, minding his own business," the clinical director said. "Nothing about his behavior indicated he was dangerous," the psychiatrist continued. "Only his history showed cause for concern."

The cops were not alarmed either. "We have two or three persons a week escaping from the mental hospital," a captain explained. He expected strays since the grounds were not fenced. "They're usually picked up wandering the streets and returned in a few hours or in a day or two. It's pretty routine."

Leslie broke the pattern. Almost two days later, on Thursday morning, the San Antonio police decided they needed help and issued a statewide pick-up order for Leslie Douglas Ashley and Mary Lou Wiederkehr, whose friend changed her tune about the personable patient and her borrowed station wagon. Cora Lee Hobbs wanted her Lancer back, and the all-points bulletin included a stolen-car alert. Her guardian did not believe Mary Lou was a willing passenger. "I think she's a hostage," Cora Lee Hobbs said. "I've known her long enough to know she wouldn't go anywhere with him voluntarily."

In a letter, left inside the Lancer abandoned near the Continental Trailways bus station in Tulsa, Oklahoma, Mary Lou did not sound like a hostage.

Lee,
Please forgive us and try to understand. We did what the

Lord willed. Sorry to have worried you. We borrowed your
car with no criminal intentions. We are leaving it here for
authorities to take possession of, hoping it shall be returned
in top shape.

Please find enclosed $10 toward rental of the car and
return expenses. More will come as soon as we're able. May
God bless you and yours. PRAY FOR US. Sincerely in Jesus
name,

Leslie Douglas and Mary Lou Ashley

The joint signature gave Leslie another "wife" without the benefit
of a ceremony, and the "rental fee" was the uncashed ten-dollar
check that her stepmother had sent Mary Lou after the upbeat
telephone call to Missouri. They could afford to be generous
because Leslie had saved about eighty dollars in cash from a hospital allowance his mother gave him.

They slammed the Lancer's doors and took off without wheels.
The station wagon sat undiscovered, gathering dust in Oklahoma,
and the note inside remained unread.

The bulletin from San Antonio infuriated Frank Briscoe. Leslie
was supposed to be locked in a maximum security hospital for the
criminally insane, not coddled in a country club asylum. "The possibility that Ashley will hurt or kill someone while at large is very
real," Briscoe wrote in a letter asking Governor John Connally to
investigate the escape.

His stepfather downplayed Leslie's departure. "He's not dangerous, he's just stir crazy," Jim Ayres said. "He's spent three and
a half years in a cell the size of a bathroom."

"We had discussed the possibility of hearing his case soon. He
may have got a hint of it," a staff psychiatrist revealed. "We came
to the conclusion that he no longer needed hospital treatment."
The psychiatrist called Leslie's breakout "an attempt to solve his
own problems."

Heads rolled in San Antonio. The director of male treatment
quit, and the superintendent who ran the entire hospital was
fired. "Being a mental hospital, we've got a great many people
going in and out," the former superintendent said. "There are a
great many keys. We just had too many keys."

Hospital authorities suspected Leslie had inside help. "This is the only way we can figure he got out," the clinical director reported. He said the same key that opened the ward 8 doors also opened a closet where a patient in pajamas could find street clothes.

Leslie's orderly friend was one of the attendants watching in ward 8 so he was questioned, but he denied being involved and the doctors trusted him. The clinical director even noted Leslie's lover had been the orderly responsible for returning the patient to ward 8 because he warned them Leslie might try to escape.

No secret was safe with the good-looking orderly. Leslie claimed later that he made his move because he heard that he was about to be transferred to Rusk, the obsolete prison which had been converted into a maximum security mental asylum. His orderly friend had leaked the rumor to him, Leslie said. The orderly was going to run away too, according to Leslie, but changed his mind because he did not want to destroy his dream of becoming a doctor.

"The man gave me the keys and turned me over to the girl," Leslie recalled, grinning.

32

Eight days after she disappeared, Mary Lou Wiederkehr walked into police headquarters in Denver. She quietly waited her turn at the information desk, then stepped forward. "I'm tired of running," she said. "I helped a murderer escape in Texas."

Mary Lou was no longer blond like the pick-up bulletin read. Her hair was dark and tied in a twist. In her gray jumper with a wide white collar, she looked too prim to be on the lam with an accused killer. She explained to the police officers that she and Leslie had been in Denver for two days. An argument in a Woolworth's aisle pushed her over the edge. "This can't go on," she claimed she announced in the dime store, "I'm getting out."

When the Denver police checked Mary Lou's story, the stolen car charge popped up. To get herself off the hook, she dialed her guardian at the beauty school in San Antonio. "It was collect and we just talked a couple of minutes," Cora Lee Hobbs said.

"He forced me to go with him," Mary Lou pleaded. Cora Lee believed her and dropped the car theft complaint. Police in Tulsa retrieved the abandoned Lancer, along with the apology note and the uncashed ten-dollar check.

Cora Lee's benevolence did not apply to Leslie. He was still wanted as an auto thief, as well as for being a homicide fugitive, and the cops could not decide if they should hit him with kidnapping as well. They did not have anything against Mary Lou after she ironed out the stolen-car charge, but they were not certain she told the truth about being abducted. She tried to convince them by leading the police to Leslie.

Leslie claimed Mary Lou lost her temper in Denver because he wanted to break up with her and return to his handsome orderly in San Antonio. When she stormed out of the Woolworth's store, he knew she would turn herself in and he expected her to help the police identify and capture him. He hurried back to their hotel room and saw a squad car drive by when he peeked out a window. Leslie believed the cops were circling the building, trying to close in on him, and he did not stick around to see if his assumption was correct. He slipped out a back door and started walking. He said that he hiked alone in the cold for miles before he finally found the courage to stick out his thumb and hitch a ride.

Denver was dark, and Leslie was gone by the time Mary Lou brought the police to the hotel. His clothes were still in their room. Mary Lou believed he had left his entire wardrobe except the outfit he was wearing. She also thought he was down to the last twenty dollars of the getaway fund he had saved from the allowance his mother gave him while he was in the mental hospital.

Mary Lou helped the police hunt for Leslie in downtown Denver as the temperature hovered near freezing that Wednesday night, but their efforts were futile. They released her and she left town as soon as her bus fare arrived. The money came from her sister, who lived in Austin, and Mary Lou had dropped out of sight before an agent from the Texas Department of Public Safety reached Denver to take custody of her.

Being a step behind a mental patient made the Texas law enforcement agency look bad, but Mary Lou's sister assured the DPS that Mary Lou would come to Austin. She arrived on schedule Friday, but she did not have any answers. Mary Lou said she did not know how Leslie had snuck out of the San Antonio hospital or where he went after they separated. Her psychiatric record made her difficult to prosecute, so the DPS let her return to her guardian.

Mary Lou receded into obscurity. Her final words about Leslie were relayed to the press a month later. "We haven't heard from him," Cora Lee Hobbs said. "We don't want to hear from him."

When he left Denver, Leslie hitched a ride due south to Colorado Springs. Next, he used part of his last twenty dollars to grab a bus, still due south. Just across the New Mexico border, he decided to stop in the small town of Raton.

Raton, *mouse* in Spanish, was a prosperous crossroads when the Santa Fe Trail from Missouri was the major route for trade between the East and West, a hundred years before Leslie found refuge in a church run by a female minister who welcomed him to her tiny congregation. She only needed one hand to count the worshipers who showed up to hear her preach at Sunday services, so she had plenty of time to spend with the new candidate for her flock. Leslie stayed to pray and look for guidance from her. He enjoyed the peace and quiet in the high, clear country. He believed that he would not be caught in the remote town, but he could not find any work so he decided to leave after just three days.

Prayer and consultation with the woman minister revealed a path to him. Instead of heading for the warmth of the West Coast, he decided to brave the winter wind and bought a bus ticket for Chicago. He said the fare east cost thirty-three dollars, more than the cash he had left, but he refused to reveal how he financed the trip. "I sure as hell didn't steal the money," he said. "The good Lord provided the money," Leslie claimed. "The good Lord has always provided it." Even in a remote mountain town, Leslie knew how to earn quick cash without holding a job.

Working on stage in drag was still his dream; being an "entertainer," he said. Unable to crack Chicago's transvestite world, Leslie took a job washing pots and pans at a posh private club for $1.25 an hour, the minimum wage. He dabbled in sidewalk politics, passing out buttons and campaign literature supporting Barry Goldwater's doomed presidential bid. Leslie agreed with the Arizona conservative's campaign slogan, "In your heart, you know he's right." The emphatic policies that put Goldwater on the fringe of the mainstream appealed to Leslie, so did the mix of Jewish and Protestant heritage they both shared.

Leslie settled into a Polish section of Hyde Park, an inner city neighborhood near the University of Chicago. He revived his favorite interior decor, filling his rooms with Buddhas and artificial flowers.

On the run, he switched aliases often. This time, he called himself C. D. LaMonte, putting a masculine identity on his favorite drag persona; he also introduced himself as Edward Elizondo, a monicker stolen from the handsome orderly in San Antonio. Once he became comfortable in Chicago, Leslie stuck with one name, Louis Douglas Green.

"Green is Jewish, you know," he said, adding a tribe to the Old Testament roll call.

The security of his minimum-wage dishwashing job gave Leslie the incentive to apply for his first Social Security card as he turned twenty-seven years old. When he was not scrubbing dirty dishes, Leslie said he hung out in coffee shops with his constant companion, a Polish housewife whose immigrant husband had not mastered English. Leslie repeated his old patterns—filling his apartment with kitsch, killing time in tolerant restaurants, and attaching himself to a woman who laughed at his antics. His current goof was a new spin on a familiar habit. Again, he split his identity and deceived unsuspecting listeners. In Chicago, he started telling people he was half black, half white.

After nearly five months in Hyde Park, Leslie became uneasy. Nothing specific; just a feeling. He left his dishwashing job at the fancy club and moved to a different apartment. He said that he turned up his nose at an offer to be stock boy at seventy dollars a week because he preferred to work in swank surroundings. Instead, he took a fifty-hour-a-week job as a bus boy at the Chicago Athletic Club for a dollar an hour plus tips. One of the managers, a sympathetic woman, liked him and gave him extra work as a food runner for private banquets, but Leslie soon realized he had been tricked. Busboys and food runners did not earn tips; they peaked at a buck an hour. After four days, he quit.

Leslie then found a job as a short-order cook, but boiling water was the limit of his culinary skills. He did not even know how to fire up the grill. The boss offered to teach him how to cook, but Leslie was too nervous to listen to the lesson. He barely finished his second day.

In February, the worst of winter blew in the bitter wind. Leslie was floundering so he decided to move on. He took his favorite Buddha, a large one, to the bus station with the idea of buying a ticket for Detroit since it was the nearest big city and the fare was cheap. Looking down the schedule, he saw that a redeye was scheduled to leave for Miami around 4 A.M. He could afford the ticket, so Leslie decided to treat himself and his Buddha to an early spring and sat through the fourteen-hundred-mile ride to sunshine and blue water.

In March, the Texas Department of Public Safety released the results of an investigation at the San Antonio mental hospital. The handsome orderly had admitted bringing Leslie street clothes and letting him climb down a fire escape.

The DPS uncovered wider problems at the hospital. All the doors in the male wards unlocked with a single key and two hundred copies of that key had been made. The lax security went beyond hardware. Besides taking patients off the grounds for beer and cocktails, the orderlies let them leave with friends and relatives. The DPS learned Sylvia had taken Leslie out for dinner when she came to visit him.

Leslie's first week in Miami was a struggle. He only had a few dollars left when he arrived in the middle of the night. He spent fifty cents for a bed in a skid row flophouse to stretch out and sleep on his back for the first time since he carried his big Buddha onto the bus.

During his first week, he only landed one payday, washing dishes at a dollar an hour on a fifteen-hour shift. The job was open, but the work was too hard for such bad wages so he did not return. Although he knew the WANTED bulletins listed him as a transvestite and often included photos of him in drag, performing on stage was a risk Leslie was willing to take. He looked for "entertainment" work, but found nothing. If he could not be in the spotlight, Leslie decided to dress only in male clothes. Hustling was off limits. Prostitution, in drag or out, was a good way to get busted.

Gradually, his luck improved. A day-labor employment service sent him to a couple of restaurants in Coral Gables. He liked the Jewish atmosphere in the neighborhood, so he agreed to stay at a place called Chippy's, where he worked as a busboy for thirty dollars a week plus tips. The salary was small, but the casual kibitzing suited him. He struck up a friendship with the manager, a woman he only remembered as Mrs. Diamond. She quickly promoted him to counter boy with a twenty-dollar-a-week raise.

His promotion brought new responsibilities; Leslie took orders and served beverages. Drawing Cokes and pouring coffee was no problem, but more complicated tasks gave him trouble. A stern waitress criticized his soda fountain technique. "I had never made a milk shake in my life," Leslie defended himself. He burst into tears during the squabble, and threatened to turn in his apron before Mrs. Diamond assured him that she had the patience to let him learn his craft, but he never got the chance.

Leslie had been in Florida barely two weeks when he saw his picture in a local newspaper. On April 6, exactly six months after he escaped from the mental hospital, the apprentice soda jerk discovered he was on the FBI's list of the Ten Most Wanted Criminals in America.

33

On April 3, 1965, just three days before the FBI added Leslie Douglas Ashley to the Ten Most Wanted list, Carolyn Ann Lima made the final payment on her debt to society. On a perfect spring Saturday, right after eight o'clock in the morning, she walked away from prison. The *Houston Chronicle* put the news on the front page: TORCH DEATH SLAYER CAROLYN LIMA FREE. Photographers surrounded her as she stepped through the door with her possessions in a shoe box. From her knit handbag to her pleated skirt and crepe blouse, almost everything that she wore was brown. The only other tint in her outfit was a mustard scarf tied around her neck.

"For days and days I've been looking forward to seeing the beautiful outdoors. I have a lot to be thankful for," she sighed. "It's so pretty outdoors. I thought this day would never get here." She was hungry because she had skipped her last prison meals. "I just couldn't eat," Carolyn said. "I was so nervous I thought it would make me sick, so I just had a Coke." But fresh air and freedom restored her appetite. "I want to eat me a hamburger and have me a bubble bath."

Carolyn had kept up her cosmetology skills in the matrons' beauty shop at Goree and she had also become interested in gardening. "I want to grow flowers and vegetables," she said. "Who knows what the future will bring?" Carolyn wondered. "I just want to stay home with my mother, sleep peacefully at night, and take one day at a time."

Saturdays are busy at beauty parlors, but Mae Lima closed her shop and made the trip to meet her daughter at the prison door.

Carolyn gave her mother every cent that she possessed: a dollar fifty in cash left over from her depleted commissary account, and a fifty-dollar discharge check. "It makes me nervous handling money," Carolyn explained.

Mae's hair was frosted silver. She smiled through jubilant tears, "It's the happiest day of my life." She was as radiant as the crystal spring sky. "I drove to Huntsville this morning, the sun was shining, the weather was just right, the music on the radio was lovely." The world around her seemed flawless. "I was floating on air," Mae said. A strawberry cake was waiting for the family celebration at her house on cinderblocks in the Heights. "It certainly is a pretty day for the end of a nightmare," Mae beamed.

Carolyn was free; she was not on probation or parole. She was only twenty-two years old, and her sentence was completely served, while Leslie was on the run to avoid a trial that would begin the path she had already finished. "He's completely out of my mind," Carolyn said. "I don't want to have anything to do with anything he has to do with."

Leslie got out of Miami fast when he learned he had made the FBI's Ten Most Wanted list. He left his dime-store treasures and the big Buddha he had brought from Chicago. He did not even stop to collect his last check from Chippy's, which was around forty dollars, almost a full week's salary.

Leslie wanted to go to Atlanta, but he was so nervous and confused at the bus station he bought a ticket for Augusta, Georgia, instead. The mistake especially miffed him because the fare to the wrong destination cost five dollars more than a ticket to Atlanta. He knew his mind was mixed up, and he was so scared when he stepped off the bus that he hung around the Augusta terminal until hunger and the sorry state of his finances flushed him out to find a free breakfast at a skid row mission. A full stomach cut his anxiety and gave him the energy to explore. He wandered around town where he remembered seeing lots of soldiers and an army base. He only stayed in Augusta for a day before he got his bearings and headed for his original destination.

In Atlanta, Leslie made ten dollars delivering papers and then heard about jobs with a traveling carnival. Fred's Playland was not exactly the greatest show on earth. Strings of lights and rickety kiddy rides were set up on a parking lot in an African-American

neighborhood near downtown. Leslie used an alias with a southern ring when he introduced himself to the carnival manager as
Leslie Lynn Lamar. He hid his identity, but he was not concealing his background.

He held out his hand and said, " 'I'm one of the FBI's ten most
wanted men,' " according to the carnival manager, who put his
own cynical spin on the confession. "I figured with a crack like
that he'd make a pretty good clown, so I hired him."

Leslie had jazzed up his disguise with fake horn-rimmed glasses
and dyed his hair a dark shade somewhere between red and
brown. He carried a Bible when he began his new career on
Monday, April 19. "He giggled for no reason and acted funny,
then he'd quote from the Bible and make predictions," a young
carny said. Leslie knew a lot of psalms by heart. "He always acted
like some kind of kook," the carny recalled. "I guess you'd have to
be to be Bobo the Clown."

For his job, Leslie painted over his pockmarks with white
greasepaint and added bright red lipstick, traditional funny-face
clown makeup, but his costume was rubber because Bobo sat on a
perch above a vat of water. Customers shelled out twenty-five
cents to sling balls at a bullseye that triggered a spring dunking
him into the shallow tub below.

Bobo tried to strike up a rapport with his show-business colleagues. The carnies called him Lynn. "He told more hard-luck
stories than you can count," a teenager in the troupe said. "He
looked tired and ragged, and said he'd looked for work as an
entertainer from Miami to Chicago, but he couldn't find a job."
The teenager's older brother, also a carny, continued, "Sometimes
he acted a little bit like a mental patient, just kind of funny."

The carnies shared an old bus converted into a home-on-wheels
and they stayed up late during a bull session just two days after
Leslie joined the carnival. One worker remembered, "We were
sitting in the bus and he had his suitcase open." Leslie had saved
a souvenir of his dubious fame. The carny said, "I saw the
WANTED poster and we all dumbed up. Man, we acted like we
didn't know nothing." Besides catching a glimpse of the wanted
poster of himself that Leslie kept, the carny said he spotted a
woman's black wig too. Despite Leslie's claim that he was not
wearing women's clothes while he was on the lam, the carnies
said they discovered Bobo's luggage was filled with dresses after

they seized their chance to rummage through his belongings when he was out of the bus.

Thursday morning, one of the carnies went to a post office to see if the WANTED poster was real or just a mock-up memento from a penny arcade. Sure enough, Bobo's portrait was on the wall. Four of the carnies huddled to discuss their bunkmate. The WANTED poster revealed he had escaped from an asylum. "I don't like to see people who need treatment running around," a carny said. "I knew he needed help when I saw that poster."

But another motive influenced their final decision. "I need money," a squealer admitted at the time. "We thought there might be a reward."

Five days after joining Fred's Playland, Leslie was relaxing in his bunk, nodding on and off inside the bus around three o'clock on Friday afternoon. He was drowsy, lying flat on his back when five FBI agents stepped through the door.

"I asked him if he was Lynn," Chief Agent Joseph Ponder reported. "He said yes, then I asked him what his real name was and he said Lamar." Leslie did not giggle or try to run away. "When I asked him if he was Leslie Douglas Ashley, he denied it a couple of times," Agent Ponder said.

An officer grabbed Leslie and pushed up the sleeve on his white shirt, exposing a scar on his right wrist from a teenage suicide attempt. "Within thirty seconds, he said, 'I'm Ashley,'" Agent Ponder explained. "He looked exactly like his picture in the poster." After more than six months at large, the FBI snared Leslie less than three weeks after he had made the Ten Most Wanted list.

His fake ID read Leslie Lynn Lamar, and he had an application for Georgia unemployment compensation that he never submitted. Fred's Playland did not pay well. He said the change in his pockets was his only cash and the total came to less than a dollar. Leslie refused to tell the FBI agents where he had been or what he had been doing since he escaped from the asylum, but he opened up slightly when he used his one phone call to speak with his mother.

"I'm so grateful and relieved he's alive and no harm has come to him." Sylvia was crying again. "It's like I've had a big stone tied to my heart and now it's suddenly lifted away." She was proud that Leslie was not stealing or loafing, "I knew he'd be working and earning a living."

They talked about his different jobs on the run, cook, busboy, dishwasher. Leslie, however, denied he was a clown. He told his mother he merely took the tickets for Bobo's act, and he complained that he was stiffed out of his earnings by the carnival manager. "I was supposed to get fifty percent of the profits from the show," Leslie griped. He thought he had around twenty-five dollars coming, but his plunges into the water tank netted him nothing. Leslie was busted before his first payday arrived at Fred's Playland and the manager kept Bobo's salary in the carnival treasury.

Carolyn was surprised when she learned about Leslie's most recent occupation. "I think he remarked one time that he liked circuses, but I don't think he ever worked in one before." She was gardening and helping her mother in the beauty salon to prepare for her long-delayed cosmetology exam.

She did not harbor any animosity toward Leslie. "I believe he should have another chance like I did," she said. "Everybody should have a chance, a second chance."

34

"I want to go back to Texas and stand trial," Leslie Douglas Ashley told a judge at an extradition hearing in Fulton County Superior Court. He stood alone, without a lawyer at his side in Atlanta; he had waived his right to have his own attorneys at the hearing. "They tried to railroad me to the crazy house," Leslie groused. "I'd rather stand trial for murder." He thought he understood the strength of his case. "There's no weapon and no confession," he said. "They'll never put me on death row again if I stay off the witness stand." He knew his personality had a bad influence on juries. "That'll be hard though because I want to tell my side of the story."

Although Lloyd Lunsford raced to Georgia, he arrived too late to block the extradition order. Authorities in Texas were working quickly as well. The chairman of the state hospital board said the exams to send Leslie back to a courtroom had been nearly finished before he escaped six months earlier. The new superintendent at the San Antonio asylum backed up his boss, claiming a review of the records showed Leslie had been ruled "not psychotic" before he climbed down the fire escape. A certificate of sanity was already in the works while Leslie was in Atlanta.

This maneuver meant the court in Wharton regained jurisdiction over Leslie. That county's chief deputy showed up in Atlanta looking like the picture of a Texas lawman, wearing a straw cowboy hat and a tin star pinned to his western-cut shirt. He quickly shipped Bobo the Clown across the width of the old Confederacy to Wharton, where the obligatory cenotaph honoring veterans of the rebel army shared the courthouse lawn with a monument

271

praising a frontier sheriff who had been ambushed by a cowardly outlaw.

The legal brokers greased the wheels for a murder trial. A grand jury in San Antonio swiftly declined to indict Leslie for stealing Cora Lee Hobbs's station wagon, and a new sanity hearing was ordered. Despite the clean bill of health from psychiatrists, a jury had to declare Leslie sane because the verdict from the hearing that had sent him to the San Antonio hospital still remained in effect.

A replay in Podunk did not interest Frank Briscoe. The Houston D.A. decided to skip the trip to Wharton and turned the case over to his assistant, Neil McKay. Although Briscoe bowed out, Lloyd Lunsford revved up again. The defense attorney papered Texas with subpoenas. He even sent a process server to the capitol with a summons for Governor John Connally, instructing the state's chief executive to bring along a copy of the Department of Public Safety report about Leslie's escape, but the governor managed to get himself excused. On Tuesday, June 1, Leslie strolled into the courtroom popping gum between his teeth. He blew a few bubbles as he smiled at spectators in the gallery and wiggled his finger at familiar faces. A panel of eleven men and one woman, a mother with eight children, was quickly seated. They had a single option to decide. Their predecessors at the first Wharton hearing ruled Leslie was sane at the time of the shooting and that verdict was permanent. The only open issue was Leslie's mental condition at the present time. If the jury declared him insane, he went back to an asylum for more treatment. If not, he was ready for a murder trial.

Leslie gave his mother a big kiss during a lunch recess, then he giggled while she sobbed on the witness stand. The parade of psychiatrists started again, led by Dr. Eaton Bennett, the ex-superintendent at San Antonio who had been fired after Leslie escaped. Dr. Bennett said he had never rendered a final decision about Leslie's sanity. The prosecution countered with staff psychiatrists from the hospital, as well as a letter from the new superintendent stating that files showed Leslie was "without psychosis" when he ran away.

Every medical opinion presented by each side was at least a year old until the jury heard from a court-appointed psychiatrist who had seen Leslie on May 31, the day before the hearing began. Such a recent opinion carried extra weight, and the psychiatrist testified that Leslie was legally sane.

Closing arguments were scheduled for Thursday, June 3. That morning in Florida, two astronauts were fired into orbit, a launch in NASA's Gemini project to narrow the gap in the space race with the Soviets. Eyes around the world were lifted toward the sky. A reporter asked Leslie if he watched the rocket blast off on TV. "I'm not interested in space," he said, scowling.

"You've heard of his obsession with flowers and statues, of transvestite tendencies, that he was a female impersonator, and of his suicide attempts," a Wharton lawyer assisting Lloyd Lunsford recapped the testimony for the jury. "All this put together indicates he was over the line." A remedy was required. "The law indicates that he must be cured or kept."

The local D.A. emphasized a more recent chapter in Leslie's biography. "He left the state mental hospital in San Antonio and was gone for six months," Bob Bassett, the Wharton prosecutor, said. "Any man who can stay that long with all the officers in the United States looking for him certainly ain't crazy." Neil McKay, the assistant D.A. from Houston, said the year-old verdict was false. "Somebody hoodwinked twelve good citizens of Wharton County when a jury found him insane the first time."

Lloyd Lunsford spoke last, and he drew a vivid picture of insanity. "It's like in Biblical times when they cast out devils, and this man is full of devils. He has a history of homosexuality, he wears ladies' clothes." A queer transvestite possessed by Satan was not likely to find mercy, but Lunsford tried anyway. "I want you to think about that, and come back and do what should be done."

The jurors got the case on Thursday. By Friday afternoon at 12:15, after deliberating for ten hours, they had their verdict. Leslie was found legally sane at the present time. He showed no reaction to the decision, he just chatted quietly with his mother and his lawyers for a few moments before he went back to his cell in the Wharton jail.

Three weeks later, he wrote a letter to Judge Gupton. Leslie said he was willing to plea-bargain for the same sentence Carolyn had received: five years, plus credit for back time. If he could not cut that deal, he wanted the judge to set bail, "with each passing day being pinned up is cruel and unusual punishment for something I didn't do and am being treated like an animal solely to character purposes!"

Leslie's offer was not taken seriously. Lloyd Lunsford's legal wrangling stalled the murder trial all summer. Then Judge Gupton joined the list of people who had run out of patience with the case. Like Judge Love before him, he ordered a change of venue on his own motion, declaring two sanity hearings and publicity generated during the past four years from Houston, just sixty miles away, created "a great prejudice against the defendant" that ruined Leslie's chances for a fair trial, not only in Wharton County, but in every adjoining county as well. Judge Gupton moved the case two hundred miles away, where another small-town judge agreed to hear the big-city torch-murder trial.

35

Gatesville borders the northern edge of Fort Hood, approximately 350 square miles reserved for thousands of soldiers and the hardware for their war games. The vast army complex might have brought permanent prosperity to the seat of Coryell County, except craftier politicians in rival locales put the main entrance to the gigantic military base on the opposite end of the acreage. Towns on the south side of Fort Hood boomed; Gatesville picked up the scraps left at the back door.

In 1966, Gatesville was best known around Texas as the home of the state's reformatory for juvenile delinquent boys. (Now transformed into a women's prison.) "Going to Gatesville" was the underage euphemism for jail, but Leslie's trip had nothing to do with the reform school. On January 3, 1966, he turned twenty-eight in Gatesville's jail for grown-ups, an old-fashioned hoosegow facing raised sidewalks on the town's square. A sign on the weathered facade still warns pedestrians DO NOT CONVERSE WITH PRISONERS.

Across the street, the Coryell County courthouse remains a postcard model of pioneer Victorian rectitude. Blind justice holds her sword and scales on the roof; four clocks tick off the time on each side of the cupola. Courthouse insiders said Leslie Douglas Ashley's trial came to Gatesville because a local judge had statewide political ambitions. The grapevine gossips believed Judge Truman Roberts was eager to run for the Texas Court of Criminal Appeals. A small-town jurist needed to expand his name recognition to be a viable candidate, so Judge Roberts accepted changes of venue for high-profile trials from major cities.

Although an illness in Lloyd Lunsford's family delayed the trial further, the defense attorney did not hold off his bombardment of subpoenas. Lunsford sent a summons to Carolyn Lima at her mother's house, but she was gone. He tried to find her for three weeks before she finally surfaced. Carolyn said she had been on the road promoting a low-budget film based on the shooting. The title was lifted from a slogan born during the previous summer's Watts riots: *Burn, Baby, Burn.* Carolyn said she had made a quick stop to see her mother between publicity trips to hype the exploitation flick, then she was heading to Dallas for a personal appearance at a convention for drive-in theater owners.

Lunsford aimed another salvo of subpoenas at Frank Briscoe's relatives; ranchers and farmers and agents for the state Department of Agriculture living in the countryside south of Houston. Lunsford claimed the Briscoe clan made money off crops and livestock grown with inmate labor at prison farms in the fertile Brazos River bottomlands. The defense attorney contended his opponent's family had a history of turning a profit by sending people, innocent or guilty, to the penitentiary.

On January 31, 1966, Lucky Lunsford's charge became moot when Frank Briscoe resigned as Harris County district attorney. He had fought off the perjury indictment two years earlier, and he suffered another embarrassment the next year when the 1965 Code of Criminal Procedure took effect. The revised code carried explicit language about a D.A.'s obligations: "It shall be the primary duty of all prosecuting attorneys, including any special prosecutors, not to convict, but to see that justice is done. They shall not suppress facts or secrete witnesses capable of establishing the innocence of the accused." Briscoe's enemies said the new language was a response to his behavior when he shelved Dr. Crow's psychiatric report.

Despite the criticism he took within his profession, Frank Briscoe was not quitting under a cloud. He believed that he was going out on top, still popular with voters, and he was ready to test his political strength. Within a week of his resignation, he announced his plan to seek a seat in the U.S. Congress. Briscoe wanted to represent a newly created silk-stocking district on the shady side of Houston, where azaleas hedged the clipped lawns in front of immaculate homes. In the era before Republicans took over this constituency in Texas, Briscoe was sure that his best bet was a spot on the ballot in the Democratic primary scheduled for May.

Lucky Lunsford had been lobbing slurs about Fred A. Tones's reputation from the time he joined the case. Whenever he could, the defense attorney spread the story about the obscene phone calls Tones had made and how the real estate man had responded to the fake invitation from the woman he was harassing. Lunsford cranked up his innuendoes before the Gatesville trial and said Tones had escaped from a Connecticut prison in 1937 when he was being held on a burglary conviction before he changed his name from Salvadore Pasquale. Lunsford also alleged Tones was in a Florida prison on a sex offense in 1938. And, he accused the dead man of having a long list of vice arrests, ranging from child molestation to gay activity with adults.

In a different scenario, Lunsford said the victim was really Salvadore Noticelli, an illegal immigrant who had sneaked into the United States during the 1940s using dog tags stolen from the body of a dead GI named Fred A. Tones. It didn't seem to bother Lundsford that the years in his tales were inconsistent. Tones could hardly be Salvadore Pasquale, a convict in America during the Great Depression, as well as Salvadore Noticelli who slipped into the country after pilfering a new identity off a combat casualty during World War II, but Lunsford was not trying to make sense. The defense attorney just wanted to create doubt and confusion.

Besides his contradictory smears, Lunsford was fighting to postpone the trial. He made futile motions to overturn the change of venue, then asked the judge to order his client's release because Leslie Douglas Ashley had already spent four years in confinement, the same sentence Carolyn Lima had served. Judge Roberts said no, informing Lunsford the delays keeping Leslie behind bars were caused by the defense attorney's incessant motions and objections during the preliminary hearings.

Lunsford got so mad at being stymied that he called Judge Roberts "an arm of the prosecution," a jab that incensed the traditional Texan who had spent his career in small towns where the frontier was still alive for the generation that had raised and trained him. Judge Roberts was not inclined to let a slur pass and he asked if Lunsford was serious about the insulting outburst.

"I'm serious about defending my client," Lunsford fired back.

The pretrial maneuvering became an angry feud. "I don't know what got into Judge Roberts," a courthouse veteran recalled. "He just couldn't get along with that Houston lawyer." Neil McKay, the assistant D.A. from Houston, was still on the case, and he put the blame on his opponent. "Lloyd Lunsford couldn't get along with anybody," McKay said.

To get the case back on track, Judge Roberts granted Lunsford a "running bill of exceptions," sparing everyone in the courtroom from sitting through endless interruptions by giving the defense the right to cite anything in the transcript as the basis for an appeal. No judge likes to grant a blanket objection, but political ambitions can flounder if a jurist loses control of a high-profile case. Judge Roberts decided a drastic solution was necessary to move the trial forward.

Lunsford was still making motions on Monday, May 23, unable to stall any longer when jury selection finally began. The new Code of Criminal Procedure that chastised Frank Briscoe contained another section that caused a fundamental change in Texas trials, bringing the so-called bifurcated system of justice to the state. In the bifurcated system, juries decide between guilt or innocence, and if the answer is guilty they return to the courtroom to hear more testimony about the defendant's character before voting on the punishment.

Lawyers in Texas were still learning the new system in 1966. Lunsford had not tried a capital murder case under the new code. He was wary of traps he could not foresee and he put every potential juror through a grueling, convoluted series of questions. At times, he seemed to veer off into a stream of consciousness, reeling off any inquiry that crossed his mind. Judge Roberts finally had enough. "Mr Lunsford, the court doesn't even understand the question," he roared at one non sequitur.

While the judge and the lawyers argued, Leslie sat puffing one cigarette after another in the courtroom. The dark paneled walls, brass spittoons on the floor, and ceiling fans that swept his smoke out the slatted windows created a model setting for rural justice while Leslie twitched and giggled—like "laughing at a funeral," Lloyd Lunsford remarked.

The first week ended with only seven jurors seated. The slow pace did not bother Leslie. He smiled and posed for photos as he was shuttled back and forth to his jail cell. Except for his persistent giggle, he never caused any trouble. "His mama tried though," Judge Roberts said later. "That mama of his was something else." Sylvia gave a running commentary from the gallery, blurting her opinions of the tactical jousting to the other spectators.

"I told her if she opened her mouth one more time I'd bar her from the courtroom," the judge recalled. After the warning, Sylvia remained silent.

It took almost two weeks to select the all-male jury. The panel was a mixture of ranchers, a merchant, a young high school chemistry teacher, government employees, and workers for Pentagon contractors at Fort Hood who preferred to live on the quiet side of the big army base. They made their homes in a part of the country where guns were common, even tanks and heavy artillery howitzers were part of the landscape, but female impersonators were harder to come across.

36

Carolyn Lima could not avoid her subpoena forever. She was in Gatesville, but unwilling to testify for either side so she invoked her "spousal privilege." She and Leslie had lived together and passed themselves off as husband and wife; she had signed "Carolyn Ashley" on the Rental Agreement for the .22 pistol. Under common law in Texas, they were married, so Carolyn could not be compelled to testify. She was dismissed by Judge Roberts without having to answer a single question.

Another reluctant witness could not evade questioning. Madeline Harlan hid inside her duplex on Griggs Road and refused to answer the door the first time a process server came to her home with a summons requiring her presence in Gatesville. The tragedy on her property had been a long humiliation; just two days after starting their investigation, a team of male homicide detectives dropped by to ask her for a pubic hair specimen. After five years, she did not want to cooperate anymore, but she could not dodge her subpoena. In Gatesville, she testified that she thought hammering caused the noise she heard on the other side of her wall during the evening her tenant was killed.

Betty Gutierrez, the bookkeeper who was in the duplex shortly before the shooting, had given a pubic hair sample too; the HPD put her specimen in a box normally used for confiscated narcotics. At the first trial, she was certain Leslie and Carolyn were the couple who came through the door that wet afternoon; five years later, she was not sure. She only saw the pair "for half a minute," she hedged. "I wouldn't want to swear it was them."

Lucky Lunsford jumped on the opportunity; a prosecution witness was no longer certain that she had seen the defendant at the murder site. Lunsford also tried to discredit the positive identification of the victim. He asked Kenneth Swatzel, the HPD ID expert, about an item sent to the police lab during the dead man's autopsy. The victim's severed left hand was in the plastic bag and Swatzel matched prints lifted from the singed fingers with records in police files taken from the right hand of a man known as both Fred A. Tones and Salvadore Pasquale. The conclusion was flawed, Lunsford argued, because the prints were made by different hands.

Forensic experts might disagree with him and consider the technique perfectly acceptable, but Lunsford wanted to weave doubt through the jurors' minds. He waved an FBI report and contended the bureau's archives exposed the victim's criminal history, but Judge Roberts refused to release the uncensored report. The copies he made public only contained the subject's two names, his physical description, and right-hand fingerprints. Every other entry, whether innocuous or incriminating, was rendered unreadable.

Lunsford lost his fight to enter the FBI report, so he fought harder to prevent the jury from hearing the transcript of the testimony given by Richard Ramirez at the original trial. Lunsford argued the devastating testimony was false, coerced by cops and prosecutors who had threatened to use the drifter's criminal record against him if he did not cooperate with them. Lunsford claimed Ramirez had repudiated his lies in conversations with the first defense attorney who had tried the case.

Jack Knight was willing to help Lunsford since Clyde Woody's work as Carolyn's attorney was finished and Woody was no longer part of the defense team. Knight had filed a $100,000 libel suit against Woody for derogatory comments his replacement had made about him in Houston newspapers after Woody became Carolyn's lawyer. His suit never went to court, but Knight got a measure of retribution by agreeing to be a rebuttal witness for the prosecution at Carolyn's retrial. His answers could discredit her attempt to retract the testimony she gave while he represented her. Judge Love refused to let the jury hear him, but the bad blood festered. Black Knight, Woody called him.

Lunsford did not share that sentiment, at least not publicly. With Carolyn free and Woody's work finished, Knight came to

Gatesville. Judge Roberts sent the jury from the courtroom while the original defense attorney repeated the results of private meetings with Richard Ramirez just weeks after his clients received death sentences.

Knight said Ramirez went along with the revisions that the prosecution put into his testimony because he did not think the verdicts would be so harsh. The death sentences rattled Ramirez, Knight said, and convinced him to reveal the truth.

Knight had told his story before, but this time he claimed that he had proof. He said that he had recorded a meeting at which Ramirez recanted his perjured testimony and a tape recorder was set up in the Gatesville courtroom. Everyone fell silent as Knight's tape hissed and scratched. Listeners strained to hear mumbled words that were noises without meaning. The golden evidence was inaudible. Knight's attempt to redeem himself turned into another belly flop, and the five-year-old testimony Ramirez gave in Houston was read to the jury.

The case in Gatesville had an impact on other trials around the state, and Judge Roberts blamed the defense attorney because Lunsford sent out more subpoenas than for any other case the judge had heard before. Too many of the defense attorney's potential witnesses were lawyers and jurists to suit Judge Roberts' taste. He said Lunsford's subpoenas "damn near closed the court system."

The case in Gatesville briefly stalled a murder trial about to begin in a county near Houston, where an airport mechanic was charged with raping and killing a woman he had abducted. Her body was found with threads matching the mechanic's coat in her dead grip; her hair was discovered in his car. The case against the mechanic looked strong, but his lawyer was Racehorse Haynes, who called the evidence circumstantial. Jury selection for the trial took a recess while Haynes went to Gatesville to describe his short, peripheral involvement in Leslie Ashley's case as the lawyer who almost represented Carolyn Lima.

A Houston court was slowed too. Judge Miron Love came to Gatesville to answer questions about a private conversation he had during the original murder trial.

"Didn't you once express an opinion when this man was in your court that he was nuts?" Lunsford asked.

"Yes," Judge Love replied. "I wouldn't mind being quoted on it." Being a transvestite indicated that Leslie was "crazy," Judge Love said, "somewhat crazy."

If the judge thought a defendant was incompetent, Lunsford contended the trial was invalid. Since the Houston trial was the opening link of a long chain, the defense attorney argued every procedure that followed was tarnished and the current trial should be stopped.

Judge Love explained his opinion was personal, not judicial, and had not influenced his behavior on the bench. He had no qualms about having read death sentences to Leslie Douglas Ashley and Carolyn Lima. "Their guilt had been judicially determined in my court," he said. "I had no other duty but a ministerial duty to pronounce sentence despite my personal opinion."

The jury was not allowed to hear Racehorse Haynes or Judge Love. When the panel returned to the courtroom, Lunsford focused on generating double doubts. He emphasized the prosecution's trouble putting Leslie at the scene of the crime, and he steadily questioned the victim's identity. Neil McKay called Mrs. Tones to erase any lingering suspicions about the burned body found on Avenue I. McKay had to nail down a positive ID of the dead man. After Carolyn's light sentence and Lunsford's aggressive defense tactics, the assistant D.A. wanted to make sure this verdict did not slip away from him, so he took a risk he had avoided for five years—he showed Mrs. Tones a photo of the scorched corpse.

The gruesome picture crushed her. She sank low in the witness stand and sobbed. Judge Roberts sent the jury from the courtroom while Dorothy Tones struggled to regain her composure. The defense immediately motioned for a mistrial. Ample evidence and plenty of testimony proved a charred body was found on Avenue I, Lunsford argued. The photo was "prejudicial and inflammatory, with no probative value." Provoking sobs from a witness to influence the jury was the only reason the prosecutors introduced the photo, he raged.

The prosecution had walked a thin line with the snapshot; Lunsford's charge was the reason the picture had not appeared during the previous trials. Prosecutors were more confident then; they did not need the grisly photo. The risk of a mistrial was not worth taking when the verdict was more certain; now Carolyn's surprising sentence and Lunsford's cagey defense changed their minds.

To block a mistrial, McKay turned Lunsford's objection against him. The defense was challenging the name of the man found in flames on Avenue I, so the prosecution was entitled to let the jury hear a positive, definite identification. Mrs. Tones could recognize the burned face, damaged but not destroyed by the fire. Besides, the widow's crying was not extreme enough to tilt the jury. She was a strong woman who had done her best to control herself.

Judge Roberts agreed. "There was no emotional outburst on the part of the witness," he ruled. "Only a few small tears." The judge denied the motion for a mistrial. Because Lunsford had risen with his motion before Mrs. Tones identified the body, the judge let the prosecution show her the photo again when the jury returned to the courtroom.

The widow did not cry when she looked at the awful picture a second time. "It's Fred," she whispered. "It's Fred Tones." Her voice never rose, "My husband."

The judge gave the defense one meager concession. He refused to let the jury see the photo because the horrible snapshot might prejudice them and create grounds for an appeal. Judge Roberts ruled the panel members would have to paint their own picture of the charred corpse from the widow's reaction.

Out of court, with no rules constraining him, Lunsford drew a twisted picture of the victim. With Mrs. Tones on the witness stand, he asked about her husband's background and their courtship, when her groom was allegedly in and out of prisons from Connecticut to Florida on charges ranging from burglary to sex offenses. Lunsford's questions raised objections from the prosecution and denials from the witness as he worked to prove Salvadore Pasquale became Fred A. Tones to hide a criminal history.

Mrs. Tones said she asked her husband to change his name. "I thought it was a cumbersome name," she testified. Fewer syllables might open more doors for him.

Lunsford launched onto another safari, tangling oblique questions into snarls the witness could not follow. Neither could Judge Roberts, who had reached the limit of his patience. He sent the jury from the courtroom and asked Lunsford what he was trying to accomplish with his cross-examination.

"It goes to the question of the deceased changing his name,"

Lunsford replied.

"No, it doesn't, Mr. Lunsford," Mrs. Tones interrupted. "The change of name was my decision, and that's the way it's going to be." Her voice was louder than before. "Does that answer your question, Mr. Lunsford?"

The defense attorney punched back. When the jury returned, he got Mrs. Tones to admit for the first time in open court that she never saw her husband's body after his death. Family friends went to the morgue to identify the corpse, she said. The funeral was a closed-coffin ceremony. Fred A. Tones was still alive when they spoke their final farewell before she rode off to the bus stop with her oldest son on a wet, winter morning.

The revelation restored life to Lunsford's claim that prosecution witnesses were creating certainties where the truth was more vague. The widow might identify a picture of a scorched corpse, but she never saw the body. Fingerprints from one hand were matched with prints lifted off a different hand. Lunsford claimed the prosecution could not even prove Fred A. Tones was dead. The victim's reputation and criminal history made Tones the kind of man who could pull a disappearing act, according to the defense attorney.

Lunsford's moment to back up his insinuations with proof was near, because the prosecution followed the pattern from previous trials and rested after Mrs. Tones finished her testimony. Lunsford had a hotel full of people to question waiting nearby. He had been scolded for sending out so many subpoenas, so he shocked everyone when he rose on Thursday morning, after four days of prosecution testimony, and rested without presenting a single witness.

"A poker-playing proposition," he said. His gamble was not impulsive. Lunsford realized testimony from rebuttal witnesses nearly killed his client at the original trial, and resting without calling any defense witnesses prevented the prosecution from mounting a rebuttal. The state had trouble putting Leslie at the scene of the shooting; if Neil McKay expected to fix that problem on rebuttal, he would not get the chance. Lunsford's stunning tactic was a slick maneuver that slammed the brakes on the trial, bringing an early finish with a screeching halt.

Sylvia Ayres gave another lawyer credit for the inspiration. "Racehorse Haynes talked Lunsford into resting that way," Leslie's mother said. She believed the famous defense attorney had convinced Lunsford to go for broke with the unusual strategy when Haynes came to Gatesville for the sidebar during the trial.

Leslie claimed he knew why Haynes made his suggestion, and the weakness of the prosecution case was not the reason. If Lunsford presented any witnesses at all, Leslie would have to testify to give a self-defense strategy credibility. Leslie believed Haynes could see that he made a terrible witness.

"Juries hated me," Leslie said, frowning.

Lunsford's abrupt curtain caught everyone by surprise and caused Judge Roberts to delay closing arguments until Friday morning, when Coryell County D.A. Byron McClellan blasted the defense attorney for turning the victim into a culprit. "Trying to try Fred Tones with every innuendo known," the local prosecutor told the jury. Lunsford was not only guilty of slander, waste was also one of his vices. The local prosecutor tried to count the outrageous number of witnesses that his rival had subpoenaed. "You couldn't have got them here with a Greyhound bus," the Gatesville D.A. scoffed. "Where are those witnesses?" he wondered, contending the defense quit early because its case was so flimsy.

The local D.A. then turned to Leslie. "What more loathsome motive can there be than shooting a man, robbing him, burning his body, then being found as a female impersonator in New York?" Neil McKay picked up the same thread. Leslie had murdered the real estate salesman because he "wanted to go back to the bright lights of Broadway." The killers proved their depravity after they shot their victim; they "took him to the dumping ground and threw him face down in a muddy ditch, poured gasoline all over him, and lit him up."

Lloyd Lunsford spoke for an hour and ten minutes, struggling to save Leslie by leading the jury back through the trial. "The state has failed of its proof," the defense attorney said. "It's gone on for four and a half years and it's time to end it." Actually, the case was more than five years old, but Lunsford started the clock when he came aboard. He claimed his opponents could not confirm the victim's identity, yet they withheld information about him that should influence the verdict.

"Have they been fair?" Lunsford asked. "Have they told you all the facts about this man?" Once more, the defense attorney waved police reports the jury was not allowed to see, "Did they tell you he was an escaped burglar?" Lunsford did his best to make the jury believe the missing links in the victim's background were filled with criminal mysteries.

He smeared Tones, then labored to redeem his client. "The prosecution has tried to make this man out to be a fiend," Lunsford said, aiming a finger at Leslie. "They say this man was in disguise," referring to the Hell's Kitchen bust in drag. "They say he was dressed in a long black dress, long black gloves, long black stockings, and moccasins." A gloom-and-doom ensemble. "Does that sound like a man of sound mind and discretion?" Lucky Lunsford offered his own verdict, "This man is pitiful."

37

After the closing arguments, Judge Roberts delivered his charge to the jury. The lecture sparked more fireworks, angering the defense attorney because the judge did not include instructions about murder without malice. The omission meant Leslie was not eligible for the lesser crime that matched Carolyn's conviction. He was going back to jail for murder with malice or he was not going back to jail at all.

The jurors started their deliberations around 1:30 Friday afternoon. Shortly after 5:00, Judge Roberts received a note telling him they wanted to quit because they were hopelessly deadlocked. Trials were fast in Texas, so were verdicts. Juries did not take long to make up their minds, even when they were deciding they could never agree.

Lunsford immediately motioned for a mistrial, but Judge Roberts refused to give him or the jury what they wanted. A stalemate for one afternoon was no reason to give up. The judge sequestered the panel for the night, telling them to sleep on their dilemma and get back to work at seven o'clock Saturday morning.

Rest recharged them. Muffled words from an angry argument were overheard in the hallway outside the jury room Saturday morning. Shortly after 10:00 A.M., they settled their differences. Leslie tried to stand up straight, but his posture slouched and his eyes blinked away tears when he heard the verdict: guilty of murder with malice. His mother sobbed loudly as Judge Roberts polled each member of the panel to confirm their unanimous decision.

The trial quickly shifted gears, moving into the penalty phase.

The prosecution called a procession of Houston police officers who said their sleuthing proved Leslie's reputation was "bad." What caused them to label him bad? He was a homosexual, they explained. On cross-examination, Lunsford wondered how they knew Leslie's sexual preferences. His effeminate mannerisms? Their personal experience? One by one, they admitted their conclusions about Leslie's sexual preference came from stereotypes and hearsay, but Lunsford did not try to challenge the link between being "bad" and being gay.

When he took over, the defense attorney put Dr. Neil Burch on the stand. Over the years, the psychiatrist had examined Leslie for both the prosecution and the defense. He always thought Leslie was sane, with mental problems below full-blown lunacy. "He is dependent on somebody else," the psychiatrist told the Gatesville jury, defining Leslie as "a passive dependent" who leaned on others. Lunsford wanted the panel members to believe Leslie's family could manage his passive streak if he was given probation, an option on any sentence of ten years or less.

Lunsford called Leslie's mother again. Sylvia Ayres was still sobbing from the guilty verdict when she said Leslie could work at his uncle's camera store if he did not have to go back to prison. Ted Kipperman testified that he was willing to place his nephew on the payroll at his new location in a shopping center on the south side of Houston if the jury gave Leslie probation.

The defense attorney finished by questioning the woman who managed the plant and pet department at the store where Leslie had bought his tall philodendron two days before the shooting. "I couldn't ask for a more polite person as a customer," she said.

Neil McKay would not let her paint a killer so kindly. Did she know Leslie was wearing a dress when he was arrested in New York? The witness answered no. Was she aware of this defendant's long list of drag busts before the shooting? No, again. Did she know her polite customer's divorce was due to his homosexual preferences? The manager of the plant and pet department replied no, she did not realize Leslie lost his wife because he would rather be with men.

After two hours of testimony, the attorneys made their closing speeches for the penalty phase of the trial. Leslie was "morally rotten from within," Neil McKay charged. "This man doesn't deserve to live among decent convicts," he said, reworking a pitch from the original trial, "or walk the sacred soil of Texas again as a free man," McKay ridiculed the sentence his opponent suggested. "I'm sure you won't give him probation and give him one free killing on the house."

Lunsford attacked the prosecution's case, "held together with bailing wire and chewing gum," he said. No one should be executed when the evidence was so feeble. Leslie deserved leniency. "There is no way this man can survive a long sentence in the penitentiary," Lunsford lamented.

The jury began to deliberate Leslie's sentence on Saturday afternoon. Again, an immediate impasse halted their progress and the foreman sent out a letter asking if the judge could grant probation without their recommendation. He could, but Judge Roberts did not give them a direct answer; he merely told the members of the panel to read his charge more carefully. The note was good news for Leslie because it implied the jury was haggling over a sentence in the ten-year range, the maximum penalty that could be probated by either judge or jury under the latest Code of Criminal Procedure.

The stalemate continued all afternoon. Judge Roberts received another note from the foreman saying they could vote on a punishment "until doomsday" without reaching an agreement. Lunsford filed another mistrial motion urging the judge to admit the panel was frozen. When the jurors had claimed to be hung over guilt or innocence, the judge had refused to dismiss them and they had found a middle ground, so he did not bend to them now.

"I'm going to lock you up tonight," Judge Roberts told them, "and let you get up tomorrow, maybe around seven o'clock, and start deliberating again."

The jury convened an hour after Judge Roberts suggested, and he stayed away from the courthouse until 5:30 Sunday afternoon before checking on them. Although the panel could not reach a unanimous decision, he saw a ray of hope because the latest split was ten to two. The judge would not reveal the specific punishment that was close to creating the consensus, but the foreman was not optimistic. The vote was not as narrow as it looked. The count had been shifting all day, he said.

Judge Roberts asked them to "try a little harder." Within thirty minutes, just before six o'clock, the jury returned without a decision, and a mistrial began to look like Leslie's best hope. The case became harder to prosecute as the years progressed, time was his ally. He and Sylvia were all smiles when the jury was gridlocked, but Judge Roberts destroyed their good mood when he refused to dismiss the jury.

"Gentlemen," he told the all-male panel, "this case has to be decided by someone sometime, by twelve reasonable people, and I don't know any place in the state of Texas where you could find more reasonable men than we have here." He finished the day with a final command, "Try it again tomorrow."

Lunsford believed the judge's Sunday-night decree gave the defense more grounds for a mistrial. He said the case did not have to be "decided by someone sometime." Any case could end with a hung jury, Lunsford argued. The judge's order "amounted to a comment on the weight of the evidence in this case, contrary to law," Lunsford said, but his latest motion for a mistrial was rejected. A jurist who wanted to run for a seat on a higher bench couldn't run on his record if his record was marred by bowing to indecisive juries or cranky defense attorneys.

The jury still remained in a knot before lunch on Monday. Lunsford made another mistrial motion, contending any decision now would be invalid, reached by a "captive jury" willing to shave their principles to get rid of a case Judge Roberts was determined to resolve. "A compromise verdict in violation of the law," the defense attorney said. The judge told the jury to keep voting.

The endurance Judge Roberts forced on the panel was finally rewarded. (So was he; in 1970, he was elected to the Texas Court of Criminal Appeals, where he sat for twelve years.) After three murder trials, a trio of sanity hearings, two cross-country dragnets, five years of legal maneuvering, stacks of subpoenas and transcripts, hotels filled with witnesses who never testified and others who came halfway across the country to the obscure, tiny town, the exhausted jurors doled out their punishment on Monday afternoon. For the crime of murder with malice, Leslie Douglas Ashley was sentenced to fifteen years in prison.

His skin, already pale, grew paler. He tried to stand up straight, but he could not hide his disappointment. His spine seemed to curl, bending under a burden stretching into his future.

"It's not fair," Sylvia wailed. Her son's punishment was three times harsher than Carolyn's. "She got five years, he got fifteen," Sylvia moaned as she pushed toward her only child.

At the center of their despair, Lloyd Lunsford was happy. He instantly dropped his combative tactics and accepted the entire verdict, waiving all of his motions for a new trial. Lunsford proclaimed that he would not appeal, and asked Judge Roberts to give Leslie credit for the jail time already served. The judge compromised too, promptly deducting four years, eight months and twenty-six days from the fifteen-year sentence. Leslie got credit for his time in the San Antonio asylum, but his months on the lam were not added to his ledger. He did his best to smile and offered his lawyer a half-hearted handshake.

"Any penalty is too much when it's inflicted on an innocent man," the defense attorney said, "but it beats the electric chair by a long shot." His high spirits combined faith and patriotism. "I'm proud to be part of the American miracle," Lucky Lunsford said, smiling.

Neil McKay had watched his original victories erode from a pair of death penalties to a couple of mild sentences. One of the defendants he nearly had executed was already out of prison; the other was facing less time than hippies who were being convicted for smoking marijuana in the Lone Star State during 1966.

In Houston, Leslie's verdict made bigger headlines than a landmark legal ruling that shared the front pages. On the same Monday, July 13, 1966, the Supreme Court announced a joint decision on four cases that would profoundly change the way police treated suspects under arrest. The high court published its opinion under the title *Miranda* v. *Arizona*, although the milestone could have been named Vignera, Westover, or Stewart, appellants in the other cases brought together in the unified ruling. They had all been convicted at trials where statements they made to police during "custodial interrogation" were allowed into evidence.

In the opinion he wrote, Chief Justice Earl Warren said the Fifth Amendment required "a full and effective warning" of the right against self-incrimination, and the new ruling specified the warnings that became known as *Miranda* rights: the right to remain silent, a caution that any statements suspects made could be used against them, the right to have a lawyer at all times during interrogation, and explicit notice of the right to be provided with a lawyer when suspects could not afford an attorney.

Leslie Douglas Ashley and Carolyn Lima had been given death sentences at a trial where the oral confession Carolyn made to the FBI was admitted as evidence. Before she talked to the federal agents, they had warned her that she did not have to speak with them and that anything she said could be held against her. She was also told that she had the right to consult an attorney before she was questioned. Carolyn waived her rights despite those cautions, nearly putting herself and Leslie in the electric chair. Five years later, those model FBI warnings were no longer adequate because they did not include explicit use of the words "right to remain silent" or notice of the right to have an attorney provided without charge.

Their lawyers found a different way to save Leslie and Carolyn since other rights had been violated to convict them. Still, they came within four hours of joining every prisoner executed prior to 1966 who gave a confession without being "Mirandized." Leslie heard his new sentence on the same day those warnings were published.

Frank Briscoe had to swallow a sour irony. He had defeated himself by suppressing the psychiatric report. After the appeal, when defense lawyers were able to use Dr. Crow's conclusions, even reinforced by other medical opinions, they still could not convince a jury that Leslie was legally insane at the time of the shooting. Also, defense attorneys made three attempts at having him declared currently insane and only succeeded once. With a solitary exception, the report had failed to persuade juries, and the psychiatric report saved the defendants *only* because it was suppressed by the D.A.

The appeal pivoted on the concealed report; all other arguments failed. If Briscoe had not suppressed the report, Leslie Douglas Ashley and Carolyn Ann Lima would have been dead for three years before *Miranda* had given them another path to pursue. The D.A. concealed evidence he did not need to hide; Leslie and Carolyn lived because he went too far. Judge Miron Love, the original trial judge, branded the behavior prosecutorial misconduct. If Frank Briscoe had played fair, the two death sentences would have stuck.

That winter, Frank Briscoe's political aspirations were stymied, but his problems did not come from his record as district attorney. As the Democrat on the ballot for a seat in the U.S. Congress, he was handicapped by President Lyndon Johnson's unpopularity with potential constitutents, conversative residents in Houston's most prosperous neighborhoods who were opposed to the Great Society's liberal giveaways and were alienated by LBJ's reluctance to obliterate Vietnam with an all-out push for military victory.

Although the ex-D.A. did his best to distance himself from the leader of his party by staking out positions to the right of his Republican rival, his campaign failed. "I've been elected to practice law," Briscoe said when he conceded. "I've always said my first defeat will be my last."

Frank Briscoe announced his retirement from politics, while his triumphant opponent—the first Republican sent to Congress from Harris County in nearly a century—began a career that took him to the top. The victorious candidate who beat Frank Briscoe was a Yankee transplant with a bright future named George Herbert Walker Bush.

38

For five years, defense attorneys had tried to sculpt memories of the dead man into the crooked image of a gargoyle. Stolen dog tags, prison escapes, hidden sexual kinks. By the end, Lucky Lunsford claimed the prosecution could not even prove the charred corpse belonged to Fred A. Tones, a.k.a. Salvadore Pasquale.

Confusion was easy to create around him after his death because he had encouraged confusion during his life. Salvadore Pasquale was not Italian, despite what his wife told homicide detectives after the shooting. Salvadore Pasquale was not quite Salvadore Pasquale, but Salvador Pascual.

The documents he used to enter the United States said he was born near the end of 1913 in Spain, along the Mediterranean shore south of Valencia, where citrus orchards gave the region its name, the Costa del Azahar (in English, the Coast of Orange Blossoms). Salvador Pascual lived with his parents in the village of Oliva, where he became a brickmason. Then, around the time he turned twenty-one, he moved up the coast to Barcelona, a city modernizing more quickly than the rest of his isolated country, but the move did not last and he was back in his native town within a year.

No one found tranquility for long during those years in Spain. In June, 1936, a few months before Pascual's twenty-third birthday, right-wing army officers rebelled. Within a month, one hundred thousand Spaniards were dead and the Civil War was just beginning. The sentiment around Valencia was strongly loyalist, remaining behind the republican government that Francisco

Franco and his fascists fought to topple. Like many of his neighbors, Salvador Pascual joined the Republican army and he stayed until the bitter end when, along with four hundred thousand other Spanish refugees, he fled into France over the Pyrenees Mountains as the last outposts against fascism fell in 1939.

Salvador Pascual was consigned to an internment camp in the deepest corner of southern France. Four months later, he crossed the Atlantic, entering Mexico as an *emigrante politico,* a political refugee, but he had his eye on the United States. An older brother had already settled in Connecticut after leaving Spain almost twenty years earlier. By 1939, Salvador's sibling, Francisco Pascual, had Americanized his first name to Frank but he had not found a pressing reason to become a United States citizen. With a little brother south of the border who needed a citizen vouching for him to enter the United States legally, Frank Pascual made the move to be naturalized.

Salvador waited in Chihuahua, a cowboy city in the northern desert, until Frank became a citizen in 1941. At the time, two backers were required for a permanent residency visa, so Salvador's older brother paired up with another naturalized Spanish expatriate, a coworker at the factory in New Britain, Connecticut, where he was employed. With their names behind him, Salvador filed his application at the United States consulate in Chihuahua. The approval took two months, but the wait for an opening in the immigration quota for Spaniards took two years.

Instead of remaining in Chihuahua or traveling north to bide his time in a border town, Salvador Pascual went south to Mexico City. By the summer of 1943, his name had moved to the top of the quota roster. However, he needed more documents to finalize his preparations, and straightening out paperwork took extra effort for a man without a country. To comply with U.S. immigration laws, he supplied an affadavit signed by two witnesses who swore that he was a twenty-nine-year-old Spaniard whose birth certificate could not be retrieved because he was a political refugee. He added another mandatory document, a report showing he had no criminal record in the Mexican capital.

On the last day of July 1943, Pascual brought his portfolio to the U.S. Embassy. Since he had no Spanish passport, he traveled on temporary papers issued by a Portuguese consular office watching over Spanish interests in Mexico. He filled out a form stating his intention to live with his brother in New Britain, then answered the requisite questions attesting that he had never been in jail or prison, and neither he nor his parents had ever been hospitalized for insanity.

An American consul looked over his papers and issued the visa that qualified an immigrant to become a permanent resident of the United States. The fee for the golden key was one dollar. A little more than a month later, Salvador Pascual crossed the international bridge connecting Nuevo Laredo, Mexico, with Laredo, Texas, where he stepped onto United States soil on September 4, 1943.

Even before he entered his new country, Salvador was going through the identity drift that blurs the biographies of so many immigrants. Because it is customary for Spaniards and Latin Americans to include the mother's maiden name on the end of childrens' formal names, he was used to signing papers Salvador Pascual Barreres, which did not alter the fact that his surname was Pascual in the Hispanic world. Because Anglo record keepers filed his papers under Barreres, his documents frequently went astray.

Eventually, he began to transpose his surnames, but he had already seen Salvador Pascual, the name he considered genuine, entered on immigration papers on the line marked ALIAS. His birth date was inconsistent as well. On a visa application filed in Chihuahua in 1941, he was born October 15, 1913; two years later in Mexico City, his birthday was November 13, 1913. Typos, mis-understandings, clerical errors. The actual date he was born, like his name, shifted constantly. His height fluctuated just above five feet. A couple of inches, a month more or less, the elements of a foreign name out of sequence, none of the discrepancies raised any red flags. Mismatched names and dates are common in immi-gration files. Salvador Pascual began to realize he could be who-ever he wanted to be in his new home.

In January 1944, as he settled into New Britain, he submitted a Declaration of Intention form, the next step on his way to natural-ization. Declaring his intention to become a U.S. citizen was easy, finding a way to become eligible could be trickier, but a new law gave him an opening. After Pearl Harbor, the U.S. Congress eased the obstacles, "to further expedite the prosecution of the war," the addition to the naturalization code began. The revision made any honorably discharged alien who served in the U.S. military during World War II immediately eligible for citizenship.

Salvador Pascual joined the army on March 20, 1944, becoming a private in a combat support unit where he was trained to pass out supplies near the front lines to the GI's who did the actual fighting. Just five months later, during the peak of the war when allied armies were pushing deeper into Europe and marines were crawling across bloody beaches in the Pacific, he suddenly became a civilian again and stepped into private life through the gates of Fort Dix in New Jersey.

His discharge was swift, but honorable. He went back to New Britain and applied for work at the factory where his brother was employed. He made sure to mention his honorable discharge on his questionnaire, but Salvador Pascual failed to include a detail about that discharge.

According to the War Department document in his citizenship file, he left the army after only five months on August 13, 1944, under Section VIII, Regulation 615–360: "Discharge because of inaptness or undesirable traits of character." Salvador Pascual was not recommended for reenlistment or induction. The glitch did not impede his citizenship; he was still eligible under the act granting quick naturalization to immigrant veterans.

Technically, his discharge was honorable despite the Section VIII stigma, although the language about "undesirable traits of character" was not consistent with oaths on affadavits that his witnesses signed to support his citizenship petition. Two neighbors, both women who listed their occupation as housewife, swore Salvador Pascual was a man of "good moral character." They had known him for two months, since his release from the army.

On his Petition for Naturalization dated October, 1944, Pascual answered "not" in front of married, and "no" before children. The son who was eighteen during the May, 1961 murder trial would have been born when these answers were given. On the final petition, when Salvador Pascual had a chance to choose a new name merely by filling in a blank line, he entered "none desired." A routine check to determine if any deportation proceedings were pending against him turned up negative, and his petition was approved.

On July 13, 1945, exactly eleven months after leaving the army, he signed an oath of allegiance to the United States. On the Certificate of Naturalization that Salvador Pascual received in Hartford, his dark eyes stared from a photo beneath the Great Seal of his new country with the American eagle clutching arrows in one set of claws and an olive branch in the other.

Salvador B. Pascual, the name he signed, was not smiling in the photo. He made a last-minute minor adjustment, scratching out the troublesome middle initial in his signature beneath the photo attached to his certificate of citizenship.

Two atom bombs ended the war less than a month after Salvador Pascual became an American. He was restless during peacetime and caromed back and forth between New Britain and Chicago. Michael Tones, the son who did not exist on the citizenship forms, recalled living "in an army base in Connecticut." He knew his father had another identity, but they used the last name Tones.

They had been living in Texas for several years before Salvador Pascual legally changed the family name. He left his past in ashes, even blurring the identity he gave up. The request to change his name to Fred A. Tones (the middle initial stood for nothing) was filed by Salvadore Pasquale, not Salvador Pascual, part of the campaign to pass himself off as Italian in a region without a large Italian community that might call his authenticity into question. During the Spanish Civil War, many of his peers on the Republican side despised the Catholic faith. Priests were brutalized; churches were destroyed. If Salvador Pascual shared those anticlerical sentiments, he abandoned them in his new guise and joined the Knights of Columbus, a brotherhood celebrating Catholicism.

The brickmason from the landscape of citrus groves was slicing his wedge from the American pie. In a foreign language, he sold an ideal—hustling shelter as a solid investment in the rising tide of postwar prosperity. Fred A. Tones fit the profile for his adopted homeland. Breadwinner, businessman, pillar of his faith, owner of the biggest car his credit could leverage. But every work-ethic virtue was mirrored by a vice. He allegedly flashed his penis at his secretary, beat up a fellow real estate salesman, and made obscene telephone calls to another man's wife.

The sharp eyes staring from Salvador Pascual's naturalization certificate looked weary years later in a mugshot pulled from the HPD file that contained matching fingerprints lifted from the hands of his charred corpse. The skin sagged from his high cheek-

bones. He had dyed what was left of his thinning hair. He lied
about his age. Salvador Pascual was born near the end of 1913,
but Fred A. Tones was a couple of years younger.

Salvador Pascual came from the Coast of Orange Blossoms. He
finished stripped to his T-shirt and synthetic socks, shot six times
just moments after showing off his erection, then left burning in
mud and weeds near the black sludge of a polluted port where
burning gas and sulfur fouled the air.

The Veterans Administration paid for the flat bronze headstone
in the Catholic section of the cemetery where he lies. Under a
small, unadorned cross raised in the metal, the history of his
immigrant odyssey is lost in the inscription for a man who could
be somebody else:

†

FRED A TONES
ILLINOIS
CPL   230 QM SALVAGE CO
WORLD WAR II   BSM
APRIL 27, 1916   FEB 6, 1961

His headstone made him a corporal in a quartermaster salvage
company that collected equipment from pockmarked battlefields.
After the war, Illinois was his temporary home, temporary like so
many places during his life. The birthdate matches none of his
records. BSM (bronze star medal) is a decoration for heroism over
the remains of an enigma.

None of his kin are buried with him. He lies alone in a hastily
purchased grave, an odd plot with no room left for any relations
to be laid to rest beside him.

A clue to the fatal traits that put him in the black ground might
be dug from the Section VIII discharge that ended his brief
stretch in the army. Serving Uncle Sam gave him his claim to citizenship, but something during that hitch may have foretold the
nature of his death. "Inaptness or undesirable traits of character."
Those records were stored at a vast federal archive in Saint Louis.
On July 12, 1973, a fire destroyed a wing of the building where
thousands of military records were filed, and the records of Salvador B. Pascual were lost in the blaze. A piece of his past, like the
man himself, went up in flames.

FIVE

Born to Live

39

"You should've seen me chopping cotton," Leslie said, laughing about sweating on work gangs in Texas prison farms, usually shortened to P-farms.

His first stop was a unit south of Houston where overcrowded cellblocks were surrounded by acres of fertile fields. Leslie had no aptitude for tilling crops under the hard discipline of stern guards, but he quickly found a way to escape the brutal stoop labor. He said a well-oiled ring was already established, trading privileges and protection, roll-call substitutes, and black-market goods for sex inside the unit. For years, Leslie had made his living on the outside as a prostitute, so he went straight to work with the leaders of the P-farm sex trade, turning the physical desires of other inmates to his advantage.

Leslie earned presents for lovers he wanted to impress and he pampered himself too. Before long, he had other inmates picking his cotton, but he still had to dump the loads from his bags into trucks headed for the gins. He claimed his sexual prowess guaranteed that the inmates who picked his cotton turned in the biggest bags. "I could hardly empty those things," Leslie groaned.

He believed that he pushed the limits of the sex ring at the unit. With his talent, Leslie said, the network hit a peak that worried the warden, who decided to transfer him. "Because I had so many love affairs," Leslie said, snickering. He was moved to a unit called Wynne, which Leslie claimed was a P-farm for "nutcases." Aging prisoners who became senile and masochistic inmates who mutilated themselves were moved there. The warden at Wynne determined Leslie needed a different style of supervision, so he was shipped to a unit with a savage reputation—Eastham, a snakepit north of Huntsville tucked between the pine trees of two national forests, one named for Sam Houston and the other for Davy Crockett.

Eastham broke hard guys. The guards built personal legends with cruelty that equaled the violence inmates had on their records. A cold eye might have predicted Leslie would wind up at the bottom of a fertilizer pile. Instead, he thrived. The warden kept a tight lid on Eastham, so there was no flagrant sex ring to create an inmate power structure that threatened his authority. Ironically, Leslie's promiscuous behavior balanced the severe discipline. His bunk-hopping softened the edge on the rigid, pressurized atmosphere.

"I was the warden's girl," Leslie bragged.

As a reward, for the behavior that made the warden's job easier, Leslie was taken out of the fields, and installed in the radio room, where he could keep up morale, broadcasting wisecrack adlibs across the penal colony. He eventually made trustee, a rank that let him wander around more freely and sidestep the scrutiny of hostile guards, but his rise up the P-farm pecking order did not help him with the parole board. Starting in 1968, his case was reviewed every year and promptly rejected in an annual ritual of futility.

Leslie did his best to take what prison offered him. He earned his GED, the equivalent of a high school diploma, through a remedial education program offered by the Department of Corrections. He also met two major heartthrobs behind bars; Leslie was partial to Latin lovers. One was a prisoner named Mendoza, but they were not completely compatible. "He was too big for me," Leslie said. The other inmate's name was Perez, and their connection was better.

Leslie could work up nostalgia for the stretch in prison. His love life was decent. The meals on the P-farm were good, mostly fresh meat and vegetables tended by the prisoners. The Texas Department of Corrections used food as a pacifier. TAKE ALL YOU WANT, EAT ALL YOU TAKE was the motto that hung in penitentiary cafeterias.

After he was off death row, he had companions in the prison population so he did not need to maintain his network of penpals. His obsession with the Bible lapsed when he had opportunities for sex.

Misbehavior only delayed Leslie's optimum "good time" schedule a few months. On December 15, 1971, exactly five years, five months and two days after his second murder conviction, he was released.

Like most ex-cons, Leslie found freedom was an abrupt transition, and he tried to ground himself by renewing old friendships. A little after 2:30 on a night in May 1972, a pair of Houston police officers pulled him over in his beat-up car on a street in the East End. They planned to cite him for driving without a light over his rear license plate, a convenient excuse to stop a suspicious vehicle.

The cops figured they had a weirdo on their hands as soon as Leslie opened his mouth because he told them he was out "testifying for the Lord," an unlikely after-hours avocation. (Much later, he admitted that he was looking for his P-farm lover Mendoza, who was living in the East End barrio.) The cops decided to radio for a warrant check and the response alarmed them — Leslie Douglas Ashley was still wanted for murder.

The police officers took Leslie into custody until the outdated HPD files were corrected with a few phone calls the next morning. Police-beat reporters jumped at a chance to chat with him. Leslie always made good copy. He told them he was unemployed, living with his mother and stepfather, preaching, and writing an autobiography. He had not tried to contact Carolyn.

Leslie gradually lost interest in his book and he did not preach often after his release from prison. He used a pseudonym to get a job in a restaurant, resuming an occupation that had fed him when he was a fugitive from the mental hospital. He was not happy with the dull work, so he tried the stage again, but wigs and gowns could not hide his past. He refused to become a freak attraction with whispered billing as the Death Row Drag Queen. Prostitution was out too. "When you're young, you can sell it." Leslie quoted an old adage of the trade. "When you're old, you can't give it away."

He moved in with Mendoza for awhile, but his P-farm boyfriend got drunk one night and held a knife to his throat. Leslie did what he had always done when he needed to pack up a load of furniture. "I called mother and moved my stuff out of there the very next day." Mendoza moved too. Leslie heard he was killed in Los Angeles.

Leslie tried to reunite with another prison lover, but Perez
could not go straight. They were sexually compatible, but Leslie
decided to give him up. Perez was into drugs, constantly surrounded by trouble. "If I'm going back to jail I'll go back for the
same reason I went, because somebody was fucking with me, not
because of no pills or cocaine," Leslie pledged.

40

Sylvia and Jim Ayres had opened their own business, called Sylvia Ayres Realty because she held the license. The irony of following Fred A. Tones's profession was not lost on Jim and Sylvia. They even moved their office into a converted bungalow, except they took the whole house, not half of a duplex. Over the years, their neighborhood became home for many African-Americans, but Jim and Sylvia did not join the white flight. They stayed to wrangle mortgage deals for homebuyers with low cash and bad credit, plus they managed rentals for absentee landlords. They kept their enterprise alive and invested their surplus in local properties.

They had enough money to help Leslie when he discovered his taste for kitsch could pay off. Jim and Sylvia gave him the cash to set up a booth at a swap meet where underfunded entrepreneurs turned a self-storage miniwarehouse complex into an impromptu flea market. Vendors sold auto parts, tools, and cut-rate razor blades. A barber clipped hair; a palm reader told fortunes. Leslie displayed his cheap treasures and business was good. A storefront in Montrose followed, then an even bigger space for a resale shop in the Heights.

Leslie and Sylvia remained close. Mother and child liked to get away together to the flamboyant drag shows in New Orleans. In the French Quarter, Leslie saw a transvestite with breast implants and the quality of the surgical procedure impressed him. "Mother, I'm gonna get me some of those!" Leslie yelled. "Where'd you get them titties?" he asked the object of his envy. Leslie acted on the information. "I got myself some knockers!" His mother and stepfather paid for the operation.

307

Leslie said the breast implant surgery was hard, "the most painful thing I've ever gone through." After leaving the hospital, he passed out in a restaurant, but the ordeal did not destroy his wish to become "a real woman," Leslie declared. In fact, Leslie said enduring the pain of the breast surgery instilled the courage to go all the way with a sex change—"sexual reassignment surgery" in medical parlance.

The urge to change his gender had always been in Leslie's thoughts. His desire for a sex change went back to his adolescence in the 1950s, when the surgery was in its infancy. Christine Jorgensen, the most famous transsexual of the era, had her operation in 1952. By 1976, not long before Leslie decided to have the procedure done, *Newsweek* estimated 3,000 transsexuals were living in the United States alone.

Around the age of forty, Leslie began taking female hormones, but could not get final approval for the procedure from a sex-change program at a hospital in Houston. Leslie did not want to go through with the normal sequence of acid peels to get rid of his whiskers and cosmetic surgery to refine his facial features into more feminine proportions. He wanted his genitals transformed, nothing more. Leslie went to Baltimore, where the Gender Identity Clinic at Johns Hopkins required a rigorous screening process that included religious and psychological counseling. He was not accepted there either.

Leslie still had a temper. At the beginning of 1981, he was arrested for pulling a pistol in a bar, a felony with prison potential because of his criminal record. He did not retain Lucky Lunsford as his attorney; his new lawyer plea-bargained a deal reducing the indictment to a misdemeanor, "rudely flashing a firearm." The prosecution dropped the enhancement paragraph that would have increased the penalty against an ex-convict, and the judge waived the standard ten-day sentence for the charge, but kept a one hundred-dollar fine and sixty dollars for court costs, a small price for a defendant with death row on his résumé.

Around the same time Leslie was resolving his latest legal problem, he finally found a doctor willing to perform the sex-change operation. John Sealy Hospital in Galveston, the original medical school in the University of Texas system, had developed an excellent burn ward, and the program created for correcting damage caused by fires spawned a surgical department with the skill to fabricate all kinds of anatomical parts.

Leslie checked into the huge healing complex. "Chop it off and throw it in the bayou!" was his command at John Sealy. He was castrated and given a penectomy, the surgical term for amputating a penis; then a shallow cavity was created for a vagina, which was lined with skin grafts and tissue saved from his scrotum to provide the possibility for erotic sensations during intercourse.

She awoke from the anesthesia as Leslie Elaine Green, retrieving a surname from Leslie Douglas Ashley's life on the lam in Chicago after he escaped from the insane asylum. She convalesced and kept her resale business, for awhile, but the operation had an unexpected effect on her. Leslie Elaine Green did not share Leslie Douglas Ashley's obsession with kitsch and clutter. She cleared the statues and flowers from her household decor. After a rainstorm collapsed the roof of her shop, she had no interest in rebuilding her business, so she sold off her inventory to a new owner.

Leslie's trademark giggle also vanished. When she laughed now, she had a reason. She did not share the invisible comedy that had kept Leslie Douglas Ashley in stitches. Her interest in sex waned as well. "She got to be like me that way," Sylvia said. Leslie had never liked penetration, and the painful surgery diminished her sexual drive and prompted her to withdraw from intimate contact since she could not have genuine female orgasms. Over a decade into her new gender, Leslie said she could count her post-operative romances on the fingers of one hand. She even claimed that she had gone ten years without sex.

Though Leslie did not regret becoming "a real woman," she was not pleased with the quality of her operations. Her left breast implant ruptured. Luckily, she had opted for saline, so she did not have to worry about side effects from silicone draining through her body, although she was left with a lopsided figure. She complained about her shallow vaginal work too. She envied the craft of deeper, flawless reconstructions done in England.

Leslie and Sylvia made a hometown pilgrimage to Hot Springs, Arkansas, not long after the sex-change surgery. "I wanted them hillbillies to see who I am," Leslie recalled. The visit did not please her father. "I disapprove of the whole situation down there," Leslie Sherman Ashley said. He had remarried and built a respected niche for himself, serving twenty-five years as an alderman on the Hot Springs city council, finally leaving office at the end of 1982.

After his retirement, Leslie Sherman Ashley continued to give something back to his community as a volunteer in a program for senior citizens. Although he rebuffed a chance to learn more about his ex-wife or his son who had become a daughter, his first family shared his interest in politics.

41

KILLER TRANSSEXUAL IN RUNOFF FOR COUNTY CHAIR. On March 14, 1990, Leslie was back on the front page of the *Houston Chronicle*, albeit near the bottom. She finished second, gaining more than one-quarter of the total vote in the primary election to choose a leader for the Democratic Party in Harris County. She no longer used the surname Green. Instead, she ran as Leslie Elaine Perez, taking her new identity from her P-farm lover.

"That Leslie, she's smart as a whip," her mother crowed. After the sex change, Sylvia quit calling her child Douglas.

The first-place finisher had a rational explanation for Leslie's strong showing, "When people are looking at the ballot without knowing the candidates, they're apt to be partial to a female or someone with a Hispanic last name."

"The only reason he's in the runoff is because of his last name," Leslie countered. "I'm as qualified as he is, except he has that last name." Leslie's runoff rival was Ken Bentsen, Jr., a thirty-year-old nephew of Lloyd Bentsen, longtime U.S. Senator, former vice-presidential nominee, who became treasury secretary under President Clinton.

Democratic powerbrokers hoped the young frontrunner would add the Bentsen luster to the local party. Stung by Leslie's success, they labeled her showing a fluke based on ethnic deception and pressured her to withdraw from the race. Despite their dismay at the prospect of being led by an ex-convict transsexual, Democratic insiders had to confess that Leslie had put in nearly ten years of legwork for them.

The seed of Leslie's late-blooming political career dated back to

311

Sylvia's frantic campaign to save her son from the electric chair by rounding up petition signatures and pleading for clemency. Sylvia discovered she had a flair for political activism. She liked making speeches and badgering bureaucrats. After she started her real estate business, Sylvia decided that organizing a voting bloc would enhance her stature in the community, maybe even channel a few tax dollars into her neglected neighborhood to prevent the properties she represented from losing their meager value. She and Jim Ayres headquartered a group called South Central Democrats at their office, where precinct maps and policy pamphlets were mixed with deeds and property-tract diagrams.

Much calmer with her gender reversed, Leslie followed her mother into the back rooms behind public forums. Her politics had changed since 1964 when she passed out Goldwater leaflets on sidewalks in Chicago; now she was a liberal. Leslie and Sylvia were among the first whites to join Jesse Jackson's Rainbow Coalition in Texas. Leslie snapped a picture of her mother standing beside Reverend Jackson. The photo hangs on the wall at Sylvia Ayres Realty.

Leslie stuck out within Democratic party circles, attracting plenty of attention with her basso profundo drawl, her outspoken leftist slant, and her obvious transsexual persona, but almost no one connected her with Leslie Douglas Ashley. The politicians who *were* aware of her history accepted her unseen drudgery when she volunteered to support them by licking envelopes or making phone calls.

Leslie earned a seat at the party's state convention in 1984 and again four years later. She also got involved in gay community issues, where she was less willing to compromise. Her knack for conflict created more enemies than allies within mainstream groups like Houston's Gay and Lesbian Political Caucus.

AIDS became Leslie's special interest. In 1988, she organized the local chapter of ACT UP (AIDS Coalition To Unleash Power) and proclaimed herself president, but her abrasive leadership caused turbulence in the group created for confrontation. The turmoil of her tenure launched her into controversy, but her fights and her past were not public until she won the spot in the political runoff.

GIVE LESLIE THE CHAIR was her secret campaign slogan, and she started to put the motto on T-shirts before she decided that a bet-

ter investment would be simple yard signs bearing her new surname in big, bold letters. With Sylvia riding shotgun, Leslie
drove their faded gas-guzzling Oldsmobile all over Houston. She
pounded hundreds of her blue and white PEREZ placards into the
roadside.

Party bosses could not scratch her name from the ballot. Her
murder conviction disqualified Leslie from public office, but the
Democratic chair was a private party position, unsalaried, with no
filing fee or restrictions to exclude candidates. Leslie had not violated any rules by running, and she could vote for herself too. In
Texas, felons regain their right to cast ballots five years after com-
pleting their sentences.

"I've worked in Democratic politics for years now, and they're
trying to force me out," Leslie griped. "I'm going to win this
thing," she vowed, although she was not considered a serious
challenger by anyone but herself and party bosses worried by the
slightest prospect of an upset in the runoff. They stacked a solid
front against Leslie, building an unbroken wall of endorsements
for Ken Bentsen Jr. The Gay and Lesbian Political Caucus backed
him, so did the county Democratic Executive Committee, which
traditionally remained neutral.

Many Latinos who had punched their primary ballots for Perez
changed their minds when they learned her true genealogy. A
crew from a Spanish-language television station interviewed her,
and realized her *castellano* vocabulary did not extend past *margarita*. Leslie denied that she switched her identity from Green to
Perez before the race to attract unsuspecting voters. Although she
tried to claim authentic roots, contending her paternal grandmother was named Mary Valdez, away from the camera she confessed, "I'll take the Fifth on that one."

Leslie wanted the coverage to disregard her past, as well as her
arbitrary name, and focus on her platform, which boiled down to
one issue—working to get Democrats elected. She refused to
believe her opponent could do the job better, despite his family
connections, and she tried to prove her point by working hard to
bring herself a victory. In a plaid cowgirl shirt, oversized dark
glasses and a ponytail dangling from beneath her ACT UP base-
ball cap, Leslie could frequently be seen jaywalking across busy
streets with her load of PEREZ signs paid for by her own family.

Although the media exposed her past, Leslie convinced herself thousand of uninformed voters were unaware she was not really a Latina. She and her small troupe, a couple of close friends, planted PEREZ signs for blocks through the East End barrio, lining Navigation Boulevard past 78th Street, right around the corner from the vacant lot where Fred A. Tones's body was burned.

Miles away in the Heights, reporters found Mae Lima still living in her cottage perched on cinderblocks. The sign for her beauty parlor stood in the lawn, and she had added a "reduction salon" to the services she offered. Mae still had the mental discipline to block out unpleasant thoughts. The shooting, the trials, the death-row vigil, the entire case was "something I've been able to put out of my mind." Carolyn was married, she said, no longer living in Houston, but Mae would not reveal where she was.

Election day was wet and gray. Leslie's adversaries in the gay community, who did not want her for a role model or a spokesperson, defaced her signs on the esplanade of Montrose Boulevard. Instead of simply stealing the placards, vandals left a message by ripping them, so limp cardboard hung on each side of the stake driven into the mud. Soaked by rain, the cardboard curled and the wreckage of her signs became a harbinger of defeat.

"They thrashed me through the coffee-grinder," Leslie said. "Whatever I get, I'm thankful for that. I've run a good campaign."

From the first flash of numbers at the county administration building where the runoff votes were counted, it was obvious Leslie would be beaten badly, but she dressed up for her defeat. She slipped on a long, flaming red wig and wore rings on every finger. Her red purse matched her flat shoes, and she pinned an ACT UP button to a white pullover blouse with colorful diagonal slashes draped loosely on her shoulders. She wore her dark glasses since she expected to be in the glare of television camera lights.

Leslie was losing by a landslide; the vote ran four-to-one against her. "I think my past is what's costing me this election," she grumbled. "The people thought they were voting for a killer, not a die-hard Democrat." She blamed the party hierarchy for "osterizing" her. Although she probably meant ostracizing, the reference to the blades of a food blender fit her coffee-grinder metaphor. "All I know is that I'm a good person," she paused, "and a good Democrat."

As the lopsided count piled up, Leslie and Sylvia nursed their wounds by ducking into a room filled with office equipment and vending machines to nurse their wounds. "Oh, my legs hurt," Sylvia sighed. She slipped off her shoes and sat at a lunch table. Leslie chain-smoked. "I really thought I'd do a lot better than this. I really did," she moped.

Rejection by voters depressed her, but her treatment by the politicians who snubbed her made her mad. Leslie had spent years working behind the scenes on their campaigns, and she was naive enough to believe they would overlook her past and repay her labor with loyalty. Thinking about the hypocrites who took her support, then turned their backs on her made Leslie hiss angrily as she exhaled her cigarette smoke.

"We shook 'em up, honey." Sylvia tried to accentuate the positive. "Oh, we shook 'em up."

"Mother, take a pill," Leslie snapped. She was ready for a margarita, and she packed her Carltons in her red purse. Tomorrow she might lift her spirits by shopping for a new wig, she said.

Sylvia was hoarse from weeks of futile campaigning, "We was underdogs if ever I saw one." She limped on her sore legs and followed Leslie from the room.

Downstairs in the dark lobby, they stopped to chat with a pair of teenage girls sitting near an elevator. They all knew each other from elections or caucuses where their paths had crossed. The girls shared an easygoing affinity with Leslie, wishing her better luck in her next race. As she strolled off for her margarita, Leslie never seemed to realize the building she was leaving sat on the exact block where she and another teenage girl with a drawl had bought a .22 pistol for $12.95 before Samuel Shainock's hockshop was demolished to make room for progress.

The defeat did not discourage Leslie very long. "I'll just keep on keepin' on," she promised. The attention during the runoff campaign boosted her appetite for publicity and her ACT UP Houston chapter became the vehicle for her agenda. She and Sylvia pressured the city's public transportation system to detour a bus route so the line stopped in front of the local free AIDS clinic, located on a backwater side street. Leslie also led demonstrations pestering a female evangelist who convinced a cable television outlet to air a film called *Todd's Greatest Regret*, which featured a terminal AIDS patient repenting his sexual orientation on his deathbed.

Leslie fought with Pentecostals who had been her allies. "I'm drawn to their way of thinking, but they're cuckoo," she said. "I couldn't stay with them. How could I, when they condemned me?" First, the fundamentalists rebuked her gay lifestyle, then they attacked her surgery. "After my operation, they said I mutilated myself." She was a confirmed atheist now, so was her mother. "There's nothing up there when you pray," Sylvia scoffed. Divine intervention to block an execution was no longer a necessity for them.

AIDS activism won their devotion. Leslie's ACT UP Houston chapter crested with around forty members before her leadership style began to drive supporters away. As president, she did not tolerate dissent and her detractors called her a dictator, but they could not wrestle the chapter from her because she had filed a DBA ("doing business as") charter for the title ACT UP Houston in her own name. "I didn't get off the boat yesterday," she remarked.

Her followers dwindled to a small loyal band, barely a handful. Leslie printed flyers accusing HPD vice cops of using entrapment techniques to bust gay men they enticed into trysts at a city park. She tried to drum up support for a boycott against Shell. The multinational oil company was being sued by an ex-employee who contended he was harrassed into quitting because his boss suspected he was HIV-positive. When Queen Elizabeth paid a visit to Houston, Leslie called for a demonstration against the British monarch for holding Shell stock. "Queens versus the queen," she threatened to call the protest. Leslie was left virtually alone on the sidewalk.

She did not confine herself to AIDS-oriented issues, and began spending time with radicals from the Revolutionary Communist Party. During the buildup before Operation Desert Storm, she and the local communist leader shredded an American flag at a rally against United States policies in the Persian Gulf. "I like to be seen," she admitted.

Texas was enforcing more death sentences than any other state in the nation and Houston juries had condemned more prisoners than any other city in the state. Leslie showed up at a tiny rally against capital punishment. She said the educated bleeding hearts

were shocked to rub their respectable elbows with a bawdy transsexual, yet she had a perfect right to protest. "I was the only one
in the whole crowd who'd ever been on death row," Leslie
huffed.

Making enemies was no problem for her. She stirred up more
anger in the gay community by obstructing a ceremony called
Crossroads '91, the tenth anniversary of the first report about an
AIDS-induced case of pneumocystitis in a U.S. medical journal.
For a five-dollar donation, patrons could become sponsors of a line
of white crosses on the Montrose Boulevard esplanade dedicated
to people who had died from the disease.

The religious symbol offended Leslie's atheism. "A cross be-
longs in a church and in a cemetery, not on city property," she
announced. She believed holding the ceremony in the city's most
prominent gay neighborhood promoted a misconception that
AIDS was a gay disease. "AIDS is everywhere," Leslie said. "A
memorial for those who died from it should be everywhere."

She spoke before the city council, citing a municipal ordinance
against signs on esplanades, a law often ignored and seldom
enforced, but her complaints convinced the council to move the
site to a less conspicuous location, a vest-pocket park where the
crosses were not as visible to passing traffic. Leslie was not happy
about the compromise and neither were three hundred people
who turned out for Crossroads '91. The resentment lingered long
after the ceremony ended.

Thirty years earlier, Leslie and Carolyn wasted time at soda
fountains and drive-in restaurants; now Leslie plotted her protests
and political moves at a Jack in the Box on Montrose Boulevard.
A defrocked Methodist minister, who lost his congregation when
he came out of the closet, was furious at Leslie after the problems
she caused for Crossroads '91. The minister had become the self-
appointed bishop of his own church in Montrose. His pastoral
compassion vanished when he walked into the Jack in the Box and
saw the athiest who ruined the plan to put crosses in the esplanade.

"You're a disgrace, a disgrace to the community," the bishop
boomed. "I rebuke you in the name of Jesus!" He hurled his best
fire and brimstone. "If you come by my church, I will lay hands
on you like Oral Roberts, but I won't be using olive oil!" Cus-

tomers stared; the African-American kids behind the counter began to chuckle. "I will meet you on any corner anywhere," the bishop raged. "You are the devil!"

Leslie could not contain herself. "You're the devil, darlin'," she hollered. "You're a phony preacher with a phony church. Your seven members, your nine members," she taunted him. "You're a hypocrite! A hypocrite!" The diatribe nearly rattled the windows. Hard feelings were making Leslie unwelcome in Montrose after the Crossroads '91 conflict.

Despite the resentment aimed at her, Leslie would not give up her small apartment in the neighborhood, which her mother also used as a voting address. Sylvia became a Democratic precinct judge for a jurisdiction in Montrose, although she really spent most of her time at the family house on the edge of the city. Even after two cancer operations, Sylvia was full of fight, but she left her real estate business to her husband. Jim Ayres held down the fort at work, haggling home-buyer deals and finagling the rent from tenants in the properties he owned or managed. He relied on bluster and charm, reinforced by the implicit threat of the miniature revolver that he always wore as a tie tack.

Jim liked to call himself the "godfather" of his realm. At home, he coddled Pepe and Chico, his two Chihuahuas. He also had a parrot named Baby Boy that liked to stand on his shoulder in the shower. Sylvia was fond of the bird too. She spent hours trying to teach Baby Boy to screech ACT UP! FIGHT AIDS!

Leslie toyed with the idea of running for a city council seat in 1991, and had a few generic signs printed. She filed the preliminary papers allowing her to raise money for the race, but her murder conviction was a problem, so Sylvia became the member of the family who put her name on the ballot. Her brother, Ted Kipperman, grumbled, but he gave his sister the filing fee.

The years had been good to Ted. After moving away from Jim and Sylvia, he relocated his camera shop and overcame the decline of the neighborhood around his new store by turning his business into a pawnshop. His enterprise prospered, and he leaped from a small storefront in a dying shopping center to a large, free-standing building near a strategic intersection. The World's Largest Pawnshop, he called his empire. His motto: Hock It to Me!

His own Las Vegas wedding gave Ted a brainstorm for getting rid of the rings that survivors of busted marriages bring to pawnbrokers. Instead of selling the discarded bands for melting, Ted put a wedding chapel in his store, the only combination pawnshop-wedding chapel in the world, he bragged. He sent off for a mail-order certificate that ordained him as a chaplain and offered free marriage ceremonies to customers who bought their rings from him. He gave a good rate to anyone else who wanted to tie the knot in an unconventional atmosphere.

Ted decorated his chapel with a mural of Niagara Falls and added a long, black limousine, along with an outdoor gazebo, then festooned his pawnshop with a huge painting of himself in his vestments. Ted even went out on calls to marry skydivers, waterskiers, and a couple who got hitched standing on a billboard catwalk. He gave himself another slogan: Have Bible, Will Travel.

Ted's prosperity affected his politics. He overlooked the philosophical differences with his liberal sister, but he kept his distance from his nephew-turned-niece. Leslie did not seek Ted's company either. "I don't associate with Jewish Republicans," she frowned.

After Ted paid the filing fee, Sylvia ran for an at-large council seat elected by all the voters across the city. At seventy-two, she was recovering from her third cancer operation; a tumor had taken over her thyroid gland. Health care was near the top of her agenda. She wanted to put the spotlight on health education for the Medicare generation as well as for kids. Sylvia believed students should have access to free condoms. "They don't know anything about venereal disease and AIDS," she argued.

She and Leslie put more signs around the city. This time, the name read AYRES, but Sylvia could not break clear of the pack. In the primary, she finished fifth, with just 6 percent of the vote in a field of nine candidates.

Although Sylvia was not on the ballot, she lost again on runoff day. So did Leslie. They both worked the polling place where Sylvia was precinct judge without realizing the election would be their last.

Leslie's enemies were Sylvia's enemies; mother and child did everything together. They antagonized identical foes, and Sylvia's race for the city council gave their adversaries an opening: Precinct judges were not allowed to run for public office, according to a Democratic party rule.

Sylvia and Leslie were oblivious to the restriction. They believed rules applied to other people and they did not pay attention to limitations that would straitjacket them, but the people who opposed them did. A Democratic party committee took the precinct away from Sylvia.

Stripped of the base with her mother in the Montrose precinct, persona non grata at the Jack in the Box on the boulevard, targeted by a barrage of hostile articles in the city's gay press, Leslie finally moved out of her apartment in the neighborhood and returned to the house Sylvia and Jim shared. "I had to pull back," she sighed.

They retrenched, but Leslie and Sylvia could not kick the political bug. They both filed to run for the Harris County Democratic chair in 1992. Outsiders thought they were feuding, but they were not running against each other. Instead, they were trying to draw as many votes as possible from incumbent Ken Bentsen, Jr. to prevent him from winning a majority. They hoped one of them would finish second. Whichever member of the family got into the runoff was irrelevant to their strategy.

"Mother and me are the same person," Leslie said, describing the bond that explained their fifty years together.

As a team, Leslie and Sylvia collected one-fourth of the primary vote, but their plan failed. Another candidate finished ahead of them, then lost the runoff. Ken Bentsen, Jr. held on to his office. "He has that magic name," Leslie said, then began plotting future campaigns. "I'm going to run mother for council again." She grinned. "God bless her, she loves to run." To them, the race was more important than the result.

42

Frank Briscoe came out of political retirement and ran for mayor of Houston twice during the 1970s. He lost both races, largely because he was unable to attract African-American voters. "Fried Chicken Frank," they called him, a nickname based on the quantity of thighs and drumsticks he gave away in vain attempts to win their support.

After twenty-five years in private practice catering to a well-groomed clientele, Briscoe became a prosecutor again. In 1991, a newly-elected D.A. in Fort Bend County convinced him to come home.

Although he was in his sixties, Briscoe had not lost a step in the courtroom. He took the highest-profile murder case in Fort Bend County; an ex-con, fresh out of prison, was charged with killing a woman who was abducted from a shopping mall parking lot. Briscoe won a death sentence, but a month after the verdict, early in the summer of 1992, a messenger delivered a one-page letter from his boss. Instead of being congratulated, Frank Briscoe was given a week to clear out his office.

Briscoe blamed his ouster on politics. His boss had tried to get a perjury indictment against the county sheriff, claiming the sheriff lied about a connection to an arson case involving a topless dancer and her ex-husband, who were accused of torching a farm. The sheriff admitted that he briefly dated the topless dancer before he discovered her occupation; under oath before a grand jury, he denied having meetings with two fellow officers about his link with her or the arson case. Briscoe's boss believed the denial was false—grounds for a perjury indictment—but the grand jury would not go along with him.

The Fort Bend D.A. gave up on indicting the sheriff, but he fired Frank Briscoe, charging him with meddling in the perjury investigation despite a direct order to remain neutral. Briscoe called the charge "a bunch of garbage," and implied he was fired because he rejected pressure from his boss to endorse the Republican sheriff's Democratic opponent.

The clash degenerated into a mutually destructive showdown. The Fort Bend D.A. quickly followed Briscoe into unemployment because the D.A. leaked a tape of secret grand jury testimony about the sheriff's liason with the topless dancer to the *Houston Chronicle*. The maneuver backfired, getting the D.A. convicted on five counts of misconduct and incompetence, forcing him to give up his office while he appealed the verdicts. His resignation left a vacuum in Fort Bend County, and Frank Briscoe's boosters began touting their man as a candidate in the next election for District Attorney.

In the summer of 1992, Leslie was left out of the planning for protests during the Republican national convention at the Astrodome. Defectors from her ACT UP Houston chapter had helped to build Queer Nation into the city's most robust militant gay activist group. Local members of Queer Nation joined forces with ACT UP from other cities to lay out the logistics for demonstrations during the convention. Leslie was not invited to participate. A few months before the convention, she and a Queer Nation rival, another ACT UP Houston defector, were arrested after a shoving match at a city council meeting that was supposed to be a protest against a proposal to cut municipal funding for AIDS relief.

Other local activists threatened to start their own ACT UP chapter. Given the size of the city's gay community, the Houston chapter was minuscule and Leslie's leadership was blamed. For awhile, the splinter group considered calling themselves ACT UP Montrose to avoid a battle over the name Leslie had chartered for herself, then they decided to use ACT UP Houston and dare her to respond. Leslie considered fighting, but held back. She could not explain why she let her opponents take the name she owned; maybe she sensed the movement would do better without her.

But she remained an ACT UPPER in spirit. She always wore

her button; so did Sylvia. Jim Ayres's voice still greeted callers on the message from an answering machine hooked to an ACT UP Houston telephone number, but the new chapter used the name at demonstrations drawing more protestors than Leslie had ever been able to muster. The weekend before the 1992 GOP convention began, she and Sylvia struck out on their own, setting up a table outside the Republican National Committee's headquarters hotel. They pinned an ACT UP button on a stuffed elephant and passed out "Sex Survival Kits" that included a Red Cross AIDS pamphlet, a condom, and a toy teddy bear.

Monday, the convention's first day, Leslie and Sylvia took on the religious right by giving away condoms at the God and Country rally. "Haven't you ever heard of abstinence?" a fundamentalist railed at them. "You can preach abstinence all you want," Sylvia shot back, "but kids will *never* be abstinent unless you put 'em in cages."

The cops cordoned off the sidewalk to clear a path for pedestrians, and Leslie danced between the two lines of police with a WHAT ABOUT AIDS sign. She and Sylvia were among the last to leave, but they were not planning to return after sundown for a joint ACT UP/Queer Nation march, a showcase to kick off a week-long schedule of demonstrations.

"I don't want to walk five miles," Leslie grumbled.

An HPD squad on horseback charged into the march as it neared the Astrodome, stopping the protest on the dark side of the stadium, well away from the entrance decorated with flags from all fifty states to welcome the GOP. Under the lucite dome that night, former President Ronald Reagan spoke from the podium. "May every dawn be a great new beginning for America and every evening bring us closer to the shining city upon a hill." The most popular Republican alive had the crowd at his feet.

Ronald Reagan celebrated his fiftieth birthday on February 6, 1961, the night Fred A. Tones was killed. In 1961, the future president had never run for office beyond the Screen Actors Guild and he was still a registered Democrat, despite his conservative tilt. At fifty, Ronald Reagan had a second life leading to the White House lying ahead for him, the culmination of an American dream, while a refugee from Spain was found in flames near a pile of garbage in a vacant lot.

Over the years that Fred A. Tones missed, Clyde Woody's legal practice had flourished. Woody had much success with First Amendment cases, expanding the limits of free speech in obscenity laws. Woody made Houston theater screens safe for *Animal Lovers*, a film about women having sex with a menagerie. He also did well with upper-echelon domestic disputes. Not long after he finished Carolyn's case, Woody represented Judy Garland in some of her stormy child custody conflicts with her estranged husband, Sid Luft.

Woody did not stay in touch with Carolyn. He knew she had married, so her last name had changed. A decade or so after she got out of prison, she came to him about a minor legal problem. "A dispute with a neighbor," Woody said. "Not worth getting into." After that, he lost track of her. Unlike Leslie, Carolyn led a private life.

Lloyd Lunsford handled Leslie's divorce from the common-law marriage to Carolyn. And Lunsford helped Ted Kipperman with professional legal problems. Ted groaned over Lunsford's fees, and he tried to save himself a few dollars with cheaper lawyers, but whenever he could not get rid of a problem he dipped into his budget and dialed Lucky Lunsford.

"We know Ted down here," Neil McKay said in a courthouse office. The former prosecutor recalled a suspicious load of CB radios that had surfaced in Ted's inventory. The assistant D.A. who had worked on the torch-murder case, the only attorney who stayed with the job from start to finish, became a state district judge a few years after the final verdict against Leslie in Gatesville. Even after he retired from his seat on the bench, McKay returned to the Harris County courthouse to sit for other judges during their vacations.

Judge Miron Love never stepped down. The judge at the original joint trial won reelection for more than thirty years. When he triumphed again in 1992, his four-year term stretched beyond the mandatory retirement age of seventy-five. He was aware of Leslie's political activity. "I hope he, she, or whatever she's become, has found meaning with the rest of her life," Judge Love remarked.

The original defense attorney, Jack Knight, passed away after toiling on the local legal scene for four decades. He lived long beyond the demise of the "stand and kill" self-defense law that he used without success at the joint trial. In 1974, Texas enacted a penal code that purged some of the frontier mentality from the books; the new self-defense statute brought Texas into line with other states, requiring citizens to prove they were unable to retreat before they could justify the use of deadly force.

The American Psychiatric Association updated its standards as well. In 1974, the APA took homosexuality off its list of mental disorders. Views on schizophrenia were being revised also. Freudian ideas like blaming maternal influences to explain schizophrenia gave way to theories based on brain physiology and chemical imbalances triggered by environmental stress.

Houston's physical environment endured its share of stress with the oil bust in 1986. Unused buildings were demolished because the tax rate was lower when property was undeveloped. The Pig Stand where Leslie and Carolyn discussed the three-way date was destroyed, leaving nothing but a cement slab. Fate also dealt harshly with the drive-in restaurant where Tones had driven Carolyn in his fancy Lincoln right after they met. Weeds poked through the concrete below a tall, rusty sign, a false promise of burgers and fries.

The building where Leslie and Carolyn rented their apartment still stood, but the address, 1205 Truxillo, had vanished. Not long after her tenants hit the front pages, the mortified landlady had the numbers pried off and replaced with different digits to confuse snoops who wanted to see where the drag queen and teenage hooker had kept house. Just six months after homicide detectives made their first search on her crumbling "estate," Madge Duncan Staples died. According to the legend that persisted with neighbors thirty years later, the scandal killed her.

Out on Griggs Road, where Fred A. Tones finished his life, the duplex beat the wrecking ball. The neighborhood was African-American now, and many of the new residents had the same aspirations that Tones brought with his family. Small busineses came and went in the duplex, Ted Kipperman said. The route from his pawnshop to his favorite cafeteria took him down Griggs Road almost every day around lunchtime. The building had been combined into a single address. By 1992, the space was a discount lingerie store.

Epilogue

Almost every evening during the 1992 Republican convention, Leslie and Sylvia came to a protest site across the street from the Astrodome where the city government put stages for speakers, lights, and portable toilets on the empty acreage that had been designated for dissent.

"A concentration camp," Leslie said.

By Wednesday, the members of Queer Nation and ACT UP had regrouped after their brief battle with the HPD during the convention's first night. They converged at the designated protest site, along with a feminist drum corps that beat a steady cadence as the demonstrators blew into whistles and chanted their angry mantra: "WE'RE ACT UP, FUCK YOU!" Riot police strapped on their helmets and a mounted squad blocked the getaway route with big horses.

Leslie and Sylvia stayed on the sidelines as a die-in began. The protestors lay on top of each other, but they never stopped chanting or chopping their hands toward the cops; pointing fingers of blame as the roll call of Republicans inside the covered stadium renominated George Bush as the GOP candidate for president. "THREE MORE MONTHS, THREE MORE MONTHS . . . THAT'S ALL YOU'VE GOT LEFT TO KILL US," the protestors yelled their prophecy.

Sylvia watched from a distance. "I wonder how many of those boys will be dead in a year?" she thought aloud.

The die-in fueled hate on both sides, and made the prone demonstrators more vulnerable to a rush by the cops, but the HPD held steady, letting the protestors pour their rage into a furious display of fragile mortality. Restraint paid off, and the rally wound down after the catharsis of the die-in. There was no fight that night. The AIDS activists got up from the grass, the drums and whistles stopped, and the protesters dispersed.

Before they went home, Leslie and Sylvia stopped for coffee at a branch of a fast-food chain called Whataburger. Leslie had started spending a lot of time at the Whataburger where the freeway loop around the city crossed over South Main, a permanent strip of blight lined with cheap motels, delapidated strip joints, and beer dives. The Whataburger was an antiseptic oasis, a remnant of one of the sporadic well-intentioned, but half-hearted clean-up campaigns that never changed South Main.

Leslie and Sylvia sat in swivel chairs on the same side of a formica table. They both thought deeply about the demonstration they had just seen. The barrier that kept Leslie from participating bothered her. The shield was built by animosity that flared during AIDS activist turf battles, struggles over status to combat an epidemic, but the root was a single word.

"I support Queer Nation, I really do," she said. "It's the youth and I'm behind them." Leslie stirred her coffee. "I was a gay man before most of them were born." Policies and personalities were not the only reasons for her feud with Queer Nation. "I just don't like that word." She paused for several seconds. "I was damn near killed by people who called me a queer."

The sentiment of counselors, cops, and her own defense attorney remained in her mind. *He is drawn to places where queers hang out and where people are queers. . . . Ashley appeared to be a "Q." . . . Two persons that you and I wouldn't walk down the street with for fear that someone would say "What's he doing walking down the street with those queers?"* Leslie could not forget the pain that word had brought her.

Sylvia was miles away. "I would never let them kill you," she proclaimed to her only child. Vindication made her thirty-year-old vow seem brand new. Sylvia said her ears still heard the shrill sirens wailing in Huntsville when she learned about the stay of execution. "Look at the goose bumps," she held out her pale arm.

Tireless lawyers, contemplative judges, prayers and donations, they all sustained the effort to save Leslie and Carolyn, but Sylvia's desperation had enlisted them and fueled the fight that stopped the executions. "I don't know how I did all that." She shook her head slowly. "When it was over, I looked up and it was me."

Every Saturday, Leslie and Sylvia drove downtown to hand out AIDS awareness pamphlets in front of a Woolworth's store on Main Street, where the sidewalk was an unofficial demonstration corner. They joined the evangelists and communists, the Black Muslims and Jehovah's Witnesses, each spreading their separate faiths to shoppers and bus riders along the busy block.

Leslie's latest mission was delivering AIDS education to members of minority communities. She and Sylvia came prepared with an array of Red Cross folders, but they no longer passed out condoms because their supply sources had cut them off.

"Nobody will give them to us anymore," Leslie bragged, "because we've passed out so many already."

During the presidential campaign, they supported the Democratic nominee, who happened to be from Hot Springs too. They did not let their dispute with local party brass prevent them from backing the national ticket, just as they never let their problems with rival AIDS activists cut the hours they devoted to fighting the illness.

On election night, Sylvia pinned an ACT UP button to her CLINTON-GORE T-shirt before she left for a Democratic bash to watch the victorious vote count. An envelope addressed to Leslie was in their mail box a few days later:

Dear Ms. Perez:
We did it!
All those months of effort—all those years of hope and commitment—have finally paid off. I am writing today simply to say, "Thank you."

Leslie realized bags of identical letters written on Democratic National Committee stationery were mailed to loyal party workers filling long computer rosters.

. . . I simply want to tell you how much I appreciate all of your help and let you know I am truly looking forward to continuing our work together in the exciting times that lie ahead.

My best regards to you and your family.
     Sincerely,
     Bill Clinton

Leslie was not fooled by the signature. "It was probably signed by a machine," she said, laughing, but a thank-you note from the president, even with an automated, impersonal autograph, was a triumph for a survivor who once listed Death Cell 6 as her address.

About the Author

Robert L. Bentley is a screenwriter and a journalist. He is currently an associate news producer for E! Entertainment TV. A native of Houston, he lives in Los Angeles.